101
Inspirational
Stories
of the
Rosary

101
Inspirational
Stories
of the
Rosary

Compiled and Produced by
Sister Patricia Proctor, OSC

Foreword by
The Most Reverend William S. Skylstad, D.D.
Bishop of Spokane

Inspirational Stories Edited by
Cathy Felty • Ann Marie Lillis
Nick Elfrink • Sr. Marcia Kay La Cour, OSC

Illustrated by
Nick Elfrink

A Called by Joy Book

Franciscan Monastery of Saint Clare
Spokane, Washington
www.rosary101.com

Although the author and publisher have made every effort to ensure the accuracy and completeness of information contained in this book, we assume no responsibility for errors, inaccuracies, omissions, or any inconsistency herein. Any slights of peoples, places or organizations are unintentional.

ISBN 0-9728447-0-8
First Printing March 2003
Second Printing May 2003 revised
Third Printing October 2003

Library of Congress Control Number: 2003103209

ATTENTION SCHOOLS, UNIVERSITIES, COLLEGES
AND CHARITABLE ORGANIZATIONS:
Quantity discounts are available on bulk purchases of this book for educational, gift purposes or as premiums for increasing magazine subscriptions or renewals. For information, please contact Sister Patricia Proctor, OSC Monastery of Saint Clare, 4419 N Hawthorne Street. Spokane, WA 99205 Phone: (509) 327-4479

Ave Maria

This book is dedicated to help all Christians find the answer to many of life's problems and difficulties through the prayer of the Rosary.

With Prayerful Thanks

I hardly ever read the acknowledgments in other books so I will understand if you as a reader skip over this section, but this book is such a testimony of so many people putting it together I almost feel I should rent a billboard and say, "Thank You" in the biggest and boldest letters I can find.

First and foremost the deepest thanks to our Blessed Mother who let me have the joy of doing this project. It has been so much fun and I have had so much help and cooperation from every source that I truly knew she was doing the driving and I was just in the back seat enjoying the trip.

Secondly, thank you to our beloved Pope John Paul II who has filled the world with the greatest gift in promoting the rosary. The whole world is blessed to have such a good and holy Pope.

Then I move to the special and wonderful sisters that I live with in community. There are only seven of us, but because we work together and support each other so fully in each project, we accomplish as much as if we were two or three times that number.

As I move now into the broader stream of my thanksgiving, I first and foremost give the greatest tribute and thanks to the Rosary Brigade. These are the wonderful friends who buoyed this project up on a sea of rosaries. This whole project from start to finish has been a tribute to prayer. On the web site we list over 19,000 rosaries prayed, but I know many more than that have been offered and continue to be prayed. To all of you I offer my deepest thanks and gratitude. In heaven we shall all join together and sing praises to God for giving us the gift of each other.

When I first received the "tap" on the shoulder to do this project, I had hoped to find a publisher who would print this book for us. I contacted our own dear brothers in Francis at Saint Anthony Messenger and the good people at Our Sunday Visitor. Both of them were very interested in doing the book but they could not get it printed before 2004. My heart was set on doing this book for the "Year of the Rosary!" 2003! So like the little red hen, I said, "Very well, then, we will do it ourselves!" Since I was blessed with the "gift of ignorance" in knowing how to publish a book I had no qualms that it couldn't be done. The sisters let me buy some books on "self-publishing" and we moved ahead.

The more I read, the more I found out how much there was to do. Like this wonderful card I once saw in which a little man sees this elephant who wants to get to the top of the mountain. Somehow, by pushing and pulling, shoving and tugging he manages to get the elephant successfully to the top. He wipes his head and has a big grin on his face. Then he looks back down from where he has come and there patiently waiting are a hundred more elephants!

This is where I truly and completely felt the wonderful supporting strength of prayer. Not once did I ever feel this project was going to fail. I had a few doubts about my sanity now and then, but those were very momentary and a good night's sleep always seemed to vanquish them. What made my heart sing through this whole project were the many beautiful and touching stories that have been sent in. I was in awe of each one. I kept telling the sisters, these stories are like precious diamonds that the Blessed Mother has dropped into my lap. I know she will take care of this book, because she wants everyone to know, Christian and non-Christian alike, that there are amazing results obtained in praying the rosary.

Along with the stories came in generous friends who have sent in donations big and small to help us to cover the costs in printing Mary's book. Their wonderful support has helped us to reach every obligation that was presented to us. Thank-you. Thank-you. Thank-you.

Now before I run out of room I have to mention a few special friends in particular who made this book so special. The wonderful editors, **Cathy Felty, Anne Marie Lillis, Nick Elfrink and Sr. Marcia Kay LaCour, OSC; Dale Duncan (layout); Mike Cox (cover); Barb Ries (everything I needed help with and that was a lot!); Cynthia Landeen (index); Fr. Richard Gribble (history); Fr. Richard Fragomeni (mysteries); Seth Murray (making a rosary) and Connie Olson (web support).** This book is the result of many hands, many prayers and most importantly many friends! Thank you!

Table of Contents

Appendices

Foreword

On October 16, 2002, our Holy Father Pope John Paul II issued an Apostolic Letter entitled "The Rosary of the Virgin Mary." He requested that from then on for a year we in the Catholic Church celebrate the "Year of the Rosary." His reflections on the rosary as prayer are an important reminder for all of us of this prayer that has such a long, rich tradition. The treasure of this tradition was enriched even more by the Holy Father with the addition of a new set of mysteries: the Mysteries of Light.

In a systematic way as we pray the rosary, we meditate upon the important mysteries of our faith. Again and again, we come back in prayer to these great moments in Jesus' life that provide an unending source of discovery and appreciation of God's goodness to us. In our most difficult and painful moments when concentration might be very difficult, the simple structure of the rosary provides a calming sense of peace and a consistent presence with God in prayer.

In his Apostolic Letter, Pope John Paul II encourages us to pray regularly the rosary as a way of keeping in contact with the depth of the Gospel message in its entirety. Even though this prayer is Marian in character, he reminds us that it is basically Jesus centered. In an increasingly complex and challenging world, the rosary is a wonderful gift to keep our lives focused on Jesus' presence and on the mysteries of faith that have touched our journey of faith so profoundly.

Each of us has his or her unique way of praying the rosary. I remember in our farm home when the family did the supper dishes, our mother would lead us in the rosary. For years I have used the Nordic Track for exercise early in the morning. Quite often I have been asked, "Don't you find it boring?" No, I don't because that is when I pray the rosary.

Sister Patricia Proctor, OSC, has collected over one hundred stories of how the rosary has impacted individual's lives. Each story carries with it a witness of faith that helps to make up our common spiritual heritage in the Catholic Church. I suspect that each of us in reading these accounts will come more into contact with our own experience of praying the rosary and appreciate even more its transforming and consoling power.

William S. Skylstad
Catholic Bishop of Spokane

Preface

When Sister Patricia suggested publishing a rosary book it seemed like a momentous task beyond a small community's ability! The more Sister worked on it and the more we shared and thought of it, the more urgent it became to do it!

Since the Contemplative vocation is principally one of prayer, almost every challenge of life comes to us for prayer. It is because of the hundreds of calls, letters and other means of communication, that we, as a Poor Clare Community, have seen the urgent need to help those seeking answers to their problems. Meditating on the life and love of Jesus and His mother in praying the rosary has been a most calming and strengthening experience for those seeking help.

The stories inspired all of the Sisters and the need to accomplish this work filled the Monastery. Sister Patricia's hours of work, prayer and trust in our Blessed Mother's help, inspired the Sisters to encourage her and offer whatever assistance was needed.

Now we pray that the many life stories and happenings related in this book will be inspiring to you the reader, as they have been to us.

It is our joy to be able to point to these stories and say to all, "Here is your answer that will comfort, quiet and show you the way—and in the end increase your joy!" May you experience many encouraging hours in these pages.

Sr. Mary Rita Dolan, OSC, Abbess
Monastery of Saint Clare
Spokane, Washington

Introduction

One of the major television networks has a news program with a special feature called "Everybody Has a Story." This feature is one of the most enjoyable parts of the broadcast. An individual is randomly chosen from the telephone book—the hosts close their eyes and point. The person who is picked becomes the show's "story of the week."

I think the Blessed Mother has brought about this book in exactly the same way. I was out taking a walk one day, praying my rosary (something I didn't do all that often before this book), and she zapped me with her finger: "Hey, you! I have a job for you to do."

I have been a Poor Clare Sister for over 20 years, and during that time I have figured out a few basic things about how God works. One is—and don't take this wrong—but I think God is kind of sneaky. He sort of sets you up. He tends to fix things and arrange things so that as you blithely go along with your life thinking you are totally in charge, all of a sudden you realize, "I have been set up!" Now, if you think this is totally unscriptural, just recall the book of Jeremiah in which he laments to God, "You duped me, and I let myself be duped!" (Jeremiah 20:7)

Not that one ever loses their choice of free will. That never happens. But there are "coincidences": meeting someone totally out of the blue and you later marry that person, or reading a book that just happens to be sitting on a shelf you normally never look at and suddenly your whole way of thinking is changed. All those little "coincidences" seem to be God working quietly behind the scenes to "set us up."

So it was that I found myself taking a quiet walk in our garden. It was only a few days after Pope John Paul had just made the startling proclamation that he was calling for October 2002 through October 2003 to be the "Year of the Rosary," and he was announcing a new set of mysteries for the rosary! I've always believed in the rosary but always felt it was like the Ten Commandments—it was just something that was. God dropped it in our laps through Saint Dominic and we were supposed to pick up the ball and go with it. (Read the history of the rosary in this book, and you will be surprised how the rosary really came about!)

The fact that the Pope could change it and did was most remarkable. It was also rather liberating. All of a sudden it became a prayer of the 21st Century. It has links to the Middle Ages but is definitely something also just for "today." With these wonderful new mysteries, the rosary was taken out of the dust and mothballs of medieval Catholicism and brought forth with new life and wonderment! There is indeed something new under the sun. Though Pope John Paul may be in his 80s, he still has a lot of life left in him!

Newly enthused about the Rosary and taking my little walk, I realized (and here is the part where I think I was set up) that I should ask the Blessed Mother if there wasn't something our community could do to promote the rosary. So I did, and the thought came back almost immediately: "Why not write a book?" A book with stories similar to those from *Chicken Soup for the Soul* or the kind that the popular ecumenical magazine *Guideposts* puts out. This book, of course, would be totally Marian with stories of personal testimony about people who have prayed the rosary and experienced wonderful results.

Now, in looking back, I rather feel that it was the Holy Spirit who popped the idea into my head to ask the question, and naturally the Blessed Mother was there with the answer. To prove this point, everything following this remarkable thought that came out of "nowhere" just seemed to fall into place: my Abbess, Sister Mary Rita, thought it was a wonderful idea, as did the rest of the community.

With a green light from them I proceeded to introduce it to the wonderful friends who subscribe to my free, daily on-line Peace Card. Their reaction was not only enthusiastic, they almost immediately started sending stories. In no time at all, I was completely over my head but paddling valiantly towards the publication shores.

The stories were wonderful. Each was totally different from the other and all truly remarkable in their witness of what the power of the rosary could obtain. Time after time, as I opened my e-mail, I would find a new story and would feel like a precious gift had been dropped into my lap. All of a sudden, I went from praying the rosary once in a while to praying it as many times as possible throughout the day. I mean after all, this stuff works!

I created a web page just about the rosary book—www.Rosary101.com—and on this new site I asked people to join with me in praying for the success of this book. Once again, I was carried away on a tide of prayer by wonderful friends. From all across the country, and from even around the whole world, offers came in to join the "Rosary Brigade." At this moment, over 19,000 rosaries have been prayed to spread Mary's little "set-up" job about the rosary.

And the Blessed Mother works fast when she wants to: from start to finish this book has taken less than six months to complete. As I write this, it is only days away from being sent to the printer, and from there it continues to be in Mary's hands to drop the books where she will. I know that each book will do its mission of promoting the rosary and the great power of prayer because it's not my work, it's Mary's work.

I can truly and completely say this was not my personal project. I only opened myself to saying "yes" to God and He took it from there. I hope as you read this book you will be filled with the conviction to say "yes" to God as well and put your next project and special need under the powerful protection and patronage of our Blessed Mother, Queen of the Rosary.

Sr. Patrica Proctor, OSC
Monastery of Saint Clare
Spokane, Washington

Shrine of Safe Return

In the early spring of 1944, with WWII fully engaged, work on an open-air shrine to be dedicated to our Lady Queen of Peace was begun in St. John's Parish in the little German/Dutch community of Leopold, Missouri. To make this an all-parish effort, even the children were recruited to bring in sparkling, quartz-encrusted stones for the walls. Thousands of stones were brought in from the local hills and creekbeds. Parish craftsmen and builders raised the crenelated walls, laid the flagstone floor, and completed the necessary concrete work. In May of that same year, the shrine of our Lady Queen of Peace was dedicated to the safe return of members of St. John's Parish serving in the armed forces. The practice of saying a parish rosary for the intention of world peace and the safe return of the servicemen of the parish was begun at that time. Every evening, as long as weather permitted, dedicated locals would gather about dusk to say a group rosary at the shrine.

Initially 44 names were inscribed in the marble tablets of the altar front, representing the young men serving in WWII. Since the ending of WWII, a multitude of parish members have served in the armed conflict around the world, through the Korean Conflict and the Viet Nam War. To this day, the rosary is still recited at the shrine, and to this day not one parish member has lost his or her life while serving our country. There were many harrowing tales of near misses, and some men were wounded, but none of the wounds were life-threatening.

Nick J. Elfrink   *Leopold, Missouri*

The Rosary and Final Exams

When I was in high school and taking final exams, a friend of mine got out her rosary and prayed the entire period. She had done all the studying she could possibly do and now was looking for help in keeping calm so she could answer the questions.

My friend got one hundred percent correct on that exam.

I was not Catholic then, but asked her to teach me the rosary. She did. I could not learn enough about our Blessed Mother from that time on. I'm sure this is what brought me into Holy Mother Church when I was 21 years old, over 35 years ago.

Sometimes I believe those born in the Faith take what we have in the Sacraments for granted. I'm so grateful for all the richness I'm afforded through them.

Marian J. Ferris   *Attica, New York*

The Amethyst Rosary

I converted to the Catholic faith 42 years ago, but I was blessed by my faith and by the Blessed Mother before I was ever born.

My mother never married. In 1942, the year I was born, she was a 38-year-old woman living with and caring for her 80-year-old parents as well as her three older brothers.

Four years before I was born, my Lutheran mother had purchased an amethyst rosary in a jewelry store because she thought it was pretty. Some Catholic friends told her what it was. Not being a Catholic, and not knowing anything about praying a rosary, she kept it in its little gold colored box in her china cabinet.

While I was growing up, my mother would often clean her china cabinet, and she would let me walk around the house, wearing the rosary around my neck, until it was time to put it back in it's little box and tuck it safely back in the china cabinet. I really enjoyed that. I guess it made me feel important.

I can remember always being drawn to things that were Catholic. I loved seeing nuns in their habits. When the movie "The Lady of Fatima" came out in the early 1950s, my mother and I went to see it. We both enjoyed it immensely. I would often play that I was the "Lady". When I was seven years old, my mother and I went with her Catholic friends to a Redemptorist Mission in their church. Again, it was something I really enjoyed.

One of my cousins converted to Catholicism and got married when I was 16 years old, and two weeks later, I met my future husband. You guessed it—he was Catholic. For the next two years, I self-taught myself a lot of Catholic prayers and read as many pamphlets from the Knights of Columbus as I could get my hands on.

On my 18th birthday, I called the priest in my hometown and explained that I wanted to take instructions. He asked if it was because I was going to marry a Catholic. When I explained my history to him, he seemed very pleased. A couple of weeks later I told my mother I wanted to buy a rosary, but, instead, she gave me the amethyst one I had gotten to know in my childhood.

What makes this story even more amazing is that my mother bought the amethyst rosary four years before I was born, and amethyst is the birthstone for February, the month in which I was born. I still pray on that same rosary, and the Blessed Mother has always been there to help me.

Growing up in the 1940s and '50s as an illegitimate child was not easy for me, nor was it easy for my mother to have a child out of wedlock. My mother and I spent many Sunday afternoons singing hymns and reading Bible stories, and I can honestly say that I wouldn't have traded places with anyone else.

The Blessed Mother got me through all the name-calling and teasing that I had to endure from other people, and my mother taught me that you don't treat other people any different than how you want to be treated yourself.

I was also blessed with a remarkable extended family in addition to my wonderful mother, with three great "fathers" who were my uncles. They supported us and loved us, and they treated me like I was the most special little girl in the world.

In the past year, I was going to a priest for spiritual direction, and I told him my story. He said that he felt the Blessed Mother had this all planned, long before I was ever born. I believe he's right.

JoAnn Eckstein   *Hector, Minnesota*

Every trifling thing
is told to her
and every great sorrow;
she is
the sharer
of all earth's joys
and griefs.

Caryll Houselander

A Rosary Laugh

When my youngest daughter, Jane, was seven years old, she fell and broke her left arm just at the elbow. In the resulting X-ray, the break looked like a right angle.

As my mother and I sat in the waiting room while Jane was being treated in the emergency room, I started to pull out my rosary, which was in a plastic case. It was my refuge in times of stress.

My mother heard the sound, and looked over at me.

"How many of those have you had today?" she asked.

When she saw what had made the sound—not pills, but my rosary—she began to laugh, and so did I.

This laughter provided us both with a release from the tension we were under. Thank you, Mary!

Patricia M. Agerton   *Fort Walton Beach, Florida*

My Best Friend

From the age of ten, I have had a very special relationship with the Blessed Mother. You may well ask why my relationship is so different, and I must add that I came from a very Protestant background.

I know my little Protestant girlfriends thought I was strange. When they wanted to play house or play with dolls, I never wanted to be the "mommie" or the "teacher." I always want to be the Blessed Virgin, or a nun, always playing with some sort of veil.

One day I went to the florist shop with my aunt, and she told me I could choose anything I wanted. The shop had some beautiful floral arrangements and music boxes, but there was one thing that drew me to the other side of the shop. I looked up at a shelf and there sat a six-inch, pastel colored bust of the Blessed Mother.

Needless to say, I had to have it. I couldn't go home without it, so my aunt generously bought it for me. But she asked, "Sheila, what is your dad going to say?" I replied that well I didn't know and didn't care.

"She will go in my room," I added.

I still have the bust today, over 40 years later, and when we have moved from one house to another, I personally carry her with me to wherever we go. No one ever dares to touch her.

After my aunt bought me the bust, I learned to pray the rosary, because, although I was Protestant, I had many Catholic friends. I finally converted to Catholicism 12 years ago, and it was at the urging of my youngest son that he and I were converted together at a private Mass, baptized, confirmed and had our first Holy Communion. I cried through the entire ceremony: And a little child shall lead them—and my son did!

I do know that the Blessed Mother is with me always, not just when I am praying the rosary, but my most wonderful experience with the rosary came when my mother, whom I had been taking care of for six years at home, passed away from Alzheimer's.

She was in a coma and had been expected to pass away the previous week, but she was not ready. On that particular night, it was bedtime and we had just finished praying the rosary. Although in the coma she could not pray, I laced the rosary between our fingers and prayed the rosary out loud so she could hear.

After the prayer, I could feel the Blessed Mother's presence so strongly that I felt her touch me on the shoulder and say "Sheila, it is time." I was so relieved and completely unafraid of what I would experience.

I got up and moved my chair away from my mom's bed, put my rosary away and leaned over my mother and kissed her good night. She died. It was the most beautiful experience I could have ever imagined. My mother had a slight smile across her lips, and I stood basking in the feeling of peace and love that I felt for this wonderful woman. And Mary said to me, "Sheila, she is at peace and will join your father. She is so happy."

And I knew this was true and that she would join the love of her life. My father had come to get his sweetheart and take her home on Valentine's Day, February 14, 2002.

Sheila D. Dowdell   *Unionport, Ohio*

The Rosary Solves All Problems

Regarding the Holy Rosary,
Sister Lucia (the lone surviving seer
of Fatima) speaking to Father Fuentes
in the authentic December 26, 1957
interview said:

"Look, Father, the Most Holy Virgin in these last times in which we live has given new efficacy *in the recitation of the Holy Rosary. She has given this efficacy to such an extent that there is no problem, no matter how difficult it is,whether temporal or above all spiritual, in the personal life of each one of us, of our families, of the families in the world,or of the religious communities,or even of the life of peoples and nations that cannot be solved by the Rosary. There is no problem, I tell you, no matter how difficult it is, that we cannot solve by the prayer of the Holy Rosary. With the Holy Rosary, we will save ourselves. We will sanctify ourselves.We will console our Lord and obtain the salvation of many souls."*

The Baby Was Coming Soon

When I was 36 weeks pregnant with my first baby, my heart thrilled with the thought that my "D-Day"—delivery day—was just around the corner. On my second-to-the-last trip to the doctor for a prenatal checkup, I could hardly see around my large belly as I awkwardly climbed onto the examining table.

My doctor whisked through the routine exam and asked if I had any questions or concerns about the birth.

I smiled confidently and shook my head. I was as ready as I would ever be. No drugs or pain relief for me. This baby was going to come naturally. Isn't that what all the pregnancy books advised? Pain was all in the woman's mind. Breathing exercises and my loving husband were all I needed to make it through.

I came out of my reverie of natural childbirth to see my doctor frowning as she pressed my belly. She saw the concern in my eyes and quickly reassured me that everything was fine. The baby had not yet assumed the birthing position and was not head down.

In medical terms, the baby was in the breech position.

"Should I worry?" I asked the doctor.

"No," she replied, adding that the baby would most likely turn before my next appointment. I also was reassured that some babies like to wait until the very last minute before assuming their birthing positions.

I put it out of my mind and spent the next week washing all the darling baby clothes and arranging them in the new dresser. There was so much to get ready! The baby was coming soon!

Every once in a while I wondered whether the baby had turned and even tried to feel my own belly, but (pardon the pun) I couldn't make heads or tails of the situation.

I lumbered into my very last appointment and waited nervously as my doctor poked around. I could tell by her expression that the baby was still in the breech position. My hopes of a natural birth began to vanish.

"What can I do?" I inquired, anxious to know my options.

I was told I could schedule a Cesarean Section and have my baby surgically, or I could undergo a procedure called an "external version."

I immediately rejected the C-Section option. I still clung to my hopes of a natural birth.

"What's an external version?" I asked.

My doctor explained that it was a procedure where she would try to turn the baby around by pressing on my stomach from the outside. I winced. It sounded painful. She gave the procedure only a 50 percent chance of success—the baby's buttocks had already dropped into my pelvic area.

"Of course, there is always the possibility that the baby could flip back into the breech position," she also added. "I should also tell you that if the procedure is successful, there are risks. The umbilical cord may get tangled up, or it may collapse."

I gasped. That sounded serious. The cord was the baby's lifeline. She also explained that she would have to do it at the hospital with an operating room available if anything went wrong. Now I was scared.

I went home to discuss this with my husband. We decided to go ahead with the external version in hopes of avoiding a C-section, but I was terrified. We prayed daily that the baby would turn around. My husband even tried talking into my belly in hopes that the baby would understand.

I tried every old wives' tale that I'd ever heard. I stood on my head. I played music into the lower section of my belly in hopes that the baby would move its head down toward the sound.

We told all our friends and family. Everyone was praying.

I was a nervous wreck the morning that I arrived at the hospital for the procedure. I had fasted according to the doctor's orders. I was dressed in a hospital gown. My doctor had arrived and was suited up and ready. The nurses assured her that the operating room was ready at a moment's notice. I smiled weakly and tried to be brave as the nurse prepared to insert the IV needle.

The doctor hesitated a moment and told the nurse to wait on the IV for a moment. She left the room and came back wheeling in a sonogram machine. She explained that she wanted to be sure of the baby's position before she began. I was hooked up to the sonogram.

The doctor and nurse huddled around the machine. Suddenly both of them gave a gasp of surprise. They smiled and told me joyfully that the baby had turned around all on its own! My heart soared. I was off that table and out of that hospital gown in the blink of an eye.

We thanked the doctor and assured her that this was the answer to prayer. She just smiled and nodded.

My mother called my grandmother the moment we left the hospital to tell her the good news. My grandmother answered the phone and rejoiced with us at the miracle. She then told us very seriously that this had happened through our Lady's intercession.

Curious, we asked how she knew. At the very moment we called, she had just finished praying a 15-decade rosary for the baby to turn!

The following week, I gave birth to a beautiful, healthy baby girl. We named her Miriam, in honor of our Lady.

Kathleen J. Happ   *Annapolis, Maryland*

Mary, the whole world reveres you
as the holiest Shrine of the living God,
for in you the salvation of the world
saw its dawning.
The Son of God was pleased
to take human form from you.
You have broken down
the wall of hatred—
the barrier between heaven and earth
which was set up by man's
first disobedience.
In you heaven met earth
when divinity and humanity
were joined in one Person,
the God-Man.

St. Bernard

The Rosary Will Bring Them Home

Going to a Catholic school for 12 years naturally gave me a chance to learn and practice the rosary. On Mother's Day and Father's Day especially, we tried to see how many rosaries we could say for our parent's special day. It was just a part of our life and our up bringing.

When I was out of school and working and living at home, it was my father, a convert, who really taught me how to appreciate my faith. My father had tremendous faith in the power of the rosary.

During World War II my two brothers-in-law, a cousin and my future husband were all overseas. My father told me he was going to get them back safely by saying a rosary a day for each one of them until they returned.

Even when my husband-to-be was a prisoner of war he told me not to worry, he would get him back to me, if it was God's will. Lots of times I would come home from work and he would be sitting in his rocking chair with the rosary in his hand.

I am proud to say they all returned home safely and my father lived long enough to walk me down the aisle when I was married. On the way down, he turned and smiled at me and said, "See, hon, I told you I would get him back for you."

He died the next year, but his spirit still lives in the hearts of my family, my grandchildren and even my great-grandchildren. My husband and I celebrated our fifty-fifth wedding anniversary this year. Thanks dad, for being such a wonderful role model and being there when I needed you.

Dorothy J. Donohoe   *Huntington, West Virginia*

O Mary,
may my heart never cease to love you,
and my tongue never cease to praise you.

St. Bonaventure

Rosary Power

About five months ago, I decided to start saying the rosary again, a practice I had neglected for a long time. For a fresh start, I even bought a new rosary. One afternoon, the power went out, so I decided to go out on the deck and pray the rosary. I started to make the sign of the cross—and bam! The power came back on. I have a new respect for the rosary. I wasn't even praying for power. Not that kind anyway! Hail Mary!

Jennie E. Desvignes   *Auburn, California*

The Healing Rosary

I was born on March 15, 1931, and live in Nova Scotia, Canada. The rosary has always been and still remains a big part of my life.

In March 1982, I discovered a lump in my breast and was horrified. I went to the doctor and he informed me I needed surgery immediately. Before the surgery, I had my rosary clutched tightly in my right hand and still had it when they wheeled me into the operating room. I had been given a sedative to prepare me for the anesthesia, which made me groggy.

As the doctors were preparing to put me to sleep, they noticed I still had my rosary clutched tightly in my hand and later told me that they had a little struggle to remove it. The surgery went fine, and I was informed that the lump itself was cancerous, but that I had no cancer.

I have been cancer-free for 19 years. Through the power of my prayers, and because my husband and daughter prayed and prayed for me before the surgery, I survived through the power of prayer.

Another occasion involves my oldest brother, who spent about 12 years in a nursing home prior to his death. I had come from a family of eight children, and our parents made sure we attended Mass and recited the rosary nightly during Lent, but as time went on my oldest brother became an alcoholic and left home. He had many bad experiences throughout his life, such as begging and sleeping in ditches.

Although he had been a very good person before his drinking began, and had served as an altar boy, he had forgotten his faith, finding himself in and out of jail. However, when he came to the nursing home, he ended up praying and always asked the nurses for his rosary.

He developed lung cancer, and as a family we stayed with him every day. He could not lift his arms at all and would make signs to us to go to his bedside to say the rosary.

At the time that he died, the family was with him, and as he was dying, he had his rosary in his hand. Staring at us, he managed to lift his rosary and look up at the ceiling. With all his might, he smiled a glowing smile and placed the rosary to his heart.

The nurse was watching and said, "He saw the face of the Blessed Virgin!"

Since all of my miraculous interventions on the part of the Blessed Virgin, I am very active in the Church. I am a Eucharist Minister and give communion to the sick. I play my guitar at Mass. My only child Sharon, an epileptic at the age of four, has now, through medication and prayers, become a reader at church.

Mrs. Marian Fitzgerald   *Yarmouth, Nova Scotia, Canada*

The heart of our good mother Mary
is all love and mercy.
She desires nothing else
but our happiness.
We need only have recourse
to her and we will be heard.
-St. John Mary Vianney

Thy Will Be Done

My 70-year-old mother Betty was dying of lung cancer. As a family, my father, Eddie (who was not even Catholic), along with my brother, Kevin, my sisters Susan and Betty Lee and I would pray the rosary with my mom as she lie in pain.

When she became incoherent, we still prayed together. The rosary united us in prayer and gave my mother the comfort she needed in those moments of pain, fear and expectation. It also provided us with a means of doing something at a time when we all felt helpless.

During one of these rosaries, I was suddenly struck by the meaning of "Thy will be done." I realized that God was in control and that He would help my mom and all of us according to what we needed best and most in our lives.

I didn't pray for healing for her, I prayed that His will be done—whatever that might be. I realized He knew best and would provide for each one of us what we needed. And He did. She died quietly in the early hours of November, 21, 1994. Her family all had the chance to be with her, to say how they felt about her and to let her know the depth of their love for her. Does it get any better than that?

Well, a little more than a month later, on Christmas Eve, I found my 69-year-old dad barely conscious in the house that he and my mother had shared. It was just three days before what would have been their 50th wedding anniversary. I just knew he wouldn't make it. I called an ambulance as well as my brother and sisters to get to the hospital. "Thy will be done."

My brothers and sisters all made it to the hospital as my father slowly slipped into a state of unconsciousness. We were numb as we awaited someone from the church to come. I had left a message, knowing how busy Christmas Eve is at St. Luke's, I was hoping that a deacon would make it out that evening. My dad was holding on…barely.

In walked our pastor, the man who visited our home during my mom's illness, who had gotten to know my dad through these visits. He told us that he had grabbed the items necessary for Baptism, then he asked, "Did your father ever express a desire to be baptized?"

As God orchestrates things, I sort of laughed and cried at the same time as I shared a conversation that I had had a few weeks prior with my dad. My dad was hospitalized with pneumonia after my mom passed on. While he was in the hospital I was asking him about what would we do with him if he died, since he wasn't baptized.

My brother and sisters can attest to this: if he was going to say no, it would have been "Hell, no, now leave me alone." However, he just looked uncomfortable and said that we'd talk about it. So I left it alone, figuring I had some time to get him to revisit this topic.

When Father Logan posed this question, I had to answer honestly and say, "He didn't say, 'Hell, no!' so I think it would be okay."

My brother and sisters agreed. At that, Father Logan took the baptismal water and said the prayers and blessed my daddy—and at that moment he flat lined and was gone. As pure as a babe just born! "Thy will be done."

It was a hard time after that for all of us, but our faith in God and His promise of eternal life keeps us all going. We pray the rosary, and our Hail Mary's and Our Father's have taken us through many a storm and will continue to do so. "His will be done."

Michele LaBarr-Haynes   *Rego Park, New York*
In Remembrance of Betty and Eddie LaBarr

Such is the greatness of Mary,
such the favor she has with God,
that he who when in need of help
would not run to her,
would wish to fly
without the aid of wings.

Pope Leo XIII

Safe in Mary's Hands

I pray the rosary daily; however, there is one particular day I will never forget. At that time, my 20-year-old daughter Jill was pregnant, in serious trouble, and about to leave town. A man she had met, and whom she hardly knew, was coaxing her to leave her family and come out to him in Nevada. This man was a gambler, and Jill's father and I feared he would try to get her into prostitution, since it is legal out there.

I convinced her to stay with me that evening, but when I awoke the following morning, I found a note saying she was leaving. She said that she loved me very much and I was not to worry, but I panicked and called her father and all her friends. Later that evening, when Jill's father spoke to this man, he was told that Jill was on a bus to Nevada.

Crying hysterically, I called from Ohio to my dear friend in Michigan who is also my "spiritual mother." My friend knew the whole story of Jill. She listened, then told me, "Let me call you back." After a little while she called and said, "I prayed about this and what comes to mind is you need to pray the rosary and consecrate Jill to Mary's Immaculate Heart." I hung up the phone and picked up my rosary. I climbed into bed (by this time it was quite late) and I started saying the rosary, sobbing. I was going with very little sleep at this point and I managed to get through two decades before falling into a deep, much needed sleep.

About 3 a.m. I suddenly awoke and jumped out of bed. I reread my daughter's letter. At the end of the letter I read these words that had not sunk into my head earlier. "Don't worry, I'm wearing my Miraculous Medal."

I laughed out loud, then thanked Mary. I got back into bed, finished saying my rosary, and fell asleep. The next morning I called Jill's father, who at this point was beside himself with worry. I told him not to worry, Jill was still here in town. He said, "How do you know that?" I told him I knew in my heart. Jill's father is not Catholic, but I told him, "I prayed about it and I have faith that she was still here." I got ready and went to Mass, feeling full of joy.

When I returned from Mass, I called her father. His wife answered, because Jill's father was on the cell phone talking to Jill! Jill was staying with one of her friends until her bus left that evening. Her father had only the phone number, and didn't know the address of Jill's friend. He was unable to convince Jill to let him pick her up and bring her home.

Eventually, my nephew, Carlo, came to the house. I managed to get Jill on the phone and Carlo convinced Jill to let him come and get her. He had guaranteed me he would have her home within 30 minutes if he could just speak to her. He made good on the guarantee!

When she came home, I asked her, "What made you not get on that first bus?"

She said, "I don't know. I had my ticket in my hand but I just couldn't go, so I exchanged the ticket for one for the following day."

The time she was about to board the bus the first time, is the exact time I had begun praying the rosary. Our Mother was truly watching over this daughter of mine. Oh Mary, conceived without sin, pray for us who have recourse to *You!!*

Karen I. Staubs   *Akron, Ohio*

*Men sometimes wonder
that we call her
Mother of life,
of mercy,
of salvation;
what are all
of these
compared
to that one name,
Mother of God?*
John Henry Cardinal Newman

Not Expected to Live

My husband had a severe heart attack and was not expected to live. I was devastated. He was only 47 years old.

Word got around the neighborhood very fast, and one of my friends arrived at the door.

She said, "C'mon and get the kids. We're going to say the rosary."

We sat down around the kitchen table and prayed the rosary. Following the rosary, my friend left without fanfare.

The next day when I arrived at the hospital, I was told there had been a great improvement during the night. Bob was going to live!

When I got home, the children were excited because there was a white dove sitting on the roof of our house. They were convinced it was the Holy Spirit bringing peace to our family.

Praise be to our Lady!

Beatrice C. Stroupe   *Charlotte, North Carolina*

Having confidence in you,
O Mother of God,
I shall be saved;
being under your protection,
I shall fear nothing;
with your help,
I shall give battle
to my enemies
and put them to flight;
for devotion to you
is an arm of salvation.

St. Peter Damian

The Flashing Yellow Light

Before my maternal grandmother died, she was bedridden for five years in our home but always had a rosary bead in her hands. My mother also eventually became bedridden, and had been for two years, and always kept her rosary in her hands, just like her mother.

On January 13, 1999, my grandmother's feast day, my mother and father were at home with my son. I was teaching at the junior college level, my second teaching assignment. I was to travel to a high school about 18 miles from home, and teach the classes there. I had never made the trip to Pleasant View before, but I knew Jesus and Mary would guide me.

The night was pitch black with fog and thick clouds. A nasty drizzle was coming down as I turned the key in the ignition of my car and asked the Holy Trinity to protect me on the trip. As soon as I hit the end of the driveway, I started my rosary tape.

Most of the road was newly paved, and I took it slow so I could be certain I would not miss my turn. It was a well-traveled road, and I met a lot of traffic.

I knew I was to turn at a flashing yellow light, but because of the fog, I saw it too late and missed my turn. I turned around at a nearby service station and onto the side street that I needed to be on—except that I was across the highway from where I needed to be.

If I went through the intersection with the flashing yellow light, I would be less than a quarter mile from the school, but the weather made crossing the intersection very hazardous. I was able to make out a very steep hill to my left as I looked for traffic.

I checked six times, once for each person of the Holy Trinity, and once for each person of the Holy Family. All was clear, so, still praying my rosary, I touched my accelerator.

I was only inches into the road when a car driven by a young woman came speeding over the hill. She smashed into the driver's side of the car, and my foot came off the accelerator. My car skidded and then bounced off her car.

What little momentum my car had was now gone. I was sitting by the side of the road, and her car was in the middle of the street. I immediately got out of my car and went to her car to see if she was all right. Another woman in a van stopped and called the police with her cell phone.

Through the grace of Jesus and his Holy Mother, no one was hurt. My car started, and again, through the grace of Jesus and His Holy Mother, all the damage to the cars was body damage and a missing headlight. My car had a dent in the back door and a dent in the side of the trunk.

The police arrived and attributed the accident to weather. The other driver, a young woman was very shook up and couldn't stop crying, so the police called her boyfriend who came and picked her up.

When the officer asked me whom he should contact for me, I told the officer he didn't need to call anyone. My father's eyes were bad, and he had trouble driving at night. However, when the officer checked my car, he couldn't get it started, and so the officer insisted on calling dad. I couldn't understand why my car wouldn't start again. I checked under the hood but nothing was loose.

Then it hit me: the inertia switch! Every Ford has an inertia switch that shuts down the gas line on impact to avoid explosion. The officer had no idea what I was talking about and gave me the impression that he thought I was inventing the "inertia switch." I went to the trunk of the car and began to feel around for the switch.

Just then, his partner came over and said, "Yeah, there's a switch right here."

He stuck his hand in the trunk, and a minute later the car was purring. The officer commented to me that I must have been through this several times, and I smiled and replied no. This was my first—and only—major car accident.

The officer shook his head and commented on how calm I was. I simply told him to listen and popped in my rosary cassette. He nodded his head. The officer then went to the school and informed the students that I would be there shortly. He and his partner still kept an eye on me until my father arrived to check on me. Then dad went back home, and I went on to the school.

The woman who hit me had no insurance, so it was three years before I found the cash to repair the body damage. During this time, it didn't bother me to drive a "wreck." I attribute my life and the life of the girl who hit me to the intervention of the Most Holy Rosary of the Blessed Virgin Mary. I also attribute the fact that the car started when I tried it to the intervention of the rosary. The gas line was already shut down and should not have started, but I believe it was simply our Lady's way of letting me know that the car could be driven and to remind me of the inertia switch in the trunk.

A year has passed since I finally had body work done. My friends tell me to get a new car, but every time I look at that car, I thank the Holy Trinity and The Holy Family for my life. When I drive it, I know exactly how blessed I am.

A few short months after the accident, I submitted my papers to join the Third Order Carmelites of Mary Immaculate. I have since been received and am in my third year of novitiate formation. I firmly believe I owe my life to The Holy Trinity and The Holy Family through the rosary. I depend on them both, simply because their will is always the same and you will never find one without the other.

Selene M. Anderson   *Clarksville, Tennessee*

I wish to go to Jerusalem,
if you will permit me,
to see the holy faithful who are there,
especially Mary, the Mother of Jesus,
who is said to be admired and loved by all.
For what friend of our faith...
would not be delighted to see and speak
to her who brought forth the true God?

St. Ignatius of Antioch

Mary's Love for Converts

Led by the Holy Spirit, my sister called one day and said I was to take a rosary and go to our local Catholic church to pray. I questioned why it had to be the Catholic church and what was a rosary. My dad had died a few months earlier, and I now realize that once he learned the truth, he was eager for all of us to know it, too.

My sister insisted it had to be the Catholic church, so I went and sat at the very back of the church around noon. Each day that I went, the more comfortable I felt and soon I was attending daily Mass and staying after to pray the rosary with others. I eventually was able to lead a mystery and walk up to receive a blessing from the priest. It was too late for me to join the RCIA program for that year, so I waited patiently for the next class to begin.

This extra time allowed me to develop an intense love for the Eucharist, Mary and His Divine Mercy. Of course, with the help of Mary I was able to join the Church during the first year of the three-year preparation for the Jubilee Celebration.

The year 1997 was year filled with many graces for my family. My sister, Jerri, was already Catholic, but my mom and other sister became Catholic just as I did, while we still wait on my brother to see the truth.

I say the rosary daily and am a substitute rosary leader at my parish. My love for Mary and the rosary is a huge gift from God. The proclamation by the Pope for this year of the rosary is such a blessing for all of us. Our loving Heavenly Mother has always wanted what is best for us.

I am the only Catholic in my immediate family, other than my step-granddaughter, Emily, who wanted, at the age of five, to go to church. My husband suggested I take her, and her parents agreed. She received her first Holy Communion last May, and her four-year-old sister will begin CCD classes this fall. My oldest step-grandson, Emily's cousin, has also expressed an interest in joining the Church.

When he visits, he goes to daily Mass with me and recites the rosary before each Mass.

I have given them all their own rosaries and know Mary is gently guiding them into the Church, just as she did for me. Since the age of six, Emily has gone in front of the parish on Sundays and led a mystery of the rosary at our monthly youth Mass.

Wendy L. Bolinger   *Vero Beach, Florida*

*Much of life must look complicated
before it is understood and
practiced—especially life on a
high level of civilization.
Take the ceremonial of eating:
the knives, forks, spoons, glasses,
napkins, finger-bowls.
Imagine a savage introduced
to all these for the first time
and then told that all this elaborate
business is used as the background,
the accompaniment, of social
intercourse, the exchange of ideas,
the gathering of friends.
"Much simpler," he might say,
"to have the talk without the food,
or the food without the ceremony."
Much simpler, certainly;
much less civilized.
The rosary is a very intellectual,
very civilized, form of prayer.
Once understood, it fascinates.*

Maisie Ward

Marian Memories

When I was a child, each night when our family of twelve retired for the night, we gathered together to say the rosary. We lived in a small town and farming community, and it was a practice in those days.

During the months of Mary—May and October—our church community gathered together for the exposition of the Blessed Sacrament and the veneration of the rosary. At school and through our mother we learned a lot about Mary, so much that we came to love her as our mother.

I remember walking one mile every evening during May and October to go to the church for the rosary. We were also told that saying three Hail Marys before falling asleep would assure us that Mary would be with us at the time of our death.

When I was a teenager, and away from home, something happened that I was not quite as faithful to the rosary as I had been when younger. But Mary was always with me, waiting for the day I would remember her.

I did return to Mary, and today I'm very grateful for the teachings I got from my family and the school I attended. Our church community was a big influence in those days, and today you don't see the Blessed Sacrament being exposed on the months of October and May to venerate the months of Mary.

Mary will always remain my protector and someone I can trust who will be with me always. Believe you me, I say my rosary every day, and I also ask Mary to pray for me at night when I'm sleeping.

Louise Moline   *Prince Albert, Saskatchewan, Canada*

*This prayer is perfect because of the praise
it offers, because of the lessons it imparts,
because of the graces it obtains, and
because of the triumphs it achieves.*

Pope Benedict XV

Six Cardiac Arrests

My husband Patrick is a retired police sergeant who served 32 years on the force.

In October 2000, we were in our favorite spot, Niagara Falls, Canada. We have been visiting there for 39 years and were visiting friends on this occasion.

The night before we came home, my husband had a massive heart attack in our hotel room. He suffered six cardiac arrests. The paramedic squad was there in three minutes and used shock paddles.

The hospital trauma unit said we would never get him home alive. I started begging our Lord and Padre Pio to let me keep him a bit longer. Pat was asking for a priest. We could not find a priest to come until the next day when a very beautiful priest came, and anointed Pat.

We got to bring him home ten days later, and when we arrived, Pat demanded to go to Mass. He had not been to Mass in over 40 years. I am so very thankful. Then lo and behold—Pat asked me for a rosary.

You cannot imagine the beautiful image I saw at Mass. This beautiful man, having given so much to so many, saying his rosary with such sincerity. It brings tears to my eyes, just reliving this story.

I think our Lord hears Pat's prayers, with a very loving heart. It seems to me sometimes our Lord has to hit us over the head to get our attention. I am so very grateful for the time we have had together, and I hope for much more. But as many of you know, I am sure our Lord and our Lady never do anything half way.

Barbara L. Barlow   *Reynoldsburg, Ohio*

When the Holy Rosary is said well, it gives
Jesus and Mary more glory and is more
meritorious than any other prayer.

St. Louis de Montfort

Told to "Make Rosaries!"

My miracles of the rosary began in 2001. I was very ill with an illness that medical science could not solve. I had numerous medical tests, including CT scans, abdominal x-rays, blood work-up, upper and lower GI series, colonoscopies, gastric scopes, gallbladder tests, liver scans. Nothing helped. All the doctors could offer me was narcotic pain medication to ease the pain. My life was totally consumed with trying to ease the pain. Depression and suicidal thoughts began to creep into my thinking. My husband Richard, unable to help, became as frustrated as I was with this illness. Our marriage began to suffer.

But my life was about to change. My husband was going to the Pentecostal church and happy with his faith and beliefs. I was raised a Southern Baptist, but had slipped away from that and tried other religions. Finally I just gave up on all of them.

But *miracle one* was about to happen. Unable to sleep, I got up early one morning and turned on the television while waiting for my tea water to heat. I was weak and in a lot of pain. I laid down on the sofa. The station that came on was EWTN. This irritated me but for some reason I did not change channels.

The "Rosary" came on and I listened to it, then the "Mass" came on. Again irritated, I listened. Finally the Mother Angelica show was on and I listened. This one I actually liked. I found her funny. By this time my husband woke up and he changed channels. I got up to make another cup of tea and just as I got to the kitchen doorway I heard a voice. It was so clear. A quiet, but insistent voice, it said "Make rosaries."

Realizing that strong pain medication can do strange things to the mind, I chalked it up to that. But twice more that voice spoke to me, and finally I decided to test this voice, as absurd as I thought it was. I turned on the internet and typed in *Make rosaries*. Up on the screen popped "Our Lady's Rosary Makers."

Before I called Our Lady's Rosary Makers in Louisville, Kentucky, I decided to tell them I didn't have any money, thinking that if they heard that they wouldn't send any rosary making supplies to me. Instead a lady with the sweetest voice answered the phone and asked me what type of rosaries I wanted to make, cord or chain ones? When I said I didn't know, she took my name, phone number, address, and gave me an ID number. When I asked her the cost she said it would be about $15.00. Now was my chance to tell her I didn't have any money! But she surprised me. She said, "That's okay, Honey, you have 30 days to pay for them and if you don't have all the money send whatever you can until it's paid off." I was so surprised, I don't even remember if I thanked her. She told me it would take a week to ten days for the supplies to arrive and to be patient.

The next morning the supplies were in my mailbox! This was the *second miracle*.

That week my husband Richard and I made over a hundred rosaries.

The *third miracle* was that I started to turn on the Rosary each morning and began to pray it still not knowing why I was doing it. By the end of nine days I was completely healed. I did not know what a Novena was at the time but I had just made one! On the 10th day I called our parish in Arcola and made an appointment to meet with Carol Bauer and Fr. Joe Allen to begin converting to the Catholic faith.

The *fourth miracle* was my husband's conversion. I had prayed for this for months. During the special Mass when I went through the Rite of Acceptance my Richard got up from the pew and went to Fr. Joe and Carol and said "I should have been up there with her!"

My husband and I went through the Rite of Election together in Springfield, Illinois. I was baptized, and we were both confirmed at the same time in 2002. Today Richard and I are Extra-Ordinary Eucharistic Ministers; we go to the Arthur Nursing Home and pray the rosary once a week. Together we conduct a Communion Service for the residents at the Home. We are both RCIA team members and soon to be Lectors in our church.

Kathryn M. Hillier   *Arthur, Illinois*

Mio Papa

My father, Alberto, was born in 1915 in San Martino di Lupari in the province of Padova, Italy. All his life, papa was a faithful man, a faith that he came by from his family.

In Italy, it was the law (as it still is) that every young man enter the military for at least two years. Before my father left for the army, my nonna, Adelina Gorgi, gave him a rosary to take with him so that he could pray as he encountered new experiences.

Papa followed his mamma's request, and he carried out his commitment in the army uneventfully. But just as he was finishing his term in the Berserglieri Corps, war broke out in Europe and papa was to remain in the army for a total period of ten years.

During WWII, my father was stationed in Africa and was under fire many, many times. In his pocket was the rosary that my nonna had given him, and when many men around him perished, he was left standing in the foxholes. Was it luck or was it the rosary? My Papa Alberto was sure it was the rosary.

Papa survived WWII with a piece of shrapnel embedded in his leg, which he carried for all of his life as a reminder. He ended up as a prisoner of war and then was released at the end to return home, grateful to have survived.

My father's life was very adventurous. He married after the war, started a family and then emigrated to Guelph, Ontario, Canada in 1951, with his young family, as did many Italians after the war. Papa was never a person to let grass grow under his feet. He started a construction company and always carried the rosary in his pocket.

On one particular construction sight, the rosary fell out of his pocket and went down into a deep wall. My father was very concerned and upset wondering how he was going to get his miraculous rosary out of the wall. Well, lo and behold—the wall fell, and he was able to retrieve it. No, he did not knock it down! He was sure it was the Virgin Mary that intervened.

On June 24, 1997, Papa Alberto passed away after a very successful life. My mother, Gemma, his life long companion of 50 years, saw to it that he was entombed with his beloved rosary that his mother had given to him, the rosary that saw him through many trials, tribulations and successes in life.

My father would be proud to have this in print as a testament to prayer and belief.

Mariella G. LeBeau   *Guelph, Ontario, Canada*

But when the little maid
of Nazareth uttered her fiat
to the message of the angel...
she became
not only
the Mother of God
in the physical order
of grace
she became
the Mother of all,
who...
would be made one
under the headship
of her
Divine Son.
The Mother of the Head
would be the Mother
of the members,
the Mother of the vine
the Mother of the branches.

St. Augustine

Devotion Above the Clouds

My wife and I were recently married in June 2002, and for our honeymoon, decided to make a pilgrimage to Medugorje and Lourdes. It was truly a blessing to be able to spend such a special time in the hands of our Lord Jesus, with the guidance of our Blessed Mother. Our time in these places greatly increased our devotion to the rosary. We knew we were taking back something special that had been written on our hearts.

We were faced with a 13-hour trip from Frankfurt to Singapore, and when you are 185 centimeters tall, it can be just a touch uncomfortable. My wife had the window seat, I had the middle seat, and beside me was a gentleman, who I think was doing his best to impersonate Crocodile Dundee. My claustrophobia was not helped by the gentleman's falling asleep on my shoulder, his arm and leg draped across me.

I turned to my wife after trying not to get affected by the situation, and said "I don't think I'm going to be able to cope with 13 hours of this!"

It may sound a touch humorous but I was getting quite distraught and very upset. In fact, I was becoming quite annoyed with the gentleman, and the whole situation.

My wife took her rosary beads from her bag and started praying for me. I too, took out my rosary beads and also started praying. My intention was for just a little bit of room to breathe.

After the first decade I noticed that my tension and worry disappeared and was replaced with a peace and calmness. As I remembered what my rosary intention was, the Crocodile Dundee gentleman removed his arm from across my shoulder and chest, and placed it behind his head, with his elbow pointing to the overhead lockers.

Filled with joy, I then asked our Lady if she wouldn't mind very much, to get the gentleman to move his leg as well. Sure enough, he rolled his leg to the aisle side, with his elbow still pointing upwards. He slept through the whole thing. I think a contortionist would have been proud of his position.

I turned to my wife with such a happiness and peace in my heart, and we both praised the Lord for the goodness He shows to us, through our Blessed Mother, even those many miles above the clouds.

John W. Duiker   *Narre Warren Sth, Victoria, Australia*

My being proclaims the greatness of the Lord;
my spirit finds joy in God my savior.
For He has looked upon His servant
in her lowliness;
all ages to come
shall call me blessed.
God who is mighty
has done great things for me,
holy is His name.
His mercy is from age to age
on those who fear Him.
He has shown might with His arm;
He has confused the proud
in their inmost thoughts.
He has deposed the mighty
from their thrones
and raised the lowly to high places.
The hungry He has given every good thing,
while the rich He has sent empty away.
He has upheld Israel His servant,
ever mindful of His mercy,
even as He promised our fathers,
promised Abraham and his descendents
forever.

Luke 1:46-55

All Is Well

I became well acquainted with the Blessed Mother when I was pregnant with my second child. In the fifth month of my pregnancy, I slipped down two concrete steps and knocked myself out.

The x-rays revealed that my baby had an enlarged head (hydrocephalus) from the fall and were going to allow us a medical abortion. I would not hear of it and fought for my unborn child. I attended Mass daily and learned to say the rosary.

As I went into labor, and delivery was imminent, the obstetrician decided he would not be part of this "bad birth" and walked out. The nurse went out into the hall and nabbed another doctor. He was upset because I would not be "put out" and wanted to have the baby naturally.

As the birth progressed, I began to pray the rosary, and there, standing in back of the doctor was the Blessed Mother, smiling at me with her hands on the doctor's shoulders. She nodded "all is well," and the doctor reached up and patted her hand and thanked her for coming.

Never had the doctor and I met, yet we both felt her presence and knew that all really was well: blessed are thou among women and blest is the fruit of her womb, Jesus.

And all was well. I delivered an eight-pound, six-ounce, beautiful baby boy with *no* big head. Today he is a fabulous 33-year-old man. Only with prayers and in faith believing did this turn out to be a true miracle of God.

Rosemary J. Hanley   *Springfield, Missouri*

***Mary is
the Mother of God,
Mother of Jesus
and our mother,
Mother of the Church.***
Mother Teresa of Calcutta

He Pled Guilty

Something wonderful and life changing happened to my son Thomas, and it is still changing the lives of many who knew him…and even some who didn't know him.

Thomas knew all about the dangers of alcohol, but he couldn't accept that his Native American/Scots-Irish background would make him an addict so quickly. Somehow he thought you had to be "old" to be addicted.

Thomas found out about addiction first hand. He started drinking at eight years old. He would sneak his Dad's beers and then later with his friends he would try out whatever they had.

When Thomas was thirteen years old, his dad and I had the final judgment of divorce—and Thomas joined a gang that day.

Just as he couldn't foresee what addiction could do to his life, he also couldn't foresee what damage could be done to himself, his family and his community by being a gang member. What followed was a nightmare. I won't give you the details, but I want to tell you of the change that Thomas had in his life.

Thomas had a very "tough" exterior. His facial expressions were hard and his attitude was unbending. But that changed on the day that he stood before the same judge who had seen him so many times before.

The courthouse was empty. His was the only case being heard that day. His defense lawyer had walked out of the courtroom and off his case, calling him a "punk" and suggesting that the judge just lock him up and throw the key away. He suggested that I should just forget that I had a son called "Thomas," cut my losses and get on with my life with my other children.

I told him that because I was a mother, I couldn't forget my son Thomas, and I asked him to pray with me for Thomas. He just laughed.

On this particular day, with no other cases, Thomas knew he had everything going against him. The judge had ordered his defense lawyer to represent him or be in contempt of court. The prosecution had already made a deal with Thomas on a previous case and had dropped some of the charges. But then Thomas went back on his word to testify. So they were ready to get him this time.

He was faced with being adjudicated as an adult and facing serious charges. When the judge asked him how he pled—much to everyone's surprise—he pled "guilty." Even his lawyer was baffled. Thomas went on to explain that he was an addict and that he couldn't be trusted with freedom.

34

He then prayed the Our Father and the Hail Mary and as his tears (he *never* cried) fell to the floor, the prosecution and defense started making incredible changes in his charges.

The final part was when the judge sentenced him to a drug rehab program, against Thomas' wishes. He just wanted to be locked up, and the key thrown away, but the lawyers for the prosecution and for the defense told the judge that they had confidence in him, and the judge agreed that he had what it took. Even the court transcriber was crying, and Thomas told them that he would not let them down.

At the detention center, as he awaited a placement in a rehab program, he volunteered for kitchen duty, something that he would never have done at home.

During one of my visits with him, he showed me the big heavy metal bases of the tables where they ate their meals. He explained that when he mopped the floor after meals, some of the strings would come off the mop and get caught around the bases of the tables. He would pick them up and put them in his pocket and later, back at his bunk, he would dry them out after he had made them into a one-decade rosary, which he then used to teach the other guys how to pray it. They all had their rope rosaries hanging on their bunks.

On another day that I visited, before he left for his program, one of the other offenders came to our table with his mother. She told me that she wanted to thank Thomas for saving her son's life. Her son had told her of an incident where the other guys in a different module had tormented her son to the point that he tried to commit suicide, and the guys kept pushing him to do it.

The staff removed him and put him in a padded cell after they had stripped him down. But he tried to put his head in the toilet he was so determined to die.

Thomas heard about the situation and asked the staff to give him a pair of underpants for the boy to preserve his dignity and let him into the cell. Thomas calmed the boy and told him that he would be his guardian while he was there and would do what was needed to work with the staff and stop the harassment. This worked and the boy was able to leave the lockdown and there was no more harassment. And Thomas prayed with him every day.

When Thomas left the detention center to go to the program, he told his "homies" that he would be back but "not in chains." He kept his promise. He became the main speaker for a program that addressed the problems of youth. He spoke to thousands.

The judge who sentenced him took time off from the bench to sneak into the detention center to listen to Tom talk to his "brothers from another mother." He would tell the young offenders:

"You are not just a bunch of black fingerprints. You are not just a statistic, you are the future and I believe in you. I will be right there with you as you get an education, turn your life around, have a family, because I am your brother and I love you. And I will keep coming back, and if only one person listens to what I'm saying, then my life is worthwhile."

Thomas had found out when he arrived at the drug program that some of his rival gang bangers were there and out to "get him." After a confrontation on arrival, Thomas ripped off his shirt and, showing his "tattoos," told the group that he "spit on these tattoos, and spit on his colors, and spit on everything that prevented them from being "brothers."

Both Thomas and the other guy were told to "take a walk and calm down." When they met up in the courtyard outside, the clenched fists and clenched jaw of the other boy gave a clear message to Tom.

As the boy turned on his heel to walk the other way, Tom jumped him from behind with his arms tight around him, preventing the boy from lashing out. Tom kept shouting over and over, "You can't stop me loving you!"

When he released the boy, and they both stood looking at each other, something "clicked" and the boy and Tom hugged as the others looked on from behind the classroom windows.

This became Tom's new weapon…backed by the rosary.

Thomas died at age 17 in an automobile accident, and for two days the church was full: ex-gang members, rival gang members, six priests, and two monsignors concelebrated his Funeral Mass and the judge who had sentenced him gave the eulogy.

The judge has since written to me saying that if he can accomplish just a small part of the good that Tom did in his short life that he will be a happy man.

Thomas openly embraced those who used to be his enemies. The local newspaper carried his story on the front page. Thomas had made a commercial for television, which was aired two days before he died, so the television aired his story in part.

He consistently spoke out against abortion as a violence worse than any war or gang violence. He even followed a Planned Parenthood speaker at The Boys and Girls Club with the aid of fetal models that he passed around. He held one on high, shouting, "Does this look like a blob of tissue to you? It looks like a baby to me."

He got a standing ovation from the youngsters that day, and they crowded our Prolife Information Table for literature and just to talk to him. The Planned Parenthood booth was left to the woman who presented their program.

Many of the young people he hung with were victims of abortion propaganda, but he helped them to see that it was really a life, and that no one had the right to take a life. Only God had that right.

He encouraged couples who were living together to get married. They still come by my house to show me their new babies or tell me they're still going to church.

Tom had signed up to go to college and wanted to be a drug and alcohol counselor when he graduated. He wanted to get married and have a family. He had hopes for the future, but he told me many times that he didn't think he would live to see eighteen.

The night before he died, one of his friends asked him as they watched a television movie, "Tom, if you were to die today, where do you think you would go"?

Thomas said, "I know I've not been an angel, but if I die today, I believe I would go to heaven because I really believe in Jesus Christ."

They had nicknamed him "Preacher Man."

Tom always loved children. Two hours before he died he had been playing with a friend's toddler. He loved to play basketball, or football. He loved to toss and catch the football. That was what he used to do before he got caught up in a world of guns, drugs and drink, and living in the fast lane.

But that fateful day he returned to the innocent game of his childhood. When he left with his sixteen-year-old friend to move the furniture of a friend whose house had flooded, he was wearing his scapular. And when his friend's truck hydroplaned on the wet curve in the street and ended at the light pole, I believe that God saw his very best quarterback, and decided he deserved a broader field, because Tom had greater games to play.

Since his death, five little boys have been named after him, some who might have been aborted if their parents had not heard Tom's message: "No one has the right to take a life."

Many make visits to his grave where they look at his picture on the headstone and in looking into his eyes, they see themselves more clearly. As a result, some have asked for help to get off the drugs and alcohol and entered programs. Others leave their gang colors or their addictive substance with a note that they are finally listening to his message and are "laying it down and doing the right thing."

I put a mail box up by his grave because I was getting all these notes that were left there, asking Tom to help them, or from parents asking Tom to help their teens and then the thank you notes for prayers answered.

On All Souls Day, we had a prayer service and a Blessing of the Graves of our loved ones after the morning Mass and a family from three rows back came and told me that they had left prayers and that they had been answered.

I showed them Tom's friend who is also buried close by. He was shot by the police, but he had put his scapular on the night before, telling his friend that he felt he should wear it because Tom had his on when he died.

I had given out scapulars and rosary beads at Tom's funeral and so I did the same at this young man's funeral, and I have already ran across some who took them and have had a "turn around" in their lives.

Our Lady told St. Dominic that one day she would save the world, through the rosary and the scapular. I have witnessed this reality in the lives and deaths of those young people so despised by society but so loved by God and His Blessed Mother.

Both their headstones have our Lady of Guadeloupe and the Divine Mercy and the rosary and scapular hanging around the necks of the statues placed there as a witness to the power of *love*. I can still hear him shout out: *"You can't stop me loving you."*

I was the director of a crisis pregnancy center when Tom died, and as I was typing this post, my eye caught the short article that I had written two years after he died. It shows how Tom's mission isn't over. It is titled "Her Worst Suspicions and Dreams Came True":

"I hope it's just the flu, I'm too old to have another baby, my kids are grown. I just kicked my husband out, he's a junkie, plus my daughter has been acting strange lately. I have this gut feeling that she might be pregnant. I'm gonna bring her with me and she can have a test also."

When they were filling out the "intake forms," the teenage daughter asked her mother what she should write for the question: "Abortion—Adoption—Parent." Her mother let her know that a baby wasn't an option for either of them.

While we waited for the test results, I shared some of my past family problems, and how God had turned things around for the good. I showed them a short clipping of a video that Thomas had made before he died, and that is when I found out that the mother knew my son. Thomas was friends with one of her sons.

She then realized that God had a plan for her baby, just as He had for my son. When her daughter's test showed "positive" also, she had already decided for life.

Her daughter has become her mother's best friend and helper in the caring and raising of the two infant children. She has improved her grades at school, and her mother has custody of her new grandchild.

We are happy for the outcome and also for the ongoing contact with them.

Rose Mary Danforth   *Jax, Florida*

The greatest method of praying
is to pray the Holy Rosary.
Saint Francis de Sales

A Sign of Love

I was very active in the Church when I was younger, then I met a divorced man who was non-Catholic. We fell in love and married with the stipulation that he would get an annulment.

My husband tried twice early in our marriage to get the annulment but was never successful. It just kept getting blocked. We never reached the stage where witnesses were requested, much less getting to the tribunal.

After two attempts, my husband gave up. He was in the military, so we worked with a number of priests everywhere we were stationed, but the result was always the same. I was devastated because I couldn't fully participate in the Church anymore, and it just seemed like I would never be able to again.

My husband became bitter. He really wanted to become a Catholic but couldn't without having the first marriage annulled. I, too, became bitter and left the Church.

Six years ago I started to pray the rosary again on my lunch hours. Three years later, I walked into St. Cecilia's Cathedral because a friend who was an artist had invited me there to view her art show in the back of the church.

I walked into the church and "Wow!"—did the Holy Spirit grab me and turn me around! I began going to church and decided to speak with the pastor about trying the annulment again.

The pastor informed me that I could not receive Holy Communion or get absolved of my sins through confession, and I was an emotional and spiritual mess. I sunk so low that I cried all that day and night, clutching my white first communion rosary and praying it.

The next morning I got up and looked at that rosary, which is over 40 years old. The links had turned golden.

I started to cry again because I realized that God really does love me and that maybe I wasn't such a horrible person after all.

My husband tried again to have his first marriage annulled. It was very slow going, but finally after four months the paperwork got off the pastor's desk and into the chancellery office, then on to a diocese in Florida. After three years, the annulment was approved.

We received the Church's blessings on November 22, 2002, St. Cecilia's feast day. (My husband picked the date not knowing how special that date is to me!)

During the past three years, I've had two more rosary's links turn to gold. It would happen when I started getting depressed about the annulment process, when I would sometimes think, "Oh, God, I must be a very bad person to not be able to receive Holy Communion or to be absolved of my sins."

Turning the links to gold was God's way of telling me that He really does love me and that I wasn't a horrible person after all.

I pray the rosary every day, sometimes with several friends. I am now praying for my husband's conversion into the Church. I'm always amazed the way my prayers and questions are answered while praying the rosary. I love praying the rosary, and I will always pray it because it makes me feel so wonderfully connected to Jesus and our Lady.

My husband and I have now been married 22 years, and we are blessed with a 10-year-old little boy who has Down syndrome.

And it feels so good to be fully back in the Church. I am so thankful.

Carol Pettis   *La Vista, Nebraska*

If you wish to convert anyone
to the fullness of our Lord
and of His Mystical Body,
then teach him the rosary.
One of two things will happen.
Either he will
stop saying the rosary—
or he will get the gift of faith.

Most Reverend Fulton J Sheen

The Rosary Is for Everyone

My church is in a covenant with two Protestant churches next door. We pray for each other weekly and sometimes share interfaith services during the seasons of Advent and Lent.

This past summer my pastor said that he had a request from the Protestant church next door for him to send over someone to say the rosary one day a week with some of the people in their elderly day-care program. Since I was unable to do this, my pastor asked me if I could make any suggestions.

I recommended my friend Liz to him. She is a convert to our faith and is very dedicated and involved in our parish.

She accepted, and I thought this was great! A few days before she was to say the rosary with this group, I received a phone call from Liz. Apparently she had never been taught how to say the rosary and asked me if I could help her.

The only time we both had available was a half-hour time slot after she dropped her daughter off for swimming lessons.

I agreed to meet her in the pool parking lot, and I taught her how to say the rosary. What a joy it was to be able to pass on this beautiful prayerful devotion to our Blessed Mother! And to know that through this way it would also be passed on to others.

She informed me later that all went so well that not only their Catholic patrons said the rosary with her, but some of the Protestants also recited the prayer.

Doris A. Forster   *Warwick, Rhode Island*

The Rosary is the most powerful weapon
to touch the Heart of Jesus,
our Redeemer, who so loves His mother.

St. Louis de Montfort

New Age and Beyond

This story goes back to my mother, who was raised Catholic and had a typical teenager's life. She married at an early age, and I was born when she was just nineteen. Possibly due to the deaths of many relatives in a very short period, she fell away from the faith, believing that some how all those deaths were her fault.

Many years, and two children later, she filed for divorce. It was during this time, that she and a friend got into the New Age Movement. This phase went on for a couple years I believe. The only thing of interest to this story that I remember, is one time when I felt in trouble and I pulled out my rosary that I had from my first communion I had made earlier that year. I remember the woman with whom we were living asking me, "Why are you bothering with that?" But somehow, in my young innocence, I think I knew that this was something I had to do. That's the last time I remember praying the rosary for a while, however.

Mom met someone, and married him three times. The first time was a "new agey" sort of ceremony at home, the second time was a couple years later, in the court, and the last time (and the one that counts) comes later on. This man eventually "adopted" me and my two siblings (please note our last name at the end of the story).

It was some time after this, that two major things happened. First, mom started realizing that she needed something more to make her life complete. At the same time, her mother, my grandmother, told her that she did not love her. That night my mom cried out to Mary, and told her, "You are my mother". So, in the transition from "New Age" to the right path, mom and I first acquired an interest in the angels, and speaking to them. Then, one morning on a talk show styled TV show, there was a "faith healer" who did the laying on of hands, etc. A little bit of searching got us to the healing service of a Charismatic Healer. It was at the first service we attended, that mom picked up rosaries and a copy of the book *The Secret of the Rosary* by St. Louis Marie DeMontfort.

That evening mom and we children prayed the rosary. Dad would have no part of it since, although he was born and baptized Catholic, he was raised Pentecostal. Mom made plans to have our home entrusted to the Sacred and Immaculate Hearts, and surprisingly, after many prayers, when the time came, dad was present for it. During this time we returned to Confession and Mass. Eventually, dad began sitting in on our evening rosary. Our Lady was pulling us along now, on the right path, using a rope, a chain, of 59 beads.

But the story does not end there. After being in the Church for awhile again, mom found out that, to make everything right, she was going to have to get an annulment. Mom and dad were almost forced out of the life of the Church, while this process took place. We still prayed the rosary during this process, went to Mass, and otherwise practiced our religion. Our Lady always intercedes with her son for her children, and although the process should've taken *years*, the final decree was received by mail in less than a year. The first marriage was declared invalid on the feast of our Lady of Guadelupe, and a week later mom and dad's marriage was blessed by the Church.

Dad attended RCIA in the meantime, and that year, I was blessed to receive the Sacrament of Confirmation, along with my dad.

We as a family try very hard now, to be pleasing to our Lord; my brother feels very called to the priesthood and so far has been blessed with the gift of being an excellent altar boy. We now have an internet apostolate to make strong, handmade rosaries at a reasonable price, so anyone can afford a rosary that will last a long time, since during conversion we went through many rosaries! I still have the broken pieces of my first communion rosary, the one that started it all for me personally.

I am now 21 years old, and I think that being the oldest child has also been a blessing to me, to witness the good and the bad in our family's journey, and to be able to recall it, for myself and others to whom God wants to make it known.

Danielle Rosario   *Chicago, Illinois*

I Needed to Pray

I was going through some very rough times in my personal life about a year ago last September. I just felt like something was missing. I had been on Prozac and was constantly crying all the time.

One Saturday I was cleaning out an old jewelry box and came across a rosary my Aunt Rita had bought me several years before. My father had passed away suddenly ten years before, and I needed a rosary to lead our family in prayer at his wake. So my aunt had bought it for me. I hadn't touched it since. I had put it away and forgot about it.

I had fallen away from my Catholic life several years before and had not looked back. But as I stood in the bedroom with that rosary in hand I felt like I needed to pray it…*right then.*

There was such urgency that it scared me. Of course, I remembered the Hail Mary and Our Father but had forgotten the rest. The next day I called my mom and asked her to send me some information on how to say the rosary. I think I scared her because she wanted to know why I wanted it, and I told her how I felt when I held the rosary in my hand.

My mother was going to send me information the following day, but she happened to talk with a friend at work who had information on the rosary in her car. Mom promptly sent it out.

The next day was Sept. 11, 2001, I don't need to tell you what happened. I cried the whole day, thinking someone was warning me to pray before anything had happened. I hadn't been to church in thirteen years, but I heard that a local church was having a rosary service the next day.

At noon the following day, I found the church, walked up the steps and felt like I had come home. I prayed the rosary, with no card to help me and remembered every word. I cried and sobbed and felt Mary right next to me the whole time.

There was a lady sitting next to me who hugged me when all was done. She had no idea who I was. I guess she just felt she needed to do this for me. I left and that day changed my life. I found a parish near my house and went to church that Sunday. I am very active in my parish and still get that coming-home feeling every time I walk up those steps.

I know Mary was talking to me. My mother told me on the phone the night that I had asked her for the prayer cards that something very blessed was going to happen to me. And my rosary would help me get through anything.

This year I sent my mother a rosary for her birthday. And I still feel something special when I hold my rosary and always will.

Laurelle T. Guck   *Mill Creek, Washington*

The Secret of the Rosary

*Both Saint Bernard
and Saint Bonaventure say
that the Queen of Heaven
is certainly no less grateful
and conscientious than
gracious and well-mannered
people of this world.
Just as she excels in all
other perfections, she
surpasses us all in the
virtue of gratitude;
so she would never let us
honor her with love and respect
without repaying us one
hundredfold.
Saint Bonaventure says
that Mary will greet us
with grace if we greet her
with the Hail Mary.*

The Motorcycle Accident

I am not a cradle Catholic. In fact, I started RCIA classes on September 10, 2001. My baptism and confirmation were on Pentecost of 2002. To say that I still have a lot to learn about my faith is an understatement; however, Catholicism has called to me for many years. It soothes my soul like no other religion.

Several years ago a friend and coworker was critically injured in a motorcycle accident. He suffered extensive head injuries and was not expected to live. As I sat at home weeping and trying to think of something I could do, I saw the rosary beads that I keep in my purse. At the time, all I knew about the rosary was the words. So, I picked up those beat-up black beads and began to say the rosary, praying to God, Mary, or any one who would hear my prayer to save my friend's life. I remember how my heart ached as I said it, how desperately I begged for my friend's recovery. The next day I visited him in the Emergency Room at the Hospital. He was unconscious and never knew I was there. He had road rash over most of one side of his body. His head was bloody and swollen from a closed head injury.

Miraculously, five days later he was in a room and was functioning independently. When I walked in, he recognized me, and we talked for quite awhile. Today, he still has some short term memory loss, but leads a "normal" life. The doctors did not think he would survive his injuries, but he did. Many people were praying for him. It is my humble wish that somehow my uninformed, but heartfelt rosary contributed to his recovery. I know that Mary heard me that night.

Marsha Stewart   *Fort Worth, Texas*

**Continue to pray
the rosary every day.**
Our Lady of Fatima to Lucia

Rosary Website Opens the Door

During the late 1960s, I was a young adult in college in San Jose, California. I converted to Catholicism but later fell away from the Church due to some disagreement I've long since forgotten.

Thirty years later, I seemed to have hit a spiritual bottom and could no longer face life as it'd been to that point. I found some on-line Catholic websites, printed out some prayers and began using them. They helped.

Then, I found a website about the rosary. I had a rosary I'd been given at my confirmation that I'd never used, so I began to pray the rosary. It helped me tremendously, and continues to do so, but only after I began to pray it daily.

Our Blessed Mother led me, through the rosary, back to her son and to the Church. I attended my first Mass in 30 years in late 1998 at Sacred Heart in Lancaster, California, after completing my first confession in 30 years. I remember that the gospel reading that day was about the Prodigal Son who came home. I was the prodigal daughter who had come home.

Today, the rosary is the most important prayer in my life, and Father Peyton's rosary prayer book has helped me learn how to contemplate the mysteries while praying the rosary. I begin my days with the rosary. It works better for me at the start of my day. My days go better that way.

The rosary helps me in ways I cannot describe. Earlier this year, I joined the Legion of Mary, which is helping me help others discover the same possible experience in their own lives through the rosary and the Church.

My mother died less than six months after my return to the Church. I don't know how I would have gotten through that experience without the spiritual strength and help I have gotten from the daily rosary and my active participation in the Church.

Darlene Lister   *Lancaster, California*

Kathy's Heart Attack

I belong to Our Lady of Mount Carmel Catholic Church in Newport News, Virginia. On Monday, December 2, 2002, I received a phone call from a friend from St. Elizabeth's Guild. Kathy Champion, a member of our guild, had suffered a massive heart attack while at work as a hair stylist at JC Penney's Styling Salon. I immediately got on the phone to ask the ladies in our guild to begin praying. I also went "on-line" and sent an e-mail asking for urgent prayers for Kathy.

Kathy had suffered massive heart failure without any warning. There were three clients in the salon; two of them were nurses. This was the first miracle. Kathy was in full arrest and they immediately began CPR. They continued CPR for ten minutes until the paramedics arrived. The paramedics attempted to revive Kathy for another 15 minutes and then transported her to the hospital. Kathy is 41 years old without any history of heart problems and we were all stunned. When someone has what they call a "sudden death" heart attack CPR must begin within two to three minutes or the person will not recover and most likely die.

On Tuesday evening some of the ladies of our guild met at my house at 9:00 p.m. to pray the rosary for Kathy's complete recovery. We told everyone if they couldn't pray with us in person to please pray the rosary at 9:00 and join us in spirit. We prayed for her to wake up so the doctors could assess her condition. Her family was at her side at the ICU unit at Hampton General Hospital. Kathy was in grave critical condition and unresponsive.

On Wednesday morning we received our second miracle. Kathy finally woke up, she was sitting up in bed and talking and asking for her father who stepped out of the room for a moment. She was very confused but she was awake! The doctors and the paramedics who transported Kathy to the hospital could not believe she was awake—a friend of mine who works at the hospital said that she had performed her CAT scan as soon as

Kathy was brought in and no one who saw her when she arrived at the hospital expected her to live. Our prayers were answered!

It was determined that Kathy's condition can be treated with medication and a defibrillator. I believe we received our third miracle since they were able to determine that the problem isn't life-threatening and is treatable. It has almost been a month since Kathy's heart attack. She is still not herself but each day she continues to improve. We believe that our prayers, especially our praying of the rosary contributed to her healing and we continue to pray for her full and complete recovery.

Paula F. Krewinghaus   *Yorktown, Virginia*

We are tossed on the tempest of the sea,
the sea which threatens to swallow us up.
Amid the winds of temptation
and the waves of tribulation,
we dread judgment
and fear because of our sins.
And sometimes we are plunged
into the gulf of sadness
as the anguish of doubt assails us.
Then,
let the name of Mary,
Star of the Sea,
be on your lips and in your heart.
She will sustain you
and give you hope.
By her help
you will reach
the port of safety.

St. Bernard

Healed Through a Rosary Novena

For 17 years I suffered from a type of migraine headache. It seemed that every year the pain would last longer and intensify. I saw many doctors who tried many techniques but to no avail. Medicine did not help.

A friend told me to ask our Blessed Mother for relief during times of pain. One night I woke up with a severe headache. Since I could not sleep, I went downstairs into the living room sat on the couch, took out my rosary and asked our Blessed Mother to please help me.

When the rosary was done, the headache was gone. I went back to bed and while I was lying there, I smelled the scent of roses. This was when I knew Mary came through for me that night.

However, I still continued to have headaches at least once each month. The headaches traveled from one side of my head then the other and lasted from two to three days.

On Christmas 1986 I had a terrific headache. The next day I decided to do a rosary novena. I asked Mother Mary if she would ask Jesus to heal me of my migraines. I promised that if she did and that if they went away, I would tell everyone I could about how she helped me.

I have not had a migraine headache since Christmas 1986. I said a rosary of petition for seven days, without realizing that a novena was for nine days. Before I even knew that the headaches were gone, I immediately followed the first novena with a rosary of thanksgiving for seven days. I still thank Mary, and, at every opportunity I have, I tell everyone how she helped me.

Maryann Boaden   *Toledo, Ohio*

There is no surer means of calling down
God's blessings upon the family...
than the daily recitation of the rosary.

Pope Pius XII

Help Up the Hill

On a cold and very snowy night a few years ago I was on my way to work at Sacred Heart Hospital. I was scheduled to be there at 11 p.m.

The roads were very slippery and had not been plowed, so I decided to drive my little blue Volkswagen Bug because it seemed to be much easier to drive during this winter weather. As I drove very carefully into town, I was fervently saying my rosary. I often pray the rosary, but even more so when I'm worried.

Things went fairly well, and as I arrived at the bottom of a hill, I noticed several cars stopped and parked at all different angles. I assumed they had tried to go up the hill but were unable to make it. I waited a bit as several cars tried again but were also unsuccessful. Oh dear, what to do? One more car, a pretty red sports car, tried to get up the hill.

As I watched, something in my mind was saying if he can do it, so can you. He didn't make it, but I figured I'd give it a try. With my rosary clutched very tightly in my left hand we started up.

I don't know for sure if our Holy Mother was working the gas peddle or the steering wheel, but we made it. I was very shaky, but thanks to my Holy Mother, I made it to work on time.

Mary Ann Colon   *Spokane, Washington*

The holy rosary is a gift
come down from heaven;
a great present that God gives
to His most faithful servants.
God is the Author of the prayers
of which it is composed
and of the mysteries it contains.

St. Louis de Montfort

Linked by the Rosary

Recently my e-mail friend, Sean, celebrated a birthday. Sean is a Catholic man who makes rosaries. He is a devoted husband and the father of three children.

After his birthday celebrations had ended, Sean sent an e-mail to the rosary-talk e-mail group, telling us all about how wonderful his day had been. He included in his e-mail a description of the gift that one of his children had given to him.

She had, without any assistance from anybody, sat down and planned out and created a rosary just for her daddy. She created it with twine, using overhand knots and hand-crafted the center and the cross from paper. A simple little rosary that most people probably wouldn't look at twice, but to Sean it was better than chocolate.

The reason I wanted to share this was to illustrate how the rosary can be the chain that binds a family together. Sean makes rosaries, his young daughter has noted this and realized just how important the rosary is to him. As the gift from her heart, she sat down and made him a rosary that I have absolutely no doubt he will treasure for the rest of his life. There is beauty in this.

I understand this common bond between family members and the sharing of the rosary. I related to Sean how my own daughter Amy loves the rosary. Amy and I love to sit down together and create rosaries. Amy makes simple cord rosaries using beads and tying a simple overhand knot between each bead. She makes some of her own centers and crosses from polymer clay, and she uses some of the metal centers and crucifixes that I purchase as well. She gives her rosaries away to other children.

As we sit and work together, we talk about so many things, everything from what to have for lunch or dinner, to what Jesus' sacrifice really meant for humankind. We talk about how cats see or how radio works, and we marvel at this world that God has given us. Together, we strengthen both our faith and our relationship during these quiet but productive times.

When Amy was born, her father, Koji, and I were practicing Buddhists. When my new husband, Isaac, and I returned to the Catholic Church, Amy's father asked me only one thing: that I let Amy decide for herself if she wished to attend Mass, receive the Sacraments, or pray.

Although Amy has never practiced any religious faith (Koji and I stopped practicing Buddhism when Amy was a few months old), she somehow developed a very strong belief system of her own during her earliest years. I will never forget my four-year-old coming to me, her then pagan mother, and telling me that Jesus died for us and that God loves everybody.

She certainly didn't get that from me, and I still wonder to this day where she picked it up from. But somehow she did, and somehow she was a Christian long before my own faith was reawakened.

At the Easter vigil of 2001, my Amy was welcomed to the Sacraments by our two beloved parish priests. She burst into tears as Father Joe baptized her, and again as Father Dan gave her her first Eucharist. It was an amazing day, and the joy of that day has stayed with us ever since. Even Amy's father is amazed at her depth of faith, and supports her completely.

These days, Amy attends Mass with me each week. She prays a rosary with me four or five times a week, and she prays with me each morning and night. I know that she also prays the rosary when she is at her father's house. This is all of her own volition, and I firmly believe that much of her desire to do these things stems from our rosary making time together, and the discussions we share during those times.

For my husband Isaac and I, the rosary has been a central part of our daily life together almost since the beginning of our marriage two years ago. We don't often pray it together, because we each have our own times that we prefer to pray our rosaries. But we make a point to occasionally "tell our beads" together, and it is a wonderfully warm and close time, something that helps strengthen our relationship with each other and with God.

As our family has grown in the last few years, bringing my new husband Isaac into the meld, as well as a stepmother and step-siblings for Amy, we have spent much time in family prayer. I sincerely believe that this prayerful time has helped us to hold each other close in heart even when separated in body. It has helped us to build a foundation for our little family, a foundation that can handle any shakes and storms that come along.

Families are bound together by love and by commitment. They are bound together by blood and by a common gene pool. But the binding that I feel makes it all more solid is being bound together in the links of the rosary, in the joy of shared prayer and commitment to our Lady, our Lord, and our Father.

May God bless you all, and may you and your family find the peace and happiness that my family and I have in our daily walk down the rose garlanded path of prayer.

Jenn Orr   *Belmont, California*

At morn, at noon,
at twilight dim,
Maria, thou
hast heard my hymn:
In joy and woe,
in good and ill,
Mother of God,
be with me still.
When the hours flew brightly by,
And not a cloud obscured the sky,
My soul, lest it should truant be,
Thy grace did guide to thine and thee.
Now, when storms of fate o'ercast
Darkly my present and my past,
Let my future radiant shine
With sweet hopes of thee and thine.

Edgar Allan Poe

Sunshine for the Pope

This year I attended World Youth Day with a group of 45 people, mostly from the Wollongong Diocese of Australia, which is south of Sydney. As a group, we prayed the rosary each day, meditating upon the different mysteries. We were praying it in different languages and each person had the opportunity to lead at some point.

On the last weekend of the World Youth Day Celebrations, we spent Saturday night at Downsview Park for evening prayers with the Pope. We were then to stay overnight for the Papal Mass in the morning. Unfortunately, at 6 a.m. on Sunday morning it began to rain, waking many people! Yes, a shower from God. It continued to rain, and some people left, not wanting to stay in the wet. However, a number of people remained for the Papal Mass.

One of my friends and I thought that we should just pray the rosary, in hopes that the clouds would disperse, the Sun would come out and dry everything, and the Mass could go ahead. So, we started to pray. Slowly but surely the rain stopped, and as John Paul II spoke his first words the Sun came out from behind the clouds.

Catriona E. Nunan   *Dapto, Australia*

A great sign
appeared in heaven:
a woman clothed with the Sun,
the Moon
beneath her feet,
and a crown of twelve stars
on her head.

Revelation 12:1

The Rainbow Rosaries

Because there is nothing like the zeal of a recent convert, I became a rosary maker a year before my confirmation in December 2001.

I recently attended a Cursillo in Australia, and made a handful of rainbow colored rosaries to take with me from New Zealand, rainbows being dear to the hearts of Cursillistas.

I gave some away on the course, but still had a number left when I arrived in Sydney for a week's holiday at the conclusion of the course. Being Spirit filled, as Cursillistas are prone to be, I prayed about what to do with them. It was decided to give them to anyone who voluntarily declared themselves to be Catholic.

And this became one of the big plusses on my holiday—finding Catholics who were proud to be Catholics, and they were not backward in coming forward, believe me.

The first one went to the driver of a "people-carrier" at Darling Harbor, who wears a Guardian Angel pin, and prays the rosary every day. God started the ball rolling by dropping my traveling companion's watch at his feet (no damage to the watch), and he started talking to us, and witnessing, too.

The next went to a couple who walked to the bus with me from my hostel. They were also Cursillistas.

A Cambodian lady in Paddy's Market sold me a driftwood carving of the head of Christ, made by her family members, and gained a rosary.

At the top of Centrepoint Tower, in the revolving restaurant, I met a wedding party. The bride and groom had had a Catholic wedding at home, then had come back to Sydney for a civil wedding for their Australian friends to attend. They received a surprise present of a rosary.

Two rosaries went to my Christian brothers in the Brothers and Sisters of Penance, as we had the first Antipodean meeting of our Association. We met in a cafe in the Sydney Botanical Gardens, with ibises pinching whatever crumbs we dropped.

My last three were still in my bag as I headed for the airport on my last morning, but they were gone by the time I got to the plane. The taxi-driver was given one, the ground-steward who pushed my wheelchair got one, too, and the final gift was to a blind lady traveling with her niece and nephew.

All were proud to drop into the conversation that they were Catholic and all received a rosary. I received blessings in abundance, and, I hope, their prayers!

Joy F. Saker   *Masterton, New Zealand*

The Scolding

Born and raised in the country, my childhood memories are gratefully those of a loving family centered around a hard working father and a faith-filled mother.

My mother was a former teacher whose insistence on saying the rosary every night at times led to a humorous ending. After the rosary, we would kneel before dad and then mom for their blessing, which ended as we kissed their hand.

In the absence of our father, we knelt before the oldest brother, who ceremoniously pronounced the blessing but would accidentally hit us on the mouth as we piously attempted to kiss his hand.

We would retaliate with a bite, instead of a kiss, which led to smothered giggles. Mother, of course, would scold us for giggling during such a sacred moment.

Sr. Lila Espinosa   *D. Lake, North Dakota*

The Rosary is a treasure of graces.
Pope Paul V

The Blessed Mother in Kuwait

I was around the age of six when my dad taught me the rosary. I kept wondering why he was playing with beads. He wasn't playing at all and I credit him, with the Lord's prompting, with teaching me this very powerful prayer.

Mary has not only helped me in my own life, but has helped save my son's life as well as the lives of his buddies during a difficult time. Although I have many stories to tell about the miracles of the rosary, I will share this one right now.

My youngest son Randy was stationed in Kuwait during Desert Storm. I was greatly concerned about his safety with all the fighting that was going on.

While he was stationed there, I attended a convention of the Diocesan Convention of Catholic Women in San Angelo, Texas. When Monsignor Rabroker realized my son was stationed in Kuwait, he and I decided we needed to have a rosary said.

We started the rosary at 11 p.m. and prayed until about 4 a.m. the next morning. (It must also be said that Monsignor often had us pray the rosary if he felt that someone needed prayer.)

Two weeks later I received a letter from Randy. He wrote:

"At 2 a.m. there were bullets flying over me and my buddies. I could *hear* them whizzing by. I was scared and started praying, and a calmness came over me, and I realized that I was gonna be all right. Some person told me I would be all right. It was a voice from the sky."

It was the same day and time that we were praying the rosary! I believe it was our Blessed Mother speaking to Randy.

I took the letter to Monsignor Rabroker and had him read it out loud at one of our meetings. Everyone was impressed with the event, and they, too, believed it was Mary's voice.

She takes care of us all. May she keep us all under her mantle and lead us to her son.

Veronica M. Hairgrove   *Beaumont, Texas*

The Visitation

Over the hillside country, Mary went,
Carrying Christ;
and all along the road
The Christ she carried generously
bestowed
His grace on all she met.
She had not meant
to tell she carried Christ.
She was content to veil
His love for her.
But all about her glowed such joy,
that into hearts of stone love flowed.
And e'en to John, unborn,
Christ's grace was sent.

Christ in His Sacrament
of love each day
Lives in my heart a fleeting space.
And then I walk life's rushing highway,
passing men who rarely think of God.
To these I pray that I may carry Christ.
For it may be
they would not ever know
Him but through me.

Sister Eileen Lillis, , OSC

60

Some Strong Prayers

My wife's number one priority was the rosary. She belonged to the Catholic Daughters "The Blue Army" and a rosary group.

She was a professional baby sitter, and one day she had a baby sitting job at the top of a mountain here in Arizona.

Some how the little toddler managed to get outside about mid-morning, and my wife went out to get the little child. When she tried to get back inside, all the doors were locked—and the parents were not to return home until evening.

She sat down and said the rosary, and when she finished picked up the child again and once more tried the doors. One opened!

When the parents came home, she told them what happened and the father asked what door did you get in and she showed him and his reply was.

"No way!" he said. "That door has not been opened or used for a long time and is always locked! You sure have some strong prayers."

My wife replied, "I sure do! It's the rosary of our Blessed Mother!"

That man still finds it hard to believe that she came into the house through that door.

My wife died at home with the rosary and brown scapular, and when the priest came to give her the anointing, she said, "I have to finish my rosary first."

The priest replied, "No problem."

Roderick D. Ferullo   *Phoenix, Arizona*

Dear brothers and sisters, recite the rosary
every day. I earnestly urge pastors to pray
the rosary and to teach people in their
Christian communities how to pray it.

Pope John Paul II

The Rosary and the 18-Wheeler

The rosary has been a big part of my life both in my single and married life. For my wife, our three grown children and me, the rosary has not only been our favorite prayer, but, also, our staple in life.

In 1955 I wrote a letter to Padre Pio in San Giovanni Rotondo, Italy, asking if he would pray for my intentions. On March 1, 1955, I received a note from his superior saying, "Father Pio will pray for your intentions and sends his blessings."

Like myself, the rosary was his favorite prayer and he said it daily. I feel very strongly that St. Padre Pio has been praying for my family for a long time and still is to this day. I pray to him very often. I am fortunate and thank our Blessed Mother for bringing St. Padre Pio into my life.

I drove semi-truck for 30 years and sometimes doubles (two trailers) for URM Stores. I drove about 2,412,000 miles in Washington, Idaho, Montana, and Oregon. I was always saying the rosary constantly throughout the day driving my truck.

In the early 1970s, I was going down the old Lewiston Highway, which had a lot of very sharp turns and a steep grade. In the 1970s, the trucks did not have too much air reserve in the air tanks for the brakes. About three-quarters of the way down the grade, the air tank developed a leak. The air gage went down to zero. For a few moments, I thought I would not be able to control the truck or, at the very least, that I would get into a bad accident.

I was thinking of whether I should jump out or not. I came around a curve and the road leveled off to some degree but was still going down hill. The truck was still moving with no air brakes. The only thing I could do was to try to slow it down with the hand brake. I pulled the hand brake and it slowed the truck a little, and while I was pulling the hand brake, I exclaimed out loud "Jesus and Mary, I need your help now!" For some reason the semi slowed down and came to a stop.

As I think back on this nightmare, the hand brake did not stop the semi-truck. To be pulling all that weight and having it stop by just the hand brake is impossible. It was the Blessed Mother who had her blue mantle around that semi-truck. Thank you, My Lady dressed in Blue!

The worst weather for driving is frozen fog and icy roads. One year I was driving to Libby, Montana. It was very cold, and the fog was very thick and freezing on the windows. It was extremely hard to see the road, and I was traveling about only 25 miles per hour. I was saying my rosary and asked the Blessed Mother for a safe trip.

As I was driving, I thought I saw the head of a horse peaking through the fog on the right side of the road. I was thinking that maybe my mind was playing tricks on me. I drove a little further, and I saw another head of a horse peaking through the fog in the middle of the road. This time it was right beside me about two feet away, just looking at me right through my window as I passed him by!

By this time I thought I might be having illusions, because I could not see a thing on the road, and it was amazing that I saw these two horses. It looked like something that wasn't supposed to be there. Why were two horses in the middle of the highway? It seemed like in a miraculous way that there was just enough room for my semi to get through between those two horses.

I kept on driving, even though it was hard to believe what I saw. I could have hit one of those horses very easily because they were so close to my truck.

On the way back from Libby the fog had lifted. Right at the spot where I thought I had seen the horses, a dead horse lay on the roadside. Someone else hit one of the horses. I said a thank-you to Mother Mary for a safe trip because she spared me from hitting one of those horses. She placed those horses miraculously so they would be out of the way to spare me from hitting them in the extremely dense fog.

In 1968, I made a trip to Twisp, Washington. The temperature was 32 degrees below zero. On the way back home, there was a very bad snow-storm. The wind was blowing ever so hard. The snow was blowing over the roadway and snowdrifts were getting high. It was very difficult to see the road. That trip took 18 hours to get home. When I made it home safely, I said, "Thank you Jesus and Mother Mary."

As I was driving to Walla Walla, Washington, reaching the crest of a hill just starting to go down the other side, the right front wheel bolt came loose. The wheel started to go back and forth on the spindle. The next few moments could have been a very serious accident. That wheel should have fallen off, but it did not. Blessed Mother to the rescue!

Just being able to drive my 18-wheeler with my rosary had its many good advantages. To enjoy God's creation was as gift to me: going over the beautiful mountain passes to see the lush forests and all kinds of trees. Driving through the Palouse and heading to Walla Walla's thousands of acres of golden wheat fields. If a small breeze was blowing and the Sun would be shining on the wheat, it resembled a thousand golden waves. Around Libby, Montana, and over the Fourth of July Pass is more beautiful scenery, and the rugged mountains and rivers of Montana are also a treat for the eyes. The great Columbia River with all the dams, low lands, high lands, rocky flat lands, sage brush, mountains, vast acres of grains, acres of fruit, forests—I have seen it all and thank God for his wonderful creation.

From Tri-Cities to Yakima are acres and acres of rich grape vineyards. They have some of the best wines in that country, along with fruit of all kinds. Traveling through Okanogan County, to Twisp, and Wenatchee there are many, many acres of apples of every kind. From Wenatchee I bought juicy, big, crispy, Red Delicious apples for the Poor Clare Nuns and when you would bite into these they would go "crunch."

Through all those years of driving, I always had a rosary with me. As I look back, I can only thank our Blessed Mother for protecting me on the highways and byways of an 18-wheeler. It is very possible that St. Padre Pio's rosaries saved me in some of these situations.

Wayne Sattler   *Spokane, Washington*

Devils flee before Mary's face
as wax melts before the fire.

St. Bonaventure

You Know How to Pray

I had a heart attack in 1987, and the surgery was a touch-and-go surgery. I slipped into a coma. At least five specialists shared the opinion that there was no hope for me.

While I was in the coma, the Blessed Mother appeared to me in the form of the Miraculous Medal, with rays coming from her feet, not her hands. She said to me, "Pray, pray. You know how to pray."

Being a person who prays daily, I answered our Blessed Mother: "Yes, I know how to pray." I talked to her casually, just as if I were talking with my family.

Then I came out of the coma and opened my eyes to find my family right there with me. They were crying, and when I asked them why, they told me I had been in a coma for three weeks.

I came out of that coma thanks to my wonderful family and many friends who prayed for me, and thanks to my trust in our Blessed Mother.

In October 1997, I went into the hospital and had surgery for tumors on my pancreas. The doctor told me that they would have turned cancerous in a matter of weeks if I had not found out at this time. Again, I feel as if our Blessed Mother was looking out for me.

It has been almost five years that I have been free from my medical problems. Although I was in a convalescent hospital and could not walk when I first came out of my surgery, I now do all my housework and cooking. My daughter must now also have surgery, and, of course, I am asking our Blessed Mother to help her in her medical procedures.

I am so grateful to our Blessed Mother, and I pray each and every day, thanking her and her beloved Son. I say as many rosaries as I can each day, and I pray that everyone else will do the same.

Catherine M. Didato   *Oakdale, Connecticut*

I Offer a Rosary

I am a 41-year-old woman who worked for two years in a private Baptist school. I am very Catholic, going to Mass everyday, since I finished "The Cursillo of Cristiandad-De Colores" movement of the Catholic Church 16 years ago.

This is the first time that I have worked in an environment that is completely different from my belief. I am learning more about how our separated brothers and sisters behave, and about their beliefs, and I show them how we Catholics love.

Shortly after starting work there, many of my coworkers began asking me to pray for them and their special needs: loved ones in jail, drug problems, divorce matters, and so on.

I explained to them that my daily prayers were based mostly on the rosary. Knowing that their belief does not venerate our Lady, the Blessed Virgin Mary, as we Catholics do, I asked them if they wanted me to offer a rosary for their needs. I also explained to them that any response would be because of the rosary and the power of it. My coworkers agreed that they wanted me to pray the rosary for them.

Many requests were answered. One lady whose son was in jail has learned that he is now free and doing well. Divorce issues were dropped in another case, and good jobs were found in another situation.

I later learned that one particular lady, Juanita, who had asked me to pray for her had previously been a Catholic. Through my prayers she was starting to feel a "call back" to her Catholic roots. Even though she has been involved in a non-Catholic church, she knows that her petitions were answered because of the power of the rosary. She even asked me to give her a little statue of "The Immaculate Conception" and one of the "Divino Nino Jesus." I did, and she placed them in a very special place in her house.

Juanita, a very good preschool teacher, agreed to let me tell her story. She has become my very good friend, as well as a friend to my family, and she often asks me to pray the rosary for her and her family. She has said she is very thankful to God for letting our paths cross and, by praying the rosary for her, I have brought God's light to her life.

I now pray that one day our Lady of the Immaculate Conception will grant me the opportunity to pray the rosary together with Juanita, and I have faith that it will be granted because our Lady and the rosary are powerful!

Maria Teresa Olivares   *West Palm Beach, Florida*

The Memorare

Remember,
O most loving Virgin Mary,
that never was it known
that anyone who fled
to your protection,
implored your help,
or sought your intercession
was left unaided.
Inspired with this confidence,
we turn to you,
O Virgin of virgins,
our mother.
To you we come,
before you we stand,
sinful and sorrowful.
O Mother of the Word Incarnate,
do not despise our petitions,
but in your mercy
hear and answer us.
Amen.

The Rosary as a Gift

On November 23, 2002 I learned that "e-mail friends" whom I had never met in person were having their two children baptized in Maryland. At the same time, I also had a good friend in Ohio who had become a Catholic and was receiving her first Holy Communion, Confirmation and was having her marriage blessed.

When I searched for the right gift, I called our adopted Grandpa Frank who is 85 and makes rosaries. He has, in fact, made over 4,000 of them and passed them on to family and friends, the poor and those in missions, as well as those who are in prisons.

I requested rosaries for everyone, and the gifts were received with great success. I gave five to the family in Maryland, and the mother was very happy and said that she will begin to teach the children the rosary. My friend Jan, the convert, said it was the nicest gift she received and is now learning to say the rosary.

The rosary is so special to me, especially as a gift, as I received one as a present on the day I married, over 20 years ago. And since then, I truly have tried to say it each day.

The rosary and saying the family rosary was so much a part of my life when I was growing up. Every Lent we said the family rosary. We also participated in the block rosary, where we would go to different people's house to share Mary's prayers.

My mother always told me if you even say it at night and do not finish it, that the angels will finish it for you. She also told me to use Mary as my model for being a mother because she would help me through my trials, joys and sorrow.

I believe with all my heart that Mary has been there for my family and me, particularly during surgeries, when the rosary is a special prayer for me. My children have had operations, and my husband has undergone quad bypass heart surgery, a leg bypass, and lung surgery. I have had two total knee replacements. I am waiting for a hip replacement on February 11, 2003, and the rosary will be my companion.

My favorite song is the "Ave Maria," and Mary is the Queen of Peace, always there to listen if only we talk to her. I feel so close to Mary because she has always been there for me with her beautiful prayer.

Helen M. Botschka   *Newaygo, Michigan*

O Mother of Jesus, and my Mother, let me dwell with you, cling to you and love you with ever-increasing love. I promise the honor, love and trust of a child. give me a mother's protection, for I need your watchful care. You know better than any other the thoughts and desires of the Sacred Heart. Keep constantly before my mind the same thoughts, the same desires, that my heart may be filled with zeal for the interests of the Sacred Heart of your Divine Son. Instill in me a love of all that is noble, that I may no longer be easily turned to selfishness.

Help me, dearest Mother, to acquire the virtues that God wants of me: to forget myself always, to work solely for him, without fear of sacrifice. I shall always rely on your help to be what Jesus wants me to be. I am His; I am yours, my good Mother! Give me each day your holy and maternal blessing until my last evening on earth, when your Immaculate Heart will present me to the heart of Jesus in heaven, there to love and bless you and your Divine Son for all eternity.

John Henry Cardinal Newman

My Life Was Spared

Through our Lady's rosary, my life was spared many times.

At age seventeen, I was riding on an a roller coaster at an amusement park, when suddenly I found myself jerked right out of my seat. The first thing I reached for was the bar in front of me, so I thought, but when it was all over, and I was back in my seat, I instead found I was holding my rosary.

My friend had grabbed me as I was going over and held on. As soon as I was lifted out of the roller coaster, I remember crying out, "Thank you, Mom Ma Mary!"

To this day I can not say how I got my rosary out of my purse and clutched on it in my hand. All I can say is it was a miracle because another young girl had been killed the day before on this same ride.

I have many beautiful stories of our Lady and her rosary. As a young woman, I asked through the rosary of my "My Beautiful Mom Ma Mary" to give me a good man. She did, and we have been married 48 years and five months. We have raised adopted twins, a boy and girl, and have five grandsons and one great-granddaughter. We also raised a second family when my husband and I took in one of our grandsons and raised him.

I would say that Mary, through her Holy Rosary, had plans for my life. I love Mary and our Lord Jesus Christ and only through them has life, with all of its ups and downs, been held together.

Loretta G. Baker   *Jonesville, Michigan*

Oh, Mary, God has chosen you
and purified you,
and elected you
above all the women of the earth.

The Koran

I've Got the Faith

"My marriage in 1944 might have been ill fated, considering its start. I suppose my mother wanted to get me "safely" married, and I recall watching in horror in the rectory office as she put her hand on a Bible and swore to an outrageous lie—I wasn't pregnant.

My husband-to-be was Catholic. I was not. It was one of those wartime affairs that required a zillion dispensations from the Bishop. And with each impediment I hoped, perhaps even prayed, that the marriage would be stopped. It wasn't.

In the late 1950s, now Catholic myself, I remembered the promises I had made to "raise the children Catholic." I took our three kids to Father Peyton's rosary crusade, and it was marvelous.

Their father stayed home, muttering, "Never marry a convert. She'll make your life a hell on Earth."

And so I bought Father Peyton's book of sweet rosary meditations, gathered the children around my knees, and taught them how to say the rosary. For me, doing so was more or less a meaningless exercise in parenting, just following through with what I had promised to do. I read the meditations to the children but had no intent in my heart.

I woke up one morning *knowing* that Jesus was real and that He loved me. I was stunned.

Just as soon as I could manage it, I drove home the 500 miles to my father, a Protestant minister's son who had yearned to be a missionary in China.

"I've got the faith, I've got the faith," I reported breathlessly to dad. "I guess there's nothing left for me to do but die," I burbled in great joy.

Dad's eyes danced with loving amusement.

"Well," he said quietly, "I guess there's always the missionary effort…"

Without my even asking for it, our Lady used her rosary to bring me into *faith*, and it's the greatest gift I've ever received. For nearly 50 years, now, without leaving the Pacific Northwest, I've lived as a missionary, burbling to anyone who will pay attention.

Carol Bergener   *Westport, Washington*

Mary's Protection

I come from a large family from Maine, and my father died when I was two years old. He left five of us little girls at home for my mother to raise. We ranged in age from two to ten years and also had two older sisters and three brothers who were married.

Being the youngest of the five left at home, I spent much of the time with my mother. I can't count the times I saw my mother on her knees praying her rosary—not including the family rosaries we prayed. We had a difficult time, and there wasn't much money to spare.

I hate to say it now, but I didn't make my mother's life very easy. I was rebellious and difficult to handle. In 1966, when I was 20 years old, I decided I was going to leave home and go to New York. Fortunately, I had a sister who was in the convent there, and she was able to arrange with the family of one of the other nuns to take me in while I looked for a job and found a place to stay.

I worked in a hospital, and about every six weeks we would have a long weekend off. I would take the bus to visit my family, and, to make the time there last longer, I would take the last bus back to New York, often getting home in the wee hours of the morning.

I recall once arriving around three o'clock in the morning. I had to walk through the long tunnel from Port Authority to get home and at that time there was no one around but me. I was loaded down with my suitcase and my portable record player (yeah—that's what it was called!) and a bunch of other stuff, so my hands were pretty full.

I had walked about half way through the tunnel, when I saw this older man with a cane coming from the other end. He wasn't using the cane to walk. He was just carrying it.

Fear sliced through me. I wanted to drop everything and turn around and run, but almost immediately I seemed to see Mary taking my hand, bags and all, and we just kept walking. We walked right by the man, and he appeared to not even see me.

I learned later that my mother couldn't sleep that night and sat in her rocking chair praying her rosary, especially for me. I still can't think of that without crying.

Thank you, ma, and thank you, Mary.

Anne B. Caron   *Hartford, Connecticut*

When we follow her
we do not lose the way;
when we pray to her
we do not despair;
when we think of her
we do not go astray.
When she holds us
we do not fall;
when she guides us
we do not grow weary.
O Mary,
your maternal heart
embraces sinners
despised by the whole world
and does not
abandon them
till they are reconciled
to their Judge.

St. Bonaventure

Miracle Delivery of Coal

When I was a young child, we were in desperate financial difficulties. Times were hard, and my father was out of a job. It was very cold, and we had only enough coal to heat the house for one more night.

At supper, our parents told us nine children about our situation and added sadly that unless we received a relief order of coal that night, we would have to go to the Children's Home the next day. We had nowhere else to go.

After our meal, we all knelt down to pray the rosary. We had nearly finished, when we heard a truck coming up the lane. We waited in anticipation and heard a knock on the door.

My father grabbed his coat, saying, "I'll help him unload it."

We finished our rosaries in great joy! But when my father came back into the house, he was puzzled.

"I don't think that was the relief order," he told our mother. "I never saw that man before, and he didn't give me a paper to sign." We all wondered who the man had been as we prepared for bed (in a house that was a little warmer).

The next day another load of coal arrived. My mother told the driver, who was her cousin, "We got a load of coal last night from another driver."

He chuckled and said, "I'm the only one around here who delivers relief orders for coal. If you got a load of coal last night, St. Joseph must have brought it!"

Whether it was St. Joseph or an angel, we don't know. We never received a bill for the coal. Our Blessed Mother didn't want her children to have to go away to the Children's Home. We thank God for the power of the rosaries.

Mary F. Pitstick   *Fairborn, Ohio*

A Special Name

I have always felt a strong bond to the Blessed Mother, and, unknown to me at the time, this all began at my birth.

My dearest mother discovered that she was expecting me at age 41. She had given birth to my brother nine years before, and given my mother's age at the time, she had some concerns about having a healthy baby. The doctor told her that she seemed okay, but that her baby would be small.

My mother started praying the rosary daily. She told the Blessed Mother that if her baby was born healthy and well, she would name me Marian, after our Lady.

The day finally came for my arrival. It was a very difficult delivery, but I arrived at a healthy and happy seven and one-half pounds. Everyone was so happy!

When my brother came to the hospital with my dad to see me for the first time, he was asked by a nurse what he thought of his new baby sister. He said that he was "flabbergasted." What a big word for such a little guy! The promise was kept to our Blessed Mother, and I was named Marian.

On the way home from the hospital, her intercession was again seen in our lives. My father was driving and my brother was in the front seat with him. My mother was in the back seat with me. At that time there were no seat belts in cars, and so my mother had me lying on her lap. She was putting a tiny miraculous medal around my neck at the time.

Suddenly, two cars came racing down the road. One car went safely past us. The other lost control and started careening towards our car. My mother said a quick prayer to the Blessed Mother for protection. The out-of-control car veered in front of our car, then turned and missed colliding with the rear end of our car by only inches.

As a newborn, I would have surely been killed or very seriously injured if the car had connected with ours. Again, the Blessed Mother offered her love and constant help.

Now, in my daily life, I constantly talk with our Blessed Mother in my prayers, and I pray the rosary at least twice a day. There have been countless ways that the Blessed Mother continues to protect us and intervene in my life, and it all began with my special name and my mother's devotion to our Lady.

Marian K. Peck   *Lebanon, Pennsylvania*

If all the devils should be arraigned
against me
before the judgment
seat of God;
if the whole of hell
should rise
up against me
and open up its jaws
to devour me;
if all the saints
should desert me;
if thou, O Mary,
wouldst only speak
one word
of intercession
I should be saved.

Francisco Suarez

A Young Bride's Vigil

It was 1966, and my high school sweetheart and I were soon to be married. We went to the hospital to get our blood tests for the marriage license. In the parking lot, Chuck turned off the ignition and the old Studebaker kind of shivered into silence. He turned to me with a dreadful look in his blue eyes and said, "Norma, we can't get married November 4."

A shock went all through me. I heard what he said, and in my mind it translated into, "We're not getting married at all!"

The fear of rejection instilled in me by an abusive father welled up inside. I struggled for the words to ask what I was afraid to hear, but then he handed me an envelope containing his draft notice. The United States Army induction date—November 4, 1966—was the same that was to be on our wedding invitations. And now the date, that seemed so lovely in script on parchment paper, would be the day he would be leaving me for the service.

He sensed my overwhelming fear and wrapped me in his arms assuring me we'd just get married a few weeks earlier and everything would be all right. I felt a brief sense of relief, but it was followed by frozen fear for his safety that I knew would not go away. It seemed that circumstances were sending our lives spinning out of control.

Then Chuck had more to tell me. Chuck had enlisted in the Marine Corps as soon as he received his Army draft notice and would depart November 3!

The wedding date was hurriedly moved up to October 29th, and we had six days together to honeymoon in frosty Niagara Falls, before Chuck left on a cold November morning to become a U.S. Marine. I watched as he walked up the street to the bus station, alone as he had requested. I wouldn't see him again until late February 1967, and I dreaded the upcoming holidays and long Pennsylvania winter. I had come so close to having the love I always wanted, and now he was gone.

I moved in with Chuck's parents and four siblings to wait out boot camp and see where the Marine Corps would send him. It was the height of the Vietnam War, and I was frightened that he would be sent there right out of boot camp.

In the months to come, I found my Catholic upbringing and devotion to the Blessed Mother were to be my solace. I decided the day my husband left, that I would pray the rosary daily. But more than that, I would pray it at the feet of the Blessed Mother's statue at my church, St. Paul's.

That is exactly what I did night after night when I was through with my workday. I would often be alone in the huge cathedral-like church— alone except for the Mother that Jesus and I shared. Each evening after the rosary, I ended with my petitions and then the Memorae: "Remember O most Blessed Virgin Mary, that never was it known that anyone who fled to thy protection, implored thy help or sought thy intercession was left unaided..." That was the awesome promise that would sustain me.

On Thanksgiving Day, a television special from Parris Island showed the rigors of Marine Corps training and an exuberant graduation class with bright, young, eager faces. Then the reporter gave the grim statistics on how many in this class would leave immediately for Vietnam and how many more would never return. I couldn't watch.

"Why did he have to join the Marines?" I cried to myself. It just seemed to be tempting fate.

My nightly rosary vigil persisted through the months, and while the prayers inspired me with confidence, I knew that other men who were just as dear to their families would be called, and I had to be ready to accept God's will. There was no guarantee the "promise" would be fulfilled as I envisioned it.

"Be it done unto me according to Thy will" were words Mary had used. In early February 1967, the orders came. Chuck would be stationed in San Diego, California, to attend radio repair school. I could join him in March, and we would at least have three months together. This 20-year-old girl, who had never seen the Atlantic, was soon on a plane headed for the Pacific coast! And as it turned out, my answer to prayer was another 12 months in San Diego, when my husband was reassigned as a radio school instructor.

My devotion to the Blessed Mother continued through my pregnancy and delivery alone in Balboa Naval Hospital, in San Diego. Chuck couldn't get off base to be with me. He was only able to call a taxi and usher me to the admitting room of the hospital at 7:30 a.m. before reporting to duty.

I was put in a dreary room with barred windows, along with another woman in the last stage of labor. She was very uncomfortable and assured me that I soon would be, too!

Alone, after my roommate was taken off to delivery, I clung to my rosary beads and passed the hours. As evening approached and the nursing shift was about to change, I was warned that the night nurse wasn't very patient and I should be as silent as possible.

Twelve hours had already passed along with countless rosaries, and five more hours were needed to deliver our baby boy, born without a whimper because the umbilical cord formed a choking collar around his tiny neck. Everyone left me to work on my child and more Hail Marys were said until I heard him cry at last.

When it was time for Charles Patrick Norris, III to be baptized, it was no surprise that the Catholic church nearest our new apartment was the Church of the Immaculate Conception, in Old Town San Diego. It appeared that we stood alone with our child as the priest poured holy water on his tiny head, but I knew we could not have had this joy without our "Mother" imploring her son to grant our prayers.

Thirty-six years later, a Hail Mary is constantly in my heart and on my lips, even if I wake through the night. In fact, just the other day I wondered, at the age of 55, how many Hail Marys have I said? And if they could all be connected, how many rosaries would be the total?

When our children, all grown now, drive home for the holidays I ask them to let me know when they are leaving so I can "pray them home." A thankful prayer follows each journey. I can't imagine my life without a special devotion to the Blessed Mother, but I believe it would have turned out differently without her protection, help and intercession.

Norma J. Norris   *Butler, Pennsylvania*

Released From Witchcraft

Ever since I was a small child, I've always believed in and trusted God. Last year, I had a huge problem involving my job situation, and even though I prayed constantly about it, I felt God had let me down because the end result was really bad and depressing.

My friend, who seriously worships idols, told me to forget about God and worship idols with her. In my desperate state, I started worshipping idols and started chanting. I offered food and gifts to the idols, burned candles, and wore amulets and lucky charms.

And, would you believe, it seemed to work! When I asked the idols to solve an important problem for me, they did. Now, I was really hooked. I stopped reading the Bible, stopped praying, stopped going to church, and stopped believing in God.

For more than a year, I was really into worshipping idols. Then, my friend introduced me to witchcraft and the occult. She told me that it was harmless, powerful and beneficial. She taught me how to cast spells and how to call upon the entities. And again it worked! I was so dedicated to worshipping idols and witchcraft that there was no way I, or anybody else, could get me out of the practice—except through divine intervention.

After a year and a half of heavy occult involvement, I was surfing the Internet and found a website about the rosary. I couldn't take my eyes off of this website. It said that the rosary is the most powerful tool available to mankind if they want to get back to God. It also stated that praying the rosary will bring the greatest sinner back into God's fold again.

Deep down inside, I desperately wanted God back into my life again.

My friend had given me a rosary several years ago, but I had never used it. I took it out and started praying the rosary every night. I asked Mary to pray for me and help me to stop worshipping idols, and to please help me out of my involvement with the occult.

Slowly, I started having an interest in the Bible and started reading it again. Once more I was praying to God, and the occult no longer held any interest for me. I saw it for what it really was: a Satanic cult ruled by the Devil himself.

I was so weak in my faith that I could not have returned to God without praying the rosary. I love the rosary and attest to the fact that it really does work miracles. I know it worked a miracle in my life!

Nok N. Napatalung   *Bangkok, Thailand*

Rosary Novena Prayer
Holy Virgin Mary,
Mother of God and our Mother,
accept this Holy Rosary which I offer you
to show my love for you and my firm confidence
in your powerful intercession.
I offer it as an act of faith in the mysteries
of the Incarnation and the Redemption,
as an act of thanksgiving to God
for all His love for me and all mankind,
as an act atonement for the sins of the world,
especially my own, and as an act of petition
to God through your intercession
for all the needs of God's people on earth,
but especially for this earnest request.
(Mention your request)
I beg you, dear Mother of God,
present my petition to Jesus, your Son.
I know that you want me to seek
God's will in my request.
If what I ask for should not be God's will,
pray that I may receive that which will be
of greater benefit for my soul.
I put all my confidence in you.

Mary's Answer

It was a cold day in a Chicago suburb, and I was pregnant with our fifth child. I was at my doctor's office, and he had just informed me he had found a lump in my breast. He also informed me that I would have to wait until I delivered the baby before I could have surgery.

It was eight weeks of tension for everyone in the family. My husband, our four other children, and I decided we would prayer the rosary every night, asking that the lump would be benign.

The day came for surgery, and we prayed very hard to Mary, asking that she ask her son to spare me to raise my children. Our prayers were answered and today, many years later, we have five beautiful children, and I have been able to see them grow up. I will forever be thankful to our Blessed Mother and the rosary.

Mary L. Rigoni   *Cape Coral, Florida*

This name,
Star of the Sea,
is appropriately applied
to the Holy Virgin.
As a star
in giving forth its light
does not lessen
its brightness,
so Mary brought forth
her Son
without losing the splendor
of her virginity.

St. Bernard

Expect a Miracle

Forty-three years ago, when I was a little girl of ten, the United States Navy moved my father to a long-awaited shore duty station in San Diego, California.

The movers packed our things and put them all onto a huge truck in San Pedro, bound for San Diego and our brand new home my parents had just bought. Everything we owned was packed onto that truck. The truck was supposed to arrive in San Diego before we did, but when we arrived, there was no truck!

We had no phone and no neighbors that we knew. It was a mile to the nearest store, and I was frightened. There was also a mix-up with the gas and electric company, and we had no lights. There was no carpet. There was nothing but bare floors, and I can still recall hearing the echo of my own breathing in our empty house!

One day…two days…three days passed, and still no truck. No one knew where our entire household and all of our belongings were. What had happened to that truck?

Suddenly, after three days of waiting, a knock came at the door. A man delivered a telegram saying that there had been a fire on our moving truck. The driver was unable to tell anyone anything, so until now they had just been tracing the families whose belongings were on that particular truck.

I looked at mama as she read the news to us without flinching. She went on to read that not everything had burned, and they would sort through everything and let us know what was left.

She put the telegram down on the bare cupboard and asked my sister and me to follow her into a corner of what would later become my bedroom. She then went to her purse and took out her pearl rosary beads.

We knelt on that hard floor, and we prayed together for a long time. Somehow I just KNEW that mama's rosary beads were more special and powerful than anything I had ever felt in my life. As we sat huddled there in silence after saying our rosary together, I asked Mama what were we waiting for.

"Expect a miracle!" she replied.

The power of praying the rosary was taught to me that day we prayed to our Blessed Mother, the Queen of the Most Holy Rosary. We received our miracle within one hour. Everything else had burned on that truck, but none of our belongings were damaged!

Bonnie N. Nicks   *Chula Vista, California*

Salute Mary,
think of Mary,
invoke Mary,
honor Mary,
commend yourselves to Mary,
remain with Mary
in your house,
walk with Mary
when you go out.
Rejoice with Mary,
grieve with Mary,
work with Mary,
pray with Mary.
With Mary
carry Jesus in your arms,
stand with Mary
at the foot
of the Cross of Jesus,
live and die
with Mary and Jesus.
Do this and you
will live.

Thomas A Kempis

I Want to be Repaid

Although this is really my mother's story, I am honored to tell it in her memory. I learned about it at my mother's funeral, when a man came up to me, offered his sympathy, and proceeded to tell me this story.

He said that when he was a young man, he became involved with a woman who was not his wife. He was having dinner with this woman in a restaurant one evening when my mother and father entered. They pretended not to recognize one another, but the next day the man received a call from my mother inviting him to her home for a piece of pie.

The man said that he went because no one ever refused my mother's pie, but he also realized that the invitation was really an order.

He arrived at the designated time, enjoyed his piece of pie, and then my mother told him that she had seen him in the restaurant with this other woman. He denied it, but no matter how often or how vehemently he denied it, my mother would not back down.

Finally she said, "Do you remember when you were out of work for several months, and I fed you and your family for all of that time?"

He said that he did remember.

My mother continued, "I want to be repaid."

The man immediately reached into his pocket to get his wallet, but my mother said, "No, I don't want any money. I want a favor."

The man agreed to do anything that he could to repay her. My mother reached into a drawer and took out a rosary. She placed it into his hand and told him to go to Mass every day for a week and say the rosary every day either before or after Mass.

She told him to say the prayer attached to each bead and think of something good about his wife, his children, or their life together.

Then she told him: "If at the end of the week you think this woman is better for you than your wife, just put the rosary in my mailbox, and I will never speak of this again, to either you or your wife. However, if you decide to go back to your wife, please keep the rosary with my prayers and blessing."

At this point in telling me his story, the man opened his hand and said, "This is the rosary your mother gave me so many years ago. My wife and I have said it every day since then."

Anna E. Paradise   *Camillus, New York*

Prayer to the Queen of the Most Holy Rosary

Queen of the Most Holy Rosary, in these times of such brazen impiety, manifest your power with the signs of your ancient victories. And from your throne, where you dispense pardon and graces, mercifully regard the Church of your Son, His vicar on earth, and every order of clergy and laity, who are sore oppressed in the mighty conflict. You, who are the powerful vanquisher of all heresy, hasten the hour of mercy, even though the hour of God's justice is every day provoked by the countless sins of men. For me who am the least of men, kneeling before you in supplication, obtain the grace I need to live righteously upon earth and to reign among the just in heaven, while in company with all faithful Christians throughout the world, I salute you and acclaim you as Queen of the Most Holy Rosary. Queen of the Most Holy Rosary, pray for us.

A Better Door

Ever since our daughter Michelle completed her studies in the United States, we have been rather eager to migrate either to the U.S. or Canada from our home in Tanzania. Every time we had a chance, like the DV lottery, we sent in our application every year, only to be disappointed.

Then, after attending Michelle's graduation, we all drove to Canada. We fell in love with British Columbia, and upon our return home to Tanzania, we submitted our application for migration to Canada. Although there were some factors (like my age) against us, we never stopped saying the family rosary daily and trusting in our Lord and our Mother. After about six months, the visas arrived for all of us.

Now came the biggest problems: resigning from the Hospital where we were working and selling our house, which was the only asset we had.

I had worked for about 23 years as the nurse in charge, and my husband worked for about 13 years in the stores of the same hospital. Our boss was a Muslim, and he definitely would not let us leave without a fight. We feared he might possibly even stop us if he could, as he was quite an influential person.

We applied for our annual leave, saying that we were taking the children for further studies abroad, and requested for all our pay as we needed the extra money for tickets and other expenses.

Just before our departure, my husband developed retinal bleeding while on duty and urgently needed treatment by a vitrous surgeon. Unfortunately there was none in our country, and the nearest was in India. To our complete surprise, our ex-boss refused to help us in spite of our working so diligently for all those years.

To our relief, our Lord opened another better door for us, and we got help from the Baldegg Sisters who are from Switzerland. On arrival in India, another friend arranged for the hospital and hotel. My husband underwent four sittings of laser treatment, and on our return, we had a good reason to resign from our place of work, saying that we no longer wanted to work for a person who would not help us in our time of need.

We then began the task of looking for a buyer for our house. I went to a computer shop to speak with someone who might be interested in our house, but there was some confusion about the size of our house not being the right size for him. Since I was in the shop anyway, I asked if he could give a job to our son who had just completed a course in computers.

He took my telephone number and said he would let me know. Two days later he called me and said that he was interested in purchasing our house after all, and asked if I could go to his shop right away. After debating for some time about the price, we settled on a reasonable figure. He had only one condition. He wanted the house in three days after paying the cash.

With the help of a few faithful friends, we packed our bags, emptied our house of about 25 years of possessions, and left the country in three days.

Fortunately, it was the month of Ramadan, in which most of the Muslims fast and, believe it or not, we passed under the very eyes of the boss's brother-in-law! He must have been in his own world or maybe the fasting made it so that he could not see clearly.

We took the night flight, and yesterday marked one year since we landed in this beautiful country, safe and sound.

On arrival to our hotel room we, the Pereira family, said just one decade (as we were very tired and sleepy) of the rosary to thank our Lord and our Mother. We look at all that happened this way: just as our Lord parted the Red Sea for the Israelites, He carried us on eagle's wings and brought us safely here. All this must have been through the intercession of our Lady as we continue praying and saying the rosary daily.

We got the news from our reliable source that our ex-boss was furious on hearing that we had emigrated.

Mary Gwendaline Pereira   *Surrey, Vancouver, Canada*

The Rosary is the weapon.
Blessed Padre Pio

Mary Finds the Missing Stone

I repair rosaries for a friend of mine who owns a Catholic store in the Denver area. His customers will bring in rosaries that are in need of repair, and I gladly fix them and get them back in working order so that they can be "back in the trenches" of Mary's army. I never charge his customers for these repairs, even if it involves extra materials like missing beads.

One day a man brought in a beautiful rosary made out of different shapes of stones I believe to have been marcasite. The repair involved replacing one stone that was missing, since there were only 58 beads. That often happens, and I usually either have a replacement bead in my little supply or can find one at a bead store.

However, this missing bead was so unusual that I was having trouble finding a replacement. I put the broken rosary back into the owner's little leather case and placed it beside my statue of the Blessed Mother. I said the 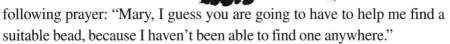 following prayer: "Mary, I guess you are going to have to help me find a suitable bead, because I haven't been able to find one anywhere."

I then continued my search for a stone but was unsuccessful. After a few months I decided that I would have to return the broken rosary to it's owner. I took the rosary from in front of my statue and looked at it one more time.

Much to my surprise, there were now enough stones to repair the rosary! Believe me when I say that I had counted many times and there were only 58 stones before I asked for Mary's help.

Instead of guiding me to a store where I could find a matching stone, our Blessed Mother gave me a wonderful gift of a miracle by placing an extra stone with the broken rosary. I then had the needed 59 beads and was able to make that rosary whole!

Karen S. Petersen   *Arvada, Colorado*

A Help for Conversion

My name is Isabella, and when I was 19 years old I moved from Sweden to Italy for study at the music-conservatory of Florence. At about the same time my godmother, who I loved a lot, died. This made me to start to reflect of the meaning with my life. I grew up as a Lutheran, but I had always felt an emptiness in the Lutheran Church.

One day, I went up to San Miniato, a Benedictine Santuary just outside Florence, and when I entered the church I suddenly knew that it was God's will that I should pass to the Catholic Church.

I talked with one of the Benedictine Fathers who gave me advice and sent me to live with some Franciscan Sisters who kept students. There, one of the sisters began to instruct me for the passage into the Catholic Church. In our first meeting she gave me a rosary along with a small booklet, because I had told her that I would like to know more about Mary. The rosary gave me help and reinforcement during this time, especially to deal with the difficulties my family felt when I told them that I wanted to become Catholic.

My joy, the day of the celebration when I received the sacraments of Confirmation and the Holy Communion was one of the biggest I ever have felt in my life. And now, one year later, I still never go anywhere without my rosary.

Isabella Lina Sodergren   *Florence, Italy*

No one has access to the Almighty
as His mother has;
none has merit such as hers.
Her Son will deny her nothing
that she asks
and herein lies her power.

John Henry Cardinal Newman

Watching My Grandmother

As a little girl, I would watch my grandmother go into the living room every afternoon and say her rosary with the deepest devotion. I would just stand there watching her in awe. Never once did she compel me to join her. However, I adored this simple woman and out of admiration learned a deep love for our Holy Mother Mary through her rosary.

I can still remember at age four receiving a small blue crystal rosary for my birthday. Although I stumbled a bit at the recitation of the Hail Mary, I tried ever so piously to imitate my sainted grandmother. The daily rosary is now a part of the fabric of my life. I believe children learn much more by what is caught then what is taught.

Mary Lou Schuster   *Joliet, Illinois*

It is in Mary's power to give you
what you wish
and what God desires for you,
so that all things
may pass through her hands.
In her God's grace
resided in such fullness
that we all can share of it.
What else should we be looking for?
Let us seek grace through Mary!
Do you want to have
an intercessor with God?
Have recourse to Mary,
for she has found recourse with God.
St. Bernard

Healing for Migraines

To those of you who suffer from migraines here is something I think you might like to read.

For years I suffered from two to three migraines a month. For those who have never experienced one, let me tell you a little about an attack. Many people have an aura, or simply put, a sign that one is coming on. In the beginning there is a visual sign which means I cannot see out of one of my eyes. It's like being blind in an instant. Within minutes, a colored light appears which looks like a jagged mirror bouncing up and down, and that lasts for several minutes. After the bouncing mirror, the terrific pain begins. There may be nausea and vomiting that can last for a few hours, though some have even had them for days without relief.

By now you are wondering, "Why is she telling us this and what does it have to do with the rosary?" After trying over-the-counter medicines and prescribed pain pills, I began praying the rosary to help relieve the pain. I have always had a very strong devotion to Mary, but the pain of migraines was nothing I had ever prayed about.

From that moment on, (over 30 years ago) I feel like a miracle happened. The pain was lessened and the headaches became more bearable. Even today, when I start to get a migraine (and they are much fewer) they go through the stages, but I am almost pain free. I cannot tell you how it feels, because you would have to experience it to know what I mean. I have shared this blessed source of relief with many family members as well as friends, because it really is something worth passing on. Praying the rosary has been my salvation.

I pray that anyone who suffers from migraines can find relief the way I have.

Janice E. Strait   *Salina, Kansas*

The Rosary Priest

My sister died of multiple myeloma. Her dying was a long painful process. She knew that a physical cure was not in the picture but she prayed for a spiritual one.

One of her friends called a rectory and asked if they would send out a priest to talk to my sister. A priest arrived a few hours later and spent time talking to my sister. He asked if they could say the rosary together. As they prayed, my sister looked at her rosary and saw that the chain links on her rosary that were previously silver had turned to a gold color.

She was very excited about this unusual occurrence, and after the priest had gone, she felt at peace. She said she felt that she had found her spiritual healing. She and her family began saying the rosary together, and every day at 3 p.m. they would recite the rosary with her. It brought the family together as well as getting them to become reacquainted with the rosary and Blessed Mother.

After my sister died, the family wanted to thank the priest who had made such a difference in her life. They went to the rectory to speak with him, but no one had any knowledge of the priest in question. To this day they have never been able to find this special angel and still wonder where he came from.

Katie M. Selle   *Dubuque, Iowa*

Smiling by night
upon her
sleeping children:
O gentle Mary
Our lovely
Mother in heaven!

Thomas Merton

My Morning and Evening Rosaries

Every night I go to bed saying the rosary.

Now, you may ask: "How special, spectacular, amazing or miraculous is that?" Many people do the same.

But I believe saying the rosary has kept me protected while being homeless and sleeping in the bushes outside of the Tacoma Community College. I am not telling you this to gain sympathy. I am telling you this so you will believe, too. I felt most peaceful, sleeping under the stars, knowing Mary's Mantle was protecting me. As the Bible tells us, we should have no anxiety at all, the Peace of God surpasses all understanding and will guide our heart and minds in Christ Jesus.

Another time I was alone in Japan. I was hired to be an English-speaking nanny for a newborn baby, assuming that I would be living in the Japanese household. On the day of arrival at night, when I was left all alone in a business apartment with strange people coming in and out during the night, I clung to my rosary. I also had my scapular on. Remember, Blessed Virgin Mary said that with the rosary in one hand and the Scapular in the other, we can achieve peace in the world.

Outside the window where I was left alone for the night, I was able to see a church. The next morning being Sunday, I ventured out to find this church to go to Mass. Not finding that particular church that I "thought" I was looking for, God guided me to a Catholic church. Without knowing the language at all, I was protected the entire time, even during a violent argument where I was threatened with the loss of my airline ticket.

The most recent "miracle" was the recovery of my husband after being rescued from wandering off in the snow for three hours. He was flown by helicopter to Saint John's Hospital. Although, during the time I was looking for him, I prayed the Divine Mercy Chaplet, when I went to sleep that night at 3 a.m. I went to sleep praying the rosary! I received a call at 4 a.m. saying my husband was awake and alert.

Then I started saying my morning rosary. I spent Saturday and Sunday night overnight in the hospital clinging to my rosary beads as I fell asleep in the chair next to my husband's bed. He was released the next Monday morning.

Margaret A. Jensen   *Stark City, Missouri*

Mother of the Redeemer,
with great joy we call you blessed.
In order to carry out His plan of salvation,
God the Father chose you before the creation of the world.
You believed in His love and obeyed His word.
The Son of God desired you for His Mother
when He became man to save the human race.
You received Him with ready obedience and undivided heart.
The Holy Spirit loved you as His mystical spouse
and filled you with singular gifts.
You allowed yourself to be led
by His hidden powerful action.
On the eve of the third Christian Millennium,
we entrust to you the Church
which acknowledges you and invokes you as Mother.
To you, Mother of human family and of the nations,
we confidently entrust the whole humanity,
with its hopes and fears.
Do no let it lack the light of true wisdom.
Guide its steps in the ways of peace.
Enable all to meet Christ, the Way, the Truth, and the Life.
Sustain us, O Virgin Mary, on our journey of faith
and obtain for us the grace of eternal salvation.
O clement, O loving, O sweet Mother of God
and our Mother, Mary!

John Paul II

Voice in the Night

Growing up in Brooklyn bestowed a cornucopia of interesting people, places and things. As a young boy from an Irish Catholic family, it meant Mass, Confession, Novenas, Parochial School and family rosary at least once a week. It was a blue-collar neighborhood, and was rich in diversity with many ethnic groups and a colorful array of street games according to the particular season of the year.

Life was good, and fun was plentiful. Much of our social interaction was contained within the several square blocks of our neighborhood, and for the older crowd, it meant the local bar and grill, represented on nearly every street corner. Of course, not everyone drank or frequented the bars, but they were certainly popular with many, including this young boy who was taken by the captivating atmosphere of interesting people, colorful sights and sounds—and, of most importance, an endless supply of beer and whiskey.

The social acceptance of these establishments and the familiarity with drinkers on my own street and own family created a fascination that lasted into my early twenties. It was legal to drink at eighteen in New York, and it was not uncommon to be able to get into bars at a younger age, sometimes without proof or sometimes with a crudely doctored draft card. Between that and the ability to experiment with booze at family functions, I was able to get an early introduction to the life of a drinker and, consequently, that of a hard core alcoholic.

In the beginning of it all, there were lots of good times: socializing, dancing, picnics, ball games and the sounds from an old fashioned juke-box. Most people briefly entertained this lifestyle and went on pursuing their careers and marriages, but there were a few of us who for whatever reason became habitual drinkers, and alcohol suddenly became a dark yet powerful force in our lives.

My own drinking changed rapidly. I quickly descended into an addictive drunk who couldn't go more than a few hours without a drink. The party had ended and the fun was over. It was the absolute worst nightmare of my life, but I didn't stop there.

Everything else changed as well. I quit going to church, my health was in a downward spiral, and my friends seemed to drop out of sight. Of course, my own family was now at a point of giving up on me. I became sicker and sicker, my liver was hardening, I had a seizure, and found myself in a hospital emergency room. Still, I wouldn't stop, and it was evident to me that now the end was not far off. I felt I was totally beyond help and death was the next step. I was plenty scared and didn't know what to do.

Then one fateful night it all hit bottom. I was out very late. It was about two o'clock in the morning, and I was beginning to go into the DT's. I was hearing voices that, at first, were annoying and then, as they persisted, became very frightening. I was in a bar a few blocks from my house, but the drinks I was having were no longer effective in stopping the shakes or calming my troublesome stomach.

In a bar on the next street, a police officer had just committed suicide by shooting himself. The quiet street had now become noisy and active with dozens of squad cars and emergency vehicles. Fear began to grip my very being. As I turned away from the sight and headed home, the voices were still there.

This is it, I thought. *I will never see the light of day again.*

Panic stricken, I made my way into my room and collapsed on my bed. I wanted to scream it was so horrifying. The voices in my head were intensifying. I knew I was about to die. I looked at my dresser, and pulled out the top drawer, and there in the back were my old rosary beads, I grasped them and lay down.

I tried to pray them but couldn't, my mind was not even capable of putting together the simple words of a Hail Mary. I put the cross in my hands and held it tightly and begged God to help me. It was the last of my sanity and strength, and it was the most powerful plea I had ever made. For the moment, my voice to God had transcended all my suffering, and I begged to be heard.

There was a short silence, then God spoke to me. All He said was, "It will be all right." A simple sentence from God, but at once, I became very tired and fell asleep.

When I awoke in the morning, I felt different. My fear was gone. The effects of alcohol on my weakened body were still there, but somehow not as bad. I survived the night, but I knew God had heard me and also knew I had to seek medical help and hospitalization.

My family was ready and whisked me off to a detoxification hospital where I stayed for a week. Ironically, it was a Catholic hospital, Mount Carmel, in Patterson, New Jersey. It was a tough ordeal for the first three days. I have been told that alcohol produces the most severe of all substances when it comes to detoxification, but I felt safe in God's hands and endured it willingly.

I have never stopped thanking God for that day, now over thirty years ago. My life has changed dramatically, but in no area as importantly as the spiritual connection with the Church, God and the Blessed Mother. There is no doubt in my mind of the miracle that took place on that dark night. I pray the rosary on a daily basis and will never forget the love and peace that I received from that voice in the night.

Thomas Berntsen   *Diamond Bar, California*

*Mary is
the ladder
of heaven;
for by Mary,
God descended
from heaven
into the world,
that by her,
men might ascend
from Earth
to heaven.*

St. Fulgentius

The Family That Prays Together

I have a precious memory that goes back to 1950, when Father Patrick Payton came to the Saskatchewan prairies, preaching on the rosary. His motto, "The family that prays together, stays together," made a great impression on many of us who lived in the region.

I know the influence it had on our family as we pledged, along with many other families, to say the rosary as a family. Kneeling on the hard kitchen floor, we gathered together (my parents and the ten of us children) for this evening prayer. Saying the rosary together is still one of my treasured family memories.

When we still gather for family events, especially in times of illness or death, the rosary is still prayed together and continues to give us renewed strength. I know it does that for me and I am sure I can include my other family members, too. All of us carry a rosary around in our pockets or purses ready for this wonderful prayer to our Blessed Mother.

For years, my brother Jacob Elder has made hundreds of rosaries, which he freely gives to others. The only request he has is that the recipient will say at least one rosary for him. His faith in this prayer, I am quite certain dates back to our family rosary. We've had many blessings as a family, and I still have great faith in Father Payton's motto: "The family that prays together, stays together."

Sr. Theresia Elder   *Scarborough, Ontario, Canada*

As mariners are guided
into port by the
shiningof a star,
so Christians are guided
to heaven by Mary.

St. Thomas Aquinas

When Mary Held My Hand

The early 1970s brought war—the Vietnam War. Yes, my young son, Dwayne, was drafted. He served here and overseas.

As his mother, I, had many conversations with God about his safety—just talks, attending Mass, and praying the rosary. I pleaded with God asking that if Dwayne's life here on Earth was to be short, please, let it be here on home ground.

Many friends would look at me and say, "Jerri, you are so calm about your son being overseas fighting. How can you be like this?" All I could say was, "I have a plea with God. I have asked for his safety. What else can I do, but wait, hope and trust."

In one of Dwayne's letters from Viet Nam, he wrote: "I will never forget the smell of blood and guts as long as I live." Then he explained that the men were given a command: if the Viet Cong soldiers who had booby trapped and hidden themselves in dead tree trunks did not come out of hiding after three calls to surrender, Dwayne and his company were to riddle the trunks with bullets.

God answered my prayers. Dwayne came home, alive and well. These were the happy and thankful times. Our family was together again. You see, we were custom farmers, a family owned business, working long hours and living the simple life.

For Lent that year, I had chosen to attend weekday Masses simply trying to share in our Lord's passion. I was also trying to prepare myself for the time that one or both of my parents would be called home.

April 5, 1974 I walked to Mass, was kneeling in silent prayer when someone knelt beside me. Looking up, I saw it was Dwayne. I was thrilled to be sharing Mass with my son. This was the last Friday of Lent. After Mass, my husband Ray, and our sons Dwayne and Gary, set out for another long hard day of work in the fields.

You see, custom work is not an eight to five job. One has to work these kinds of hours because of the weather—and customers' satisfaction is our only income.

It was after dark when the guys came in for supper. The week's work was done and Friday night is fun night! Everyone goes out, you know.

Gary took a shower and left for town. Dwayne and a friend spent some quality time with the horses. Dwayne loved his horse. It was around 10:30 p.m. when Dwayne was leaving. Ray suggested that Dwayne stay with one of his cousins in town. He asked him to please not drive home. Knowing how hard the past week had been, Ray asked again—three times—not to drive back home.

Dwayne, leaning against the front door frame, smilingly said, "Dad, I will change the irrigation setting in the north field before I come home."

We will always remember his beautiful smile and his taking of responsibilities.

It was Saturday morning as I was gathering things for breakfast. The telephone rang with news that an Umbarger man was found dead near his car that morning. Immediately, we knew that it was Dwayne, for the light was still burning that lighted his way to bed. A second call from the sheriff confirmed that they had found Dwayne dead that morning.

Needless to say, the shock was tremendous and devastating.

That evening, our family assembled all around Dwayne at the funeral home. Here is where the greatest test of all began for me. Dwayne seemed to be only sleeping, and I panicked inside. I did not say a word. I only thought, "Oh, My God, I know he is dead, but if anyone tries to close that lid, I will make a scene."

I knew that I needed help and soon! From that time until the next afternoon when our family viewed the body again, the rosary was my constant companion. Mary, my mother, lost her son in a much more difficult way with much more suffering, whereas Dwayne was killed instantly, a blessing.

The rosary never left my hand. The imprints were almost carved into my flesh. I asked Mary to intercede for me to the Trinity God for courage to let go: "Please help me."

At a time like this, my pain was so intense, I was unable to help my other children or husband.

That was when Mary took over as she held my hand, she also held theirs.

While looking at my child in his coffin, a sudden impulse rushed over me. My hand reached out to touch his forehead, as mothers do. As I did so, the shock of a hard, cold unfriendly forehead opened my eyes to see and feel that this body that God had given Dwayne no longer held his beautiful soul and spirit. It was not my warm friendly son.

Now anyone could close that lid for my son, Dwayne, lives on with Jesus, the living God in all His glory. I now understand that until God breathes life into the body, the body is just a vessel created to hold the soul and spirit.

Yes, after 28 years without Dwayne I still miss him. But I look forward to joining him again in the new Jerusalem. Thanks, Mother Mary. I love you for walking, listening and guiding me through this time of sorrow. I truly believe because of the rosary, you brought Dwayne safely home from the war and again through the rosary, you helped me realize that Dwayne is safely at home with you, and I have peace in my heart.

This was the first death and great suffering in my family—believe me, our family has had many more since that day in 1974. Sometimes in our brokenness, we are badly bent but have God, the Father, Jesus, Holy Spirit and our Catholic Church, as well as others, supporting us. Even then in our brokenness, we are badly bent. It is our choice to pray the rosary again and again. In our brokenness, our Mother Mary holds our hands close to her heart—and to the heart of her son, Jesus.

Jerri C. Gerber   *Umbarger, Texas*

*The rosary
is a wonderful instrument
for the destruction of sin,
the recovery of God's grace
and the advancement of His glory.*
Pope Gregory XII

Vain Repetition

As a former Pentecostal converting to Catholicism, I had very strong convictions about prayer, particularly our Lord's admonition not to pray with "vain repetition as the heathens do." Who were the modern-day "heathens" who prayed with vain repetition? In my mind, "they" were the Catholics who appeared to rely exclusively on liturgical, discursive prayer, the worst of which, I thought, was the rosary. As far as I was concerned, repeating all those Our Fathers and even worse, Hail Marys, could in no way be considered prayer.

How then did I pray?

Each morning when my husband and children were off to work and school, I took out my list of "affirmations" and began to pray them. "By His stripes, I am healed," I would pray. Or for my husband, "He will know wisdom and instruction and perceive the words of understanding" (Prov.1:2).

I asked God only once to give my husband wisdom and understanding. After that, I was taught that to prove my faith, I could never ask again. I had to accept that God had already answered my prayer. It was, however, acceptable to remind Him every morning of what He had already done.

When I spoke to my husband on the other hand, I was much more likely to say, "You idiot," than to praise his wisdom and understanding. Not surprisingly, I never did begin to actually experience the answer to my prayer.

"You shall have whatsoever you say," I was repeatedly told. Somehow, I thought that truth applied only to the affirmations I "prayed" in my morning prayers—not, however, to those things I said during the course of my day.

I suppose if I had ever begun to perceive "wisdom and understanding" in my husband, I could have stopped the affirmations, but since I hadn't, it seemed important to remind God every morning that He had indeed bestowed those virtues upon him.

In those days, I had a typewritten list of at least 100 affirmations that I repeatedly "prayed" over and over again each and every morning. Though I was completely sincere in my efforts at prayer, I wonder now whether I was actually communing with God or demons, or simply trying to make some mystical formula work for my own good.

"Don't pray as the heathens do, who think they will be heard for their much speaking," Jesus told his disciples. I interpreted that to mean: "Don't pray the Hail Mary, Our Father or any other prayer that doesn't come straight from your own heart."

I could see the speck in my brother's eye but was completely oblivious to the beam in my own.

Ironically, it was the Virgin Mary herself and the Holy Rosary that eventually led me to convert to the Catholic faith.

When a friend gave me a book about apparitions of the Virgin Mary, I scoffed. *I'll read it,* I thought, *but only to point out to her just how deceived she is.*

Thank God, it was my own deception that was unmasked as I read the loving words of the Blessed Mother to her children. At first, I accepted only the idea that the Virgin Mary may have appeared to these children to straighten out the Catholics' twisted thinking. *After all,* I thought, *they needed all the help they could get.* Before long, however, it was me who was on her knees. And by the time I'd finished the book, I decided to give the rosary a try.

Meditating on the mysteries of Christ was not something I had ever considered as a Pentecostal. I gave no thought at all to the suffering Christ— the Christ who willingly hung on a cross, or who clung silently to a pillar as a whip lacerated the skin from His bloody, battered body. Instead, my prayer focused exclusively on the risen Christ and the victorious life He had won—for me.

By the grace of God, I am a little less selfish in my prayers now. I've fully embraced the rosary, not as some magical formula to keep me from harm, but as an aid to contemplation of the life of Christ, that perhaps through that contemplation I might become just a little more like Him—a little more humble, a little more honest, a little more patient, a little more loving and a little more kind.

I no longer feel the need to remind God of how I think things should be. Instead, I use the rosary, the Chaplet of Divine Mercy and other prayers to remind myself of how I should be. And sometimes in the midst of my repetitions, I hear a still small voice urging me on.

"Not my will but Thine," I respond. And then I go on.

"Hail Mary, Mother of God, pray for us sinners—now."

Deborah Danielski   *Quincy, Illinois*

(This story first published in the August 1997 issue of New Covenant magazine, published by Our Sunday Visitor)

Hymn:

O Queen of all the virgin choir
Enthroned above the starry sky,
Who with your bosom's milk didst feed,
Your own Creator, Lord most high.

What man had lost in hapless Eve,
Your sacred womb to man restores;
You to the wretched here below,
Have opened heaven's eternal doors.

O hail, resplendent Hall of Light!
Hail, Gate sublime of heaven's high King!
Through you redeemed to endless life,
Your praise let all the nations sing!

O Jesus, born of Virgin bright,
To you be honor meet;
All glory through the endless morn,
To Father and to Paraclete. Amen.

The Circle Is Unbroken

As a young child I prayed the rosary every night after dinner with my family as we circled around the dining table. As we got older and got more involved in after-school programs or part-time jobs, we no longer sat down to dinner as a family as often as we had before. Still, whenever we did gather at the dining table we continued our tradition of saying the rosary together.

I missed praying the rosary everyday so I got into the habit of reciting a daily rosary myself, a practice I continue even today. I prayed this special prayer daily through high school and college and even after I got married, had a career and started a family. I had married a non-Catholic who gladly participated at Mass and our children's Catholic school but had no interest in converting to Catholicism.

At some point in our hectic lives I wanted to share the tradition of praying the rosary with my own family circle. I announced the time and place and told the kids to go get their rosary beads so we would be all ready after dinner. Julie, my oldest child, came crying out of her room holding her rosary beads—they were broken in three places. She held the pieces up to let me see, and I assured her I would get her another rosary. She was not comforted by this, however, as her grandmother had given her the rosary beads and they were very special to her.

My husband is pretty handy around the house, so I suggested that perhaps he could fix the rosary beads. He looked at the loosened links and felt there were too many parts missing to fix the beads. He laid the broken pieces on Julie's dresser and off we went to get dinner together.

After dinner, I lent Julie one of my rosaries that I had collected from traveling all over the world. She used the beads during our prayer time, but I could see that she was not happy. After finishing the dishes I went to Julie's room. My family followed behind, as was their usual practice. I thought that maybe I would take another look at the broken rosary to see if I could salvage it. I reached my hand out to the pick up the pieces and to our amazement, the parts were all connected in a perfect circle and no beads were missing!

We had all been together, so we knew none of us had been in the room to fix the rosary. We all said a little prayer of thanks to Jesus and also thanked Him for sharing His mother with us. We shared our miracle with many friends and they all loved our story and special blessing.

A short time later, another miracle occurred. After years of having no interest in joining the Catholic Church, my husband announced his intentions to become Catholic. He joined the Church at the next Easter Vigil.

My mother always told me that whatever you ask for through the rosary will come full circle.

Carmel R. Gillogly   *Fort Mill, South Carolina*

I consider nothing better
or more opportune
than to recommend and
promote this method
of prayer so that,
by the Rosary
and as a result
of it frequent consideration
of the mysteries
of salvation,
faith may be made more alive
in the hearts of men,
and the sacred fire
of prayer may be enkindled anew
and may glow
as a pledge of peace,
of moral elevation,
and of prosperity.

Pope Leo XIII

The Angel Mechanic

In Guavate, Puerto Rico, there is a shrine to our Lady called "Monte Carmelo." It has a chapel and place to pray dedicated to the Virgin Mary as she is suppose to have appeared there a long time ago. I went on a bus tour out of Arecibo with about 30 people to visit this shrine, a journey of about two and one-half hours.

We spent the whole day there, attending Mass, praying and sharing with each other until it was time to leave. When the driver started the bus for the return journey, he discovered that something was wrong with the bus and it wouldn't move. He and the other men passengers tried to find the problem to fix it but were unable to do so.

Someone suggested that we pray the rosary for a solution to our predicament. While we were praying (I think that we were on the second decade), a motorist passed by but then turned around and came back.

Stopping his car, he came over to the bus driver and said that he had done so because when he originally passed by he had looked at the wheels of the bus and noticed what he thought was something strange. He decided that something must be wrong with the bus, and he felt that he had to come back to offer assistance as he was a mechanic! He fixed the bus for free, and we returned home praying the rosary to give thanks!

Nivia Gonzalez   *Arecibo, Puerto Rico*

My children,
if you wish
for the grace
of final perseverance,
cultivate
great devotion
to Mary.

St. Philip Neri

Thank You Mary

It was the Christmas season of 2002, and my husband and I were both unemployed. He had been laid off from his job in October, and I had been laid off in early December. Our church was providing us with canned food from their pantry, but we did not have the money to continue to pay for our health insurance.

The results of my yearly mammogram revealed that I needed a sonogram, as a lump was detected on my right breast. I was not too concerned about the procedure, as I had a history of fibrocystic breast disease, and told myself it was nothing. What I was more concerned about was paying to have the procedure done. My husband and I prayed the rosary together, asking our Holy Mother to intercede. I explained my situation to the staff at the Susan G. Komen Center and a lady named Marilyn told me not to worry, that they would pay for it.

'Thank you, Jesus, thank you, Mary,' I prayed silently, breathing a sigh of relief.

The sonogram took place at the Susan G. Komen Center in St. Francis Hospital. While waiting for the sonogram, I looked up at the crucifix on the wall quietly prayed for Mother Mary's intercession on my finger rosary. The radiologist shared the results with me that day: "You have a lump. I think it is benign, but I need you to come back and have a biopsy to have it checked out just to be sure."

My silent reaction was: *Oh my, another expense! What if it is not benign?*

I immediately spoke to one of the staff members who made a phone call and then told me that they did not normally provide financial assistance for biopsies.

My thoughts drifted back to my sister, who at age 39 died after a long battle with breast cancer, leaving two children and a mountain of debts behind. I thought of my 81-year-old mother who had a mastectomy while in her 60s and how devastating it had been to her. I thought of the emotional pain and the financial strain that a diagnosis of cancer would bring to my family.

Then, I prayed the rosary and asked Mother Mary to protect my family and me. I also placed my intentions on a prayer line. The individuals on this particular prayer line are Oblates of the Community of St. John and have a strong devotion to Mary and frequently pray the rosary.

One of the people on that prayer line was a radiologist who very generously offered to do the biopsy at no cost to me. In communicating with him further, I discovered that he performed biopsies of every kind with the exception of the breast. However, he knew the radiologist Dr. R. who was scheduled to perform my biopsy and suggested I talk with him and explain my situation.

When I phoned the number on Dr. R's card, a woman answered with, "This is the Susan G. Komen Center."

I asked to speak to the radiologist, but he was unavailable. I was then transferred to Marilyn, who listened carefully to my story, and once again, told me not to worry, that the Center would pay for my sonogram. I could hardly believe my ears.

On the day of the sonogram, I arrived promptly, checked in with registration, and took out my finger rosary and began praying the rosary. It stayed on my finger as I changed into the attractive oversized pink-flowered smock and waited for the procedure to begin. As I was prepared for the biopsy, I finished saying my rosary. Then, I learned that one of the radiologist assistants was named Colleen Marie, and we began to talk about the name Mary and our Mother Mary.

Soon the radiologist appeared, but it was not Dr. R. It seems that Dr. R. was on vacation, so I had to settle for Dr. S. who was the supervisor of the radiologists, and the person on staff with the most experience. Dr. S. was very gentle. He gave me a local anesthetic and then explained each procedure step by step before doing it. The assistants commented that I was so relaxed that they thought I would fall asleep.

As all this took place, I held my finger rosary in my left hand and closed my eyes, picturing Jesus as the radiologist healing me. I felt a deep peace and a sense of comfort, as if Mary was there with me, gently reassuring me in the ways that only a mother can.

Then, I heard Dr. S. ask, " Is this a cyst? It doesn't act like a cyst. Yes, it's a cyst!"

Then he took a needle and began aspirating it. It was a benign cyst and a biopsy was not even necessary. *Praise the Lord! Thank you, Jesus! Thank you, Mary!*

As I shared the results with my husband, he rejoiced and told me that he had been praying the rosary the entire time.

Jean M. Heimann   *Chillicothe, Illinois*

Blessing of Rosary Beads

Priest: *Our help is in the
                name of the Lord*
People: *Who made heaven
                and earth.*
Priest: *The Lord be with you.*
People: *And also with you.*

Let us pray.

*For the praise and glory
of the Blessed Virgin Mary,
Mother of God,
and in commemoration of the life
of our Lord Jesus Christ,
may these beads be
blessed and sanctified
in the name of the Father,
and of the Son,
and of the Holy Spirit.*

Taken from the Liturgikon—1977

"Can Man" Dies With Rosary

Nearly nine years ago, my family made a move to Florida for a job promotion.

In my husband's hometown, where we had lived some years before, Mr. Joe "The Can Man" had known my husband all his life, and we had actually lived across the street from him for seven years. Mr. Joe was single and a loner, living with the basic necessities, even riding a three-wheel bicycle around town to get his groceries and pay his bills. After confiding in me one day that he always had a desire to own a fifteen-decade rosary, I set out to try to get one for him.

As I had four children of my own and these rosaries were costly, I purchased three large bead rosaries, took them apart and made them into a fifteen-decade rosary. This rosary was Mr. Joe's priceless treasure, but was taken from him during a stay in the hospital when he was sick.

We moved away from my husband's hometown for five years before moving to Florida but always kept in touch with Mr. Joe by mail, as he never had a telephone. In the hustle and bustle of our busy life, I forgot about Mr. Joe no longer having his rosary, until one day a letter arrived asking if there was any way possible that I could make him another.

I must confess that I did not proceed at once to purchase three more rosaries to combine them into a fifteen decade one. I guess it was the Holy Spirit that zapped me on the head one day, and I shopped our only local Catholic religious shop. Unable to find any brown large wooden bead rosaries like he had before, and special orders would have taken more time and money, I called the place in Louisiana where I had purchased the previous three and ordered three more, instructing the clerk to send them cash-on-delivery. This was before on-line ordering, trust me, and it seemed like forever before they arrived.

When the package did arrive, it was set aside for several weeks, as I no longer had the desire to accomplish this project—Satan was distracting me! It took another zap by the Holy Spirit for me to begin on the project.

Upon completing the fifteen-decade rosary, I still had to package it and make a trip to the post office to ship it to Mr. Joe. I remember thinking that he would be surprised as he had just celebrated his birthday and had been very sick. I asked him to please send a reply when he received the package so that I would know that it had made it safely.

I am not very patient when it comes to waiting for a reply, but God always knows best. About three days later, I had a phone call from Mr. Joe's niece in another town, telling me of Mr. Joe's sudden death. I asked if he had even received the rosary that I had sent, and she assured me that he had and not being a practicing Catholic, she wanted to return the rosary to me. I asked her to please keep it, as God had his reasons and it was meant for her to have it.

Later, I found out that it was a neighbor that had gone to check on Mr. Joe, and when there was no answer, he called the police who forced entry into his house. They found him in bed with the open package that I had sent, the rosary in his hands. He had died in his sleep. The neighbor, not knowing the whole story about the fifteen-decade rosary, put a short note in the newspaper, regarding Mr. Joe's perfect example for all of us to follow and a peaceful way for him to have died with a rosary in his hands.

Never a day goes by that I don't think about Mr. Joe, as my last message to him was: "I am enclosing the rosary that you so desired to replace the one that was lost. All I ask, is that you please pray for me!" I know he is still smiling down from heaven, as I often pray "to" him and ask him to please intercede for me. His niece has since been confirmed, had her marriage validated in church, baptized her daughter, and is very active in the Catholic parish where we all once lived. Mr. Joe, thank you for sharing your devotion to our Blessed Mother Mary. May your soul rest in peace.

Charlene L. Kibodeaux   *Brandon, Florida*

Among all the devotions approved
by the Church, none has been favored
by so many miracles as the
devotion of the Most Holy Rosary.

Pope Pius IX

Explosion In The Sky

My friend Don Ruff was a tail gunner in the Army Air Corps during WWII. His bomber crew consisted of 11 personnel. While flying on a mission over the China Sea, Don was praying his rosary, as was his custom. He was positioned after the bomb bay that held nine 500-pound bombs. Something triggered an explosion and Don's next recollection was coming to, 30 feet under the water, praying the Hail Mary.

The plane had been flying at 5,000 feet when the explosion occurred and plummeted a mile to the sea. Don remembers seeing wreckage and body parts as he made his way to the surface. The surface of the sea was aflame with burning fuel and he had to splash the surface to keep the flames away. There was always the danger of sharks, but after a short while Don was picked up and brought to shore to the Naval hospital.

They put a screen around Don because he was expected to die. Don fooled them all and came home to eventually marry the fiancée of his buddy who died in the crash. He is now the father of eight and grandfather to numerous grandchildren. Don was closest to the explosion, and yet he is the sole survivor from the exploded and crashed bomber. This incident is briefly covered in the military logs.

Don Koch   *Surprise, Arizona*

Let Mary never be far
from your lips
and far from your heart.
Following her,
you will never sink into despair.
Contemplating her,
you will never go wrong.
St. Bernadine of Siena (1380-1444)

Nicholas Stopped Breathing

I first have to start with my family. I was not raised as a Catholic. My family is Baptist. I converted to Catholicism about three years prior to this event. I am the second of four sons (no sisters) in my family. Though I am grown now, I am not married and I do not have any children of my own. That is not a bad thing because with three other brothers, I do not lack for any nieces or a nephew. Currently I have nine nieces and one nephew. My story is about Nicholas, my only nephew.

My family, especially my parents, were so excited to find out that my youngest brother and sister-in-law were going to have a new baby boy. He would be the first boy in the family since his father was born, over 20 years earlier. The day finally came, and it was a day I will never forget.

I live in Dallas Texas, about three hours from where my family lives. My dad called and left a message saying "he" is finally here. The labor seemed to go on for hours and hours. The following Friday, I caught the first plane to go home to see the newest member of my family and my first nephew. Being the first nephew, you can only imagine how special he really is. I thought when I arrived home, Nicholas would already be home from the hospital and beginning his new life with my family, but I was wrong.

My parents picked me up at the airport and said we needed to go to the hospital because something was wrong with Nicholas. He had lost some weight over the last two or three days, and they were not sure why. The hospital was going to release him to go home anyway, and he just needed to be closely watched.

So, already nervous, we arrived at the hospital. My brother met us at the door and told us Nicholas had stopped breathing. He said the doctors were working with him at that moment but had said they did not think it was serious. My first thought was, *He stopped breathing, how could that not be serious?*

I have worked in healthcare for 16 years, and I know when someone stops breathing it is not a good thing. It turned out that Nicholas was diagnosed with apnea, a condition where he just stops or forgets to breath. The doctors said he would be placed on an apnea monitor, a device that would sound an alarm if he stopped breathing. He would need to be on this monitor for at least one year, maybe longer, if the condition continued.

Nicholas remained in the hospital for a couple days more so the family could be trained in infant CPR, in case of an emergency. He finally went home and this began a very long and stressful year. Each time the monitor's alarm sounded, it would make your blood run cold. But, it did wake him enough to take in a deep breath and to breathe regularly again.

I had already begun praying my rosary for Nicholas on the day he was born. I asked that he be healthy, protected and grow up to be a leader in whatever career path he chose. I have no reason to believe that my prayers were not answered. So my first instinct was to turn to praying my rosary when I found out about this situation.

When my grandmother was alive, she was a very spiritual person. Health permitting, she attended church regularly and said, "Keep the Lord in your life, and there is nothing that the two of you can't do together."

I thought I could go to the cemetery where she was buried, and she would be in agreement with me when praying my rosary. Some people may think it strange, but I always find comfort in praying my rosary at my grandparents' gravesite.

Needless to say, all prayers have been answered. Nicholas just celebrated his fourth birthday. He is a typical, healthy four-year-old boy. He loves fire trucks, television, videotapes and his new little sister. He is spoiled rotten (but what four-year-old isn't) and I love him like none other. I think it is a miracle he was able to survive. I think had he not stopped breathing in the hospital and had not been diagnosed early with apnea, we would not have my nephew around today.

I continue to pray for him, as for all my family, daily and it is with the help of the Blessed Mother that we have come this far.

Michael S. Kiser   *Dallas, Texas*

Jesse's Gift of Life

Our daughter, Colleen, was already experiencing kidney failure and was on dialysis due to 20 years of suffering from diabetes. We knew that she would need an organ transplant or not live long enough to see her two young boys graduate from high school. Our devotion to our Blessed Mother through the rosary continued daily. We prayed that someone would come forward and be compatible with her blood and tissue type who could donate a kidney and part of their pancreas to her.

To our amazement, five people came forward and had the medical tests to determine if they would be eligible as donors. The doctors at the University of Minnesota Hospital chose 20-year-old Jesse as he was by far the best match, even over Colleen's brother. Jesse was a senior at St. John's University in Collegeville, Minnesota, and had no blood relationship to Colleen.

In an operation on August 16, 2000, Jesse gave Colleen a kidney and more than half of his pancreas. The medical teams that performed the operations were in awe of Jesse. Of the 5,000 transplants that had been done at the University, no living person had ever given two organs to one person. We credit the intercession of Mary of the Rosary for these precious gifts that came from Jesse to our daughter and for her continuing good health.

Elizabeth L. Kaas   *Mora, Minnesota*

O Mary, abide with us,
who are your children;
guide us along the path
which leads to God.
Be to us always a mother.
John Henry Cardinal Newman

Why Did I Get Him?

I had the duty to pray for a speaker, a priest, who was delivering his talk at a retreat. At the time, I felt anger towards this priest, and did not feel like praying for him.

Why did I get him? I wondered silently.

Still, believing that the Holy Spirit wanted me to do a good job, I walked into the chapel, and took out my rosary. It's got to be the Sorrowful Mysteries, I decided, for my mood was depressed and dark. I sat for a moment in quiet. Then, resigned to my task, I remembered that this priest's mother had died, and was watching from on high.

"How about if you help me pray for your son? You certainly loved him more than I do right now," I asked, somewhat ashamedly.

Feeling her assent, together, we began. In an instant, I forgot my presence in the chapel. I was in the garden, watching my Lord agonizing in prayer. Like a shadow against an olive tree, I saw everything, felt everything, and heard everything that happened to our Lord. The Hail Marys, Glory Bes and Our Fathers passed my lips unheard as Jesus continued through His Via Dolorosa with me at His side. My heart joined with the Blessed Mother's, and with Jesus' own. Touched with great reverence and sorrow, I was one with them.

I felt the foolishness of my selfish attitude and of sin in general. Time had no significance as I knelt with head bowed. As I finished the last prayer, the vision faded slowly…gently. I remained engulfed in the mystery for a moment.

Then, Father walked into the room in a kind of reverent silence. After a moment, he spoke. "Was it you who prayed for me as I gave my talk?" he asked.

"Yes, Father. Well … your mother in heaven, and me." I added.

"Never before have I given such a speech," he said. "It flowed forth from me, and touched many people in the room with a power I couldn't understand. Thank you."

"No, Father. Thank God." I murmured. "He and your mother, and our Blessed Mother gave us both a wonderful gift today."

I have not forgotten the power of that one rosary uttered some 15 years ago. I now approach the rosary with awe, knowing it is a timeless event uniting all generations in a mystery of love, and forgiveness.

Marianne M. Jacobs   *Hampton, New Hampshire*

Mary and Momma's Last Breath

When my mother was dying, I was sitting by her bedside praying the rosary. I was the only Catholic in my family except my mother. My father was very anti-Catholic and wouldn't let my mother practice her faith. My heart was breaking. While I was praying that rosary, right in the middle of a "Hail Mary," my mother took a last breath and slipped away. It was as if our "Mother" took her home as I prayed the rosary.

When I was a child, I would say the rosary on my fingers in bed when I couldn't sleep or when I was scared. I would have worn out a lot of rosaries, if I had had any, but my fingers are fine.

I have an autoimmune disease and because of the pain, I need to get into a very hot bathtub for at least 20 minutes, sometimes twice each day. While I'm in the tub I say the rosary, on my fingers. This way I turn my pain into prayer.

Joyce A. Iida   *Sixes, Oregon*

Her wisdom is not her own,
but His to whom
we beg her to lead us.

Bede Jarrett. O.P.

A Knock at The Door

Days always seemed to last so long when I was young, and now much too short as I get older.

When I was a teenager, my two brothers, dad and mom and I lived on a farm in Salem, Oregon. My dad was primarily a farmer, but he did have a variety of other jobs over the years as well. Before the Great Depression, dad bought and sold new automobiles. When mom had to go into town to do shopping, she would leave my brother and me at the automobile business with dad. My brother and I used to play hide-and-seek in the cars!

As a family, we always prayed the rosary every night together during Advent and Lent. Other times of the year we prayed the rosary, too, but not every night. I do, however, recall one certain week in particular when we were on our knees every night praying the rosary.

With the onset of the Great Depression, nobody had any money and our family was certainly no exception. Things were hard all over. Mom was a professional seamstress and sewed miles of fabric making vestments for the priests and cassocks for the altar boys. Dad was not able to keep his automobile business and he now bought and sold horses and later sheep for income.

The week that comes most to mind when I think about how we used to pray the rosary together was during the Great Depression. My folks were just days from losing our home. We knew unless a miracle happened that we weren't going to have a house. My folks had simply exhausted all measures to come up with the mortgage payments. For a week straight, every night after supper, mom had us all get down on our knees and pray the rosary.

We had been praying every night for almost an entire week. We knew that the bank was going to foreclose on our home the following day. My brothers and I knew that my folks were very worried. On the last day of the week, just as we were almost finished with the last mystery of the rosary, there was a knock at the door.

I got up and went to answer the door. The man asked for my dad and then said to him, "I bought a car from you many years ago, and I still owe you $10.00 on that car. I would like to pay you now."

That knock at the door that evening was a most welcome knock indeed! The $10.00 that was paid by the stranger was just enough money to keep my folks from losing their home.

William A. Trumm   *Canby, Oregon*

As told to Karen C. Hunt

Let us ask our Lady
to make our hearts
'meek and humble'
as her Son's.
It is so very easy
to be proud
and harsh
and selfish—
so easy;
but we have been created
for greater things.
How much we can learn
from our Lady!
She was so humble
because she was
all for God.
She was
full of grace.

Mother Teresa of Calcutta

Miracle on Wheels

A few years ago my husband Charles was recuperating nicely from heart surgery, so we decided to spend a week in Stowe, Vermont to help in his recovery. As we live in Canada we crossed over the border in Massena, New York, making our way to Vermont, two hours away.

As was always our custom when we traveled, we said the rosary asking our Lady to protect us on our voyage. As we finish the fourth decade, grinding sounds came from under the hood of the car and gradually got louder. By now I am getting very nervous as I knew my husband was not well enough to do very much—and we were in the middle of nowhere in the north country.

As we slowed down to pull over, I finished the last decade of the rosary. We coasted down the hill and just barely made it up to the top of the next when low and behold there was a service station and garage in the middle of nowhere, but not a house around for miles.

The car came to a stop 100 yards from the building. The owner came out to see if he could help. He told us he thought it was transmission trouble and that he wasn't equipped to fix it, but not to worry because the General Motors garage was just two miles away in the next little town. He said he could tow us there.

As we sat in our car being towed to the garage we both said a decade of the rosary in thanksgiving for all her help. We are convinced to this day that our Lady guided us all the way to a safe journey.

The transmission was fixed (cheaper than we could have had it done at home—another bonus), we were on our way the next day and had a wonderful holiday in Stowe. We attended Mass every morning and faithfully said our rosary daily.

Of course we also recited the rosary all the way back home.

We shared this miracle with many of our friends and by doing so, hope to promote the power of praying the rosary.

Bernadine M. Greffe   *Cornwall, Ontario, Canada*

Walk, Pray and Count

Every morning, when I walk
With my precious Lord, I talk.
I thank him for His patient love,
For His gifts and blessings from above.
I thank Him for nature around me I see,
And often—I pray the rosary.
To pray to His mother is a joy and a gift,
And as I honor her my own spirits I lift.

If I've forgotten to bring my beads,
I've found that's quite okay.
Cause God has helped me even in this
As I count my prayers a different way.

God gave me ten fingers on which to count.
As I say each ten Hail Marys—prayers and fingers—the same amount!
So for each ten Hail Marys, as I maintain my pace,
My fingers tuck in—so to keep my place.
When all ten are tucked in—no more to bend,
Comes the Glory Be and World without End.

The five decades move swiftly,
Soon all the prayers have been prayed.
My walk has gone quickly,
A spiritual foundation for my day has been laid.

I thank our Blessed Mother for this gift to me,
A warm wonderful prayer—her rosary.
I thank God for the rosary and my finger count way to say it,
Cause even when I'm forgetful—I can still pray it.

Diane E. Stefan—2002   *Mountain Home, Arkansas*

An Answered Prayer

About three years ago our grandson, Mark Phillip, had several febrile seizures due to upper respiratory and ear infections. While in one of the seizures, he stopped breathing and was put on life support for 24 hours. I prayed the rosary and had never cried and prayed so much in all my life. He was hospitalized and on a ventilator, and had medication as well.

Thanks to God and our Lady, he was able to breathe on his own after 24 hours and was healthy within a week or so. I was, and still am, so very grateful to God and our Lady for bringing him back to us and making him well. He will be seven years old in May 2003, and has had more seizures, but none as bad as that one. Thank you Blessed Mother and God for making him well. He is our only grandchild and is so precious to us.

Arlene Weymer   *Silver Spring, Maryland*

Holiness is union with God—
union with God depends upon two factors:
on God and on man—
on God's initiative and man's response.
All holiness, all union with God,
starts with God.
It was God who kept sin from Mary's soul
from the first moment of her existence.
It was God who chose Mary
to be the Virgin Mother of His Son.
It was God who lifted Mary,
body and soul,
to unending union with Him.
All union with God starts with God.

Walter J Burghardt, S.J.

Believing in Mary's Intervention

In the past few years, I was admitted twice to the intensive care unit of the hospital for extended periods of time due to congestive heart failure. My employer of more than 20 years—a lawyer—had personal and financial problems, and ended up shutting down his practice. Because of my medical condition, I could not work outside my home. I am a certified paralegal and needed to support myself, so I started my own business doing overflow work for attorneys.

For nearly a year I had only a couple of clients, and was struggling to make ends meet. My health continued to deteriorate, to the point where I was pretty much homebound. I began praying and, most importantly, believing that my prayers would be answered. Mark 11:24 – "Therefore I tell you, all that you ask for in prayer, believe that you will receive it and it shall be yours."

I work on the computer a great deal, and during this difficult time there were often periods when I had nothing to do. I found a website where one can pray the rosary, and I began praying it at least once a day.

Within a few months of praying the rosary, I got a new client who began giving me increasingly more assignments. That client referred another client to me, and three other current clients started giving me more work. In the interim, a client who had planned to discontinue my services due to budget constraints decided to keep me on.

There were times when I earned very little, but I never stopped believing that God would take care of things. The New Year 2003 looks much brighter, and I feel certain it is due to the power of prayer, particularly praying the rosary.

Katie L. Youngmark   *Camarillo, California*

Her Presence Is With Us

In 1987, my husband, son and I went to visit my sister and her family in Germany. While on our trip, we visited many places, one of which was the apparition site, Medjugorje. This was not my idea, but rather my husband's. Once there, we went on the tour with many thousands of other people. I did not see or feel anything and left it at that.

Several years later, while praying on my way to church, I began thinking of the Blessed Mother. I did not have a great devotion to her—it had always been only Jesus for me. So I asked her to help me to get to know her better, and to give me a devotion to her. A few days later, while eating my lunch in a small park by the river, I felt inspired to pray the rosary.

For 25 years I have belonged to a small prayer and share group with three other ladies. It came to me that perhaps we should pray the rosary at our weekly prayer meeting. I suggested it to the girls and they immediately agreed. Since that day we have prayed the rosary, bringing all our needs to her. Many, many prayers have been answered and many times we feel her presence with us. We have grown closer to the Lord, and it is due to our Blessed Mother who always directs us to her beloved Son. Praise the Lord!

Lorraine Whitworth   *Gatineau, Quebec, Canada*

...after the
Holy Sacrifice of the Mass,
the rosary is what unites us
with God by the riches
of its prayers and is what best
fosters the growth
of faith, hope and charity.
Sister Lucia of Fatima

Don't Give Up

My husband and I had been trying to conceive a baby for ten years without success. While on a vacation/pilgrimage to Italy after the first six unsuccessful years, a priest I had never met before approached me in San Marco (St. Mark) Church in Florence. He told me, in Italian, that I had not been able to conceive, and that I needed to pray to the Holy Infant. I began praying the Infant of Prague Novena and the Our Mother of Perpetual Help Novena.

Last year, four years later, I went by myself on a pilgrimage to Ireland with a Catholic tour group. When I was on the plane, I prayed a 15-decade rosary, which I try to pray every day. While praying the rosary, my eyes were closed and I saw the image of a baby in the womb. It startled me and I told a couple of people who were on the pilgrimage with me about it. I was hopeful that this was a sign, but didn't want to get my hopes up too high. A month and a half later I conceived my son, Marc Anthony, who is now eight and a half months old.

I make rosaries, and have a story about how they touched the lives of some teenagers, and a priest's as well. About a year after my husband and I were married, our pastor asked us to help teach confirmation preparation classes. A young priest who had just been ordained was in charge of the classes.

As we were preparing to go on an overnight retreat with about 40 teenagers, I decided to make them each a wire-link rosary by hand. The new priest, Father Tony, was doubtful. He didn't think they'd appreciate the rosaries, and said that he wasn't a Marian priest. I started to second guess myself, but went ahead and made the rosaries anyway.

I gave the teens an introduction to the rosary class during the retreat and they were thrilled. They couldn't believe I had spent more than 50 hours making rosaries for them. One girl even asked to stay up a little longer that night to finish praying the rosary. She was following the instruction sheet I had given them because she hadn't prayed the rosary before.

The following week we didn't have a confirmation class because of the retreat, so we weren't expecting to hear from the priest. I received a phone call in the middle of the week and it was Father Tony. He was strangely silent so I asked him what was wrong. He asked me if I knew one of the boys in the class, and on hearing the name, I said yes. He told me that the young man had been in a car accident. I asked if he was okay, wondering if the young man was in the hospital or dead.

Father Tony, after some time said, "That's the thing…He called me right after it happened and told me that he and three other teenagers were in the car when it crashed. The car was totaled but all four walked away unharmed." Father Tony then added that he had told him: "Fr. Tony, I had my rosary with me."

The young man felt he had to call the priest immediately and tell him that he had his rosary with him when they crashed. Father Tony never said anything more about it, but I think he may have changed his mind about Mary and the rosary that day.

Carolyn D. Susin   *Martinez, California*

Modern times are dominated by Satan and will be more so in the future. The conflict with hell cannot be won by men, even the most clever. The Immaculata alone has from God the promise of victory over Satan. However, now that she is assumed into heaven, the Mother of God requires our cooperation. She seeks souls who will consecrate themselves entirely to her, who will become in her hands powerful instruments for the defeat of Satan and the extension of the Kingdom of God.

St. Maximilian Kolbe

Persistence Pays Off

Our family—including my mother, father, two brothers, two sisters and me—began praying the family rosary during Lent 1950. It was usually recited right after dinner, and sometimes we prayed it in the car as we were traveling. When I left home to be married in 1964, we were still praying the family rosary. It had become second nature to me.

I tried to carry on the tradition with my children, but was not successful. My three sons are now grown and gone, and I continue to pray the rosary daily.

My youngest son, John, was born with depression. His father left us when he was only two, and life has been a struggle for him. He was imprisoned in 1992 for shooting his girlfriend, and sentenced to seven years.

In February 1995, John wrote and told me that he never wanted to have anything to do with me again. This was the son who I loved so much, the son who I had tried to help get on the right path all his life.

I was comforted by a dear friend who told me John knew it was safe to disown me because he knew my love for him was unconditional, and that I would always be there for him, no matter what.

Twice a week, as I prayed the Joyful Mysteries, at the "Finding of the Child Jesus in the Temple" mystery, I begged the Blessed Mother to soften John's heart.

On March 24, 2002 (Palm Sunday), my doorbell rang at 9:00 in the morning. I was in the basement doing laundry and couldn't imagine who would be ringing the doorbell at that early hour. I opened the door and there stood John. What joy filled my heart!

He came to tell me that he'd been doing a lot of soul searching and had come to the realization that his children had the right to know their grandmother. It was his way of telling me that his girlfriend was pregnant with his twins.

In April that year, we learned that one of the twins had been absorbed into the placenta, but the other seemed to be progressing well. The baby was due in September. Sadly, on May 24, the second twin, Alexander John was stillborn. I truly believe he was sent to do a job—bring John back into my life. He accomplished what the Lord sent him to do, and he got to go home.

My precious daddy died on December 12, 2002, and my son John is comforted with the thought that his grandpa is holding his son in his arms in heaven. No one will ever convince me that it wasn't the Blessed Mother, through the power of her rosary, who brought my son back into my life that glorious Palm Sunday 2002. Oh, how great is our God.

Ginger West   *Columbus, Ohio*

Post-Holiday Dilemma

Our children were of school age and a midwinter trip during school time did not seem feasible. Therefore, we decided to take a little trip between Christmas and New Year's. Plane tickets were purchased early and the hotel was booked and prepaid. Anticipation was mounting daily.

For good measure and for food and incidentals, my husband visited our bank and withdrew extra money. Upon returning home, he handed me the money to be put away for safe keeping, along with our airline tickets and hotel booking. I, however, was distracted by conversation and did not make a mental note of where I was placing the extra cash.

Our flight was scheduled to leave at 4:00 p.m., and shortly after lunch, I decided to pack and assemble our tickets and money. I packed our suitcases, collected the tickets and pertinent booking, but where, oh, where was the extra money?! Not wishing to alarm my family, I dejectedly searched and searched quietly. After about 45 minutes, I decided I couldn't do this alone.

Departure time was getting ever nearer.

As calmly as I could, I announced our dilemma. Quickly, everyone re-searched. Their efforts also provided no results. I assembled everyone to kneel in a circle around our bed. Prayerfully, we implored Mary to inter-cede and help us with our problem.

We prayed one decade of the rosary. My husband, who is very action oriented, needed to be doing something to bring positive results. Franti-cally, he rose to his feet and of course, our children did likewise.

My youngest child immediately announced that I should probably look in the duffel bag I had pre-packed several days earlier. It was standing only a few feet away.

Of course, the money was there. In a distracted state, I had put it where we would definitely have it with us.

Mary interceded for us and spoke to us through my child.

Josie Wasney   *Winnipeg, Manitoba, Canada*

Alma Redemptoris Mater

Mother of Christ,
Do hear your people's cry,
Star of the deep
And portal of the sky.

Mother of Him
Whose hand your glory made,
Sinking, we strive,
And call to you for aid.

Oh, by that joy
Which Gabriel did bestow;
O Virgin first and last,
Your tender mercy show.

Prayer for Good Health

I have been a member of the Legion of Mary for many years, but for the past five years I have belonged to the auxiliary of the Legion of Mary. I pray a rosary everyday to combine with the prayers of the active Legion of Mary members.

In 1999, I had a visit from three active Legion of Mary members. They usually only come in pairs, however, that day they were training a new member, so there was a third visiting. They came when I most needed a visit. The doctors told my high-risk pregnant daughter that if she carried her child full term, the baby would not be normal.

The three Legion members and I formed a circle in the middle of the room, and one member prayed for both my daughter's health and for the unborn child. They also said they would pray for the health of my daughter and her unborn baby at the next Legion of Mary meeting where the members pray the rosary together.

One month later my daughter delivered a baby she had only carried for seven months—a four-pound, perfectly formed baby boy. Although the baby did have to stay in the hospital until he gained five pounds, he and his mother were fine and healthy, and the outcome was not what doctors had predicted.

I thanked the Legion of Mary for their prayers, and now I pray a rosary every day. There are many times I feel strength from our Lord Jesus Christ who will grant any request made by His mother, the Lady of the Rosary. Jesus will answer all of our prayers, and when we pray the rosary, we have our friend, the Mother of Jesus, praying for us, too. I have developed a love for His Mother by praying the rosary, and feel she has brought me closer to her Son.

Margaret V. Taylor   *Pensacola, Florida*

Mary Gives a Sign

When my husband and I were dating 28 years ago, we started praying the rosary together. However, soon we got side tracked, and stopped praying it. Both of our lives seemed to be surrounded by many problems, so one day I prayed to the Blessed Mother. I told her that things weren't going right, and if she wanted us to get back to praying the daily rosary, that she should have my soon-to-be husband tell me something that I would immediately know was a sign from her.

My fiancé came to pick me up that day, and told me that he had been unpacking my items and had found a prayer book. Then he showed it to me. The funny thing was that he found the prayer book with my things, and I had never seen that prayer book before! Also, the Blessed Mother's picture was on the cover of the book! From that day forward, we continued to pray a rosary almost every day.

My husband died March 31, 2002, on Easter Sunday. In his last hours, as he lay semicomatose, God allowed him to tell us about heaven's presence in the room. He stated that he saw a staircase. My daughter told him to climb the stairs, and he said that he couldn't yet, because he did not have his shoes.

During his last week as he lay in bed very ill, he had become obsessed with shoes. He thought he worked in a shoe store, he spoke about going shopping at the shoe store, he kept insisting that we had to go pick up shoes at the store that he had already paid for and so on.

Just a few months ago, a friend had called to tell me of a testimonial of a family member who was present at her mother's death. The family member said that prior to her death, her mother told them not to worry, as the shoes over there (she pointed) were going to take her to heaven.

I went looking for a Bible passage pertaining to shoes and did locate in the Old Testament that God said He will give us our shoes for heaven after purification. I think my husband's two years of suffering from metastic bone cancer had purchased his shoes, and he was just waiting for God to deliver them so he could climb those stairs.

Another incident of heaven's presence during this time was that I always told my husband that I would invite our favorite saints to his death. I proceeded to call St. Therese, St. Joseph, St. Anthony, and others. As I was calling them, even though he could barely speak, he told me they were already there.

Also, the day he was dying, he told us the "lady on the wall" was calling him. The lady on the wall was a picture of our Lady of Fatima. He died with his eyes fixed on that same picture, and had a brown scapular and rosary around his neck. I know she was there with him. He had spent his life very devoted to Mary.

The picture of our Lady on the prayer book started our lives together, and the picture of our Lady on the wall was there when our 28 years together ended. The Blessed Mother was a great comfort to us as we, along with our three children, joined in unison to praise our Lady through the daily rosary. The family that prays together stays together.

Karen J. Ippolito   *Tamarac, Florida*

*...the great power of the rosary
lies in this, that it makes
the Creed into a prayer;
of course, the Creed
is in some sense a prayer
and a great act of
homage to God;
but the rosary gives us
the great truths of His life
and death to meditate upon,
and brings them nearer
to our hearts.*
John Henry Cardinal Newman

Heaven Was Flooded With Rosaries

A few years ago, my dear mother was diagnosed with a tumor in her abdomen. It showed up in the x-ray that was read by two technicians, and our doctor could actually feel the tumor by pressing his fingers into mom's abdomen.

From the time she was diagnosed until the day of her surgery, mom sat on the couch with her rosary and continuously said decade after decade to our Blessed Mother.

In surgery, the doctor operated to remove the tumor—but the tumor was nowhere to be found!

The doctor had to agree that this was indeed a miracle, and we know that it was a result of heaven being flooded with rosaries.

Mom has since passed on from this world but we continue her love for the rosary.

Anne Cox   *Ajax, Ontario, Canada*

My Parents' Prayers

In May of 1999, I was in a serious car accident. A truck veered into my lane, and I hit it going about 65 m.p.h. People at the scene said I was blessed to be alive and that I should not have survived that accident.

When I lifted my head up off the steering wheel, I saw a shimmering, transparent image of a bust of my mother who had passed away in 1985. She was rubbing her hands together and smiling with glee. I knew at that very moment that my mother had saved my life.

Not only did she save my physical life, but she saved my spiritual life as well. I had left home at the age of 17. Much to my parents' dismay, I also left the Church. For over 25 years, I refused to go to Mass, except on occasion when I went home for the holidays and wanted to keep peace in the family. I very adamantly wanted nothing to do with the Catholic religion and at times spoke out very strongly against it.

After the accident, I started to yearn to go to a shrine—something we did as a family when I was a child. So a year later, on June 30, 2000, (it was The Feast of the Sacred Heart, although I did not know this at the time) I found myself going alone to the Shrine of Divine Mercy in Stockbridge, Massachusetts. One thing led to another, and I ended up going to confession, where I had a most profound conversion back to my faith.

During confession, I had the most awesome experience! Shortly after I began my confession, the yellow light in the confessional became brighter, and then an extremely white light came down in the form of a "V." I felt a breeze on my face, which literally blew my hair back. At the same time, I had the sensation that a big door opened. Then I smelled candles and incense even though there were none in the area. I was in total awe. The next thing I knew, I heard the priest say, "So, you must be very special and very blessed." I finished my confession and left the confessional.

Since that time, my life has been turned upside-down and inside-out. I went from not going to Mass at all, to going to Mass every day. I have stopped watching all the garbage on television, and have stopped reading all the trashy books I had been reading. I watch EWTN and read only the Bible and religious books (especially books on the saints). I thirst for knowledge of God and my faith and cannot get enough. I am involved in several ministries in the Church, and I am also presently an "Aspirant" of the Third Order Carmelites.

About a year after my conversion, after sharing my experience with a new Spiritual Director, he said to me, "Sherry, do you realize what happened to you? You were literally touched by the Holy Spirit! That is a gift from God. It is not meant for just you. Gifts like this are meant to build up the community of the Church. You must share that with other people."

In all the times I had read the Bible passage: "And suddenly there came from the sky a noise like a strong driving wind, and it filled the entire house in which they were. Then there appeared to them tongues as of fire, which parted and came to rest on each one of them. And they were all filled with the Holy Spirit..." (Acts 2:2-4), I had never made the connection.

To this day, I firmly believe that the only reason why I was touched by the Holy Spirit and brought back to the Church was because my parents had prayed so fervently for me to return to my Catholic faith. My father kept me in his daily prayers, and my mother prayed the rosary for me.

So, "Thank you, dad! And thank you, mom, for asking our dear Blessed Mother to intercede and bring me back to God. You not only saved my physical life during my accident, but my spiritual life as well. I will be eternally grateful to you! May God bless you both always! And mom, I will see you again some day in heaven! I love you!"

Sherry L. Long   *Cicero, New York*

She knew,
better than anyone else
will ever know it,
that the greatest
of all griefs
is to be unable
to mitigate the suffering
of one whom we love.
But
she was willing
to suffer that,
because that
was what He asked of her.

Caryll Houselander

Red Station Wagon on a Hill

When I was 17 years old, I became a Catholic. My parents were alcoholics and didn't attend a church of any kind, but I was drawn to the Church in spite of my circumstances. I took instructions from a dear old Irish priest, Father Finley. He was very kind and wonderful to me. God sent me just the person I needed.

I was on fire for the faith. I ended up leaving my parent's home during my senior year in high school to live with my sister. I had been through the mill on more than one level and had put my full trust in God. I prayed that He would provide me with my life's mate.

This sounds much simpler than it seemed at the time. I prayed a rosary novena and never once doubted that my prayer would be answered. I knew God would provide me with His choice. On the day after I finished the novena, I met the man who was to be my future husband. We were married within nine months of our meeting. He was not a Catholic when I met him, and took instructions from the same wonderful priest. That all took place nearly twenty-nine years and five living children ago (two died before they were born and are waiting for us in heaven).

While I was receiving my miracle, my husband was receiving a tandem miracle. During the time I was praying my novena, he was having dreams. He dreamed of meeting "the girl." She had long blonde hair and lived on a hill with a red station wagon in the driveway.

Well, when he met me—I lived with my sister. No hill or red car. But, when I finally took him to meet my parents, there they were. He almost fainted. He had not told me about the dream since I did not exactly fit the mold. He then told me, and we knew there was a heavenly plan for our life together. I am nine months older than he is. I always tell him that that proves that God made him just for me.

Pamela Sue Thomure   *Exeter, California*

138

An Engaging Encounter

In today's secular culture, it is not every day that you meet a young college student seeking a husband who will live by the teachings of Humanae Vitae. So from the beginning of our courtship, I knew my fiancée was the right gal for me. There was only one problem: while she whole-heartedly embraced the Church's teaching on human life and sexual morality, she herself was not Catholic. Nor did she have any intention of becoming Catholic or exploring the Catholic faith.

At first, I felt her conversion was not far off, so we kept courting. As time progressed, however, she came to feel more and more antagonistic toward the Faith. Our relationship became increasingly strained, and I began having doubts over whether or not we would make it to the altar in the coming months.

Part of my fiancée's difficulty with the Catholic Church came from her evangelical Protestant background. Somewhat more difficult for me to admit, however, is that part of the problem also came from my graduate studies. I was studying at a pontifical university to become a canonist—in other words, one who works within the Church's internal legal system. Like our secular counterparts, canon lawyers like to argue with one another.

Moreover, in dealing with the Church's problems day after day, we also have a bad habit of forgetting the many blessings of our faith. Thus, what my fiancée saw in my Catholicism was often quite depressing.

As I sat in my apartment one morning, burdened by a heavy heart, an idea came to mind. I should set aside my canon law studies for the day and make a pilgrimage to a popular Marian site out in the country. Every weekend, Catholics from all over the region gathered there to pray to our Blessed Mother along a rosary path. Additionally, I should invite my fiancée to tag along as part of this nice little day trip.

Surprisingly, she agreed albeit with some reluctance. Without thinking twice, I rented a car and picked Sonya up at her apartment. Off we headed

into the Canadian wilderness. We listened to music along the way, alternating between secular and religious, and when we came across a quaint country teahouse, we broke for lunch. All in all, we found the morning drive pleasant as the rich autumn colors graced the scenery along the old country road.

Yet, the tension between us over the Catholic faith remained, albeit unspoken. As we pulled into the parking lot, I said a quick prayer to the Blessed Mother, and felt assured this tension would be resolved before the end of the day. Our Blessed Mother seldom disappoints.

We headed toward the first mystery, and I began reciting the words to the Hail Mary.

"Stop," Sonya said. "Where have I heard these words before?"

"Probably from the opening of St. Luke's Gospel," I replied. "The Hail Mary is basically the words spoken by the angel Gabriel when he greeted Mary, as well as the words spoken by her cousin Elizabeth soon afterward."

"Really?" Sonya asked as disbelief washed over her face. "You mean this prayer comes from the Bible?"

"Yes," I replied. "In fact, the rosary is like carrying a miniature Bible in your pocket. The prayers are for the most part the Hail Mary and the Lord's Prayer, while the Mysteries upon which we meditate are taken from certain special events in our Lord's life that we find in the Gospels."

Sonya contemplated this answer as I contemplated Our Lord's Incarnation. Her face told me that the beauty of this prayer was taking root in her heart. As we headed to the Second Joyful Mystery, she turned to me and said: "Can you teach me the words of the prayers to the rosary?"

My heart melted, and hers did as well. For the remainder of the Joyful Mysteries, I slowly recited the words to the various prayers, allowing her to repeat after me. By the time we joined a group of pilgrims at the Sorrowful Mysteries, Sonya was praying the rosary like a cradle Catholic, and none of our fellow travelers even suspected that she had yet to come into the Church.

The weather cooled off as we finished the last Glorious Mystery, and early evening rain clouds began to push away the sunny afternoon sky. As we headed toward the shelter of the car, hoping to find a nice restaurant in town for supper, Sonya asked me if we could stop at the gift shop for a moment before it closed. I replied that I was hungry and wanted to get back on the main highway before dark, but we had a few moments to spare.

Without another word, she made her way into the gift shop and toward the display case. There, the sparkle of blue crystal beads reflecting the flame of a votive candle caught her eye. She pointed this rosary out to the cashier and handed him her credit card.

"Now I can pray with you and our future children," she said as she fastened her seat belt.

I wept. Through the power of the rosary and the intercession of the Blessed Virgin, I had just witnessed a miracle. Not a miracle of physical healing or of some material good, but a miracle of the heart. For my fiancée's heart, which was open to the Church's teaching on human life when we met, now opened itself to the divine life offered by our Lord Jesus Christ. Thus the rosary saved my marriage even before our wedding day!

Almost four years have passed since this miracle of the heart. Sonya and I are now husband and wife, and God has blessed us with a beautiful daughter, the first child of what we pray are many more. Since this miracle of the heart, Sonya has faithfully accompanied me to Mass every Sunday and Holy Day of obligation, where together we pray as a family.

Pete Vere   *Nokomis, Florida*

Do not be afraid, Joseph,
son of David,
to take Mary as thy wife,
for that which is begotten
in her is of the Holy Spirit.
And she shall bring forth a Son
and thou shalt call His name Jesus;
for He shall save His people from
their sins.

Matthew 1:20

The Rosary Empowers Us

As a young girl, I was used to praying the family rosary daily. I didn't have a special devotion at that time, but we regularly ended the day with the family rosary with my parents, brothers and sisters present.

Once I joined the convent, I began to understand the preciousness of the rosary. I also learned that our founder, Fr. James Alberione (who will be beatified on April 27, 2003) had a special devotion to the rosary. He had said that without the rosary, he felt unable to even give an exhortation. He encouraged us, his daughters, to pray the rosary regularly. So, I too, began to develop a special love for praying the rosary and began carrying it with me wherever I went.

When my rosary is in my hand, I have great faith that Mary will protect me. In fact, if I go out without my rosary, I feel insecure, or as though I forgot to take something precious with me. I would like to share three incidents where I experienced the power of the rosary.

Once, two of us were visiting some big offices with our books and cassettes to share our faith. We were young then, and were feeling inferior and too shy to approach and talk to those educated men. We questioned ourselves, saying, "We were sent to serve these people by our vocation. So why should we feel shy and inferior? This fear is the work of the devil."

We decided to pray for ourselves and for those people by having an hour of adoration that included the rosary. The next day, without any inhibition, we continued our mission of visiting the offices.

Another time, I was returning home alone late one evening after a vocation tour. It was very dark and no one was on the way to meet me. I had to walk for about 15 minutes with only little lights from the town shining here and there. I was quite scared as the place was very deserted and known for drunkards. I took out my rosary and began to pray.

Without looking left or right, I walked towards my house and then started running. My fears were gone with the praying of the rosary. When

I reached home, I found my mother waiting for me with her rosary in her hand. I really felt relieved and was grateful to our Blessed Mother.

The last incident I'd like to share is from when I was on a vocation tour in October 2001. During my tour, I got the news that my priest brother was in very serious health, and I should go home at once. I was quite upset and had to travel for six hours. From the time I began the journey, I prayed the rosary, grasping it very possessively.

First I prayed the joyful and sorrowful mysteries, and then started the glorious mysteries. When I reached the Ascension of Jesus, a mystical experience came over me. I couldn't make out whether I was sleeping or in a trance. I cannot express in what situation I was. At once I felt strange. I became deeply contemplative. When I reached home, I learned that that was the very time my brother left for his eternal reward. I still feel this experience was something precious because my brother, too, had a special devotion to the Holy Rosary.

Sr. Vimala Nil Savarimuthu   *Mumbai, India*

Roses for Our Lady

As a child, my mother used to implement daily prayers into our lives. She tried to make prayer time fun for my sister and me. My mother, Peggy (may she rest in peace), came up with this idea to use when we got together to pray the rosary.

Before each Hail Mary, we would pretend that each bead was a different colored rose and dedicate it to our Lady. We would also offer it up for an intention of our choice.

This made the rosary more enjoyable for us. For example we would say: I offer up this diamond-colored rose with golden leaves to our Lady for all the rich people that they would share their wealth with the less fortunate.

After a while, and because we were so used to it, we started running out of intentions to choose from because we had covered almost every intention in the world. We also had run out of every color and sometimes even made up our own colors. My mother said that it was okay to pray for the same thing twice because the world needed plenty of prayers.

In the beginning it was a novelty, and, like all children, we tried to outdo each other by offering up the most beautiful color you could think of and for the saddest intention. As the years went by and we grew up, we came to realize the seriousness and importance of saying the rosary and for the intentions we offered. This will stay with me for the rest of my life, and I can only pray that one day I will be able to pass this onto my own children.

Georgia Alexiou   *Johannesburg, South Africa*

*Take shelter
under our Lady's mantle,
and do not fear.
She will give you
all you need.
She is very rich,
and besides
is so very generous
with her children,
especially the smallest,
like you.
So take advantage
without fear
and with complete confidence,
whenever you need anything.
She loves giving.*

Bl Raphalea Mary
Foundress of the Handmaids
of the Sacred Heart of Jesus

Gift of Life a Second Time

On March 29, 2000, my son Kelly was critically injured in an industrial accident at his work site. A hydraulic backhoe pinned him against a brick wall and was literally squeezing him to death. He was rushed to the hospital and was in the emergency room for six hours.

My daughter-in-law, my parish priest, and I sat and waited that entire time wondering if the next time we saw the doctor, it would be to receive bad news. We knew his chances of survival were pretty slim.

With a lot of prayer and after a long wait, he was finally released from the emergency room and transferred to the trauma unit where he remained in a comatose state. He was put on a respirator with a chest tube in place because of one of his lungs had collapsed and the other had partially collapsed. The doctors told us that, in their language, they did not believe he would make it through the night.

My family prayed and waited some more, while friends and family came all through the night to see Kelly, maybe for the last time. He made it through the night, the next day, another night, another day, and was still alive at day ten when the doctors finally admitted he was going to live.

I spent a lot of time in the hospital chapel, and friends spent time with me there. They brought me a rosary from our church book store, and we sat there and prayed to our Holy Mother. That same day that they brought me the rosary, I had been told that my son took a turn for the worse, and that he might die at any minute.

With tears and prayers to God, I held on to my rosary almost constantly, and kept my crucifix over his bed. He came through the ordeal, and woke up four and one-half weeks later.

Kelly made it to the rehabilitation floor, came home and learned how to walk all over again. He is now a picture of health. The doctors believed he would not live and still talk about him today.

They say that the major part of his survival and recovery was prayer, our faith, and the work of God.

I really cannot say if when I prayed the rosary that it was at that exact moment that Kelly started coming back to us. However, from that day on, I have kept my rosary with me, and have prayed every day with it.

God gave me the miracle of my son's life at his birth, and He and the Holy Mother answered my prayers and gave me the gift of his life a second time, after his accident.

To look at Kelly now you would not believe he was ever hurt in what was almost a very tragic accident. God gave me the gift of His Son and the gift of my son twice.

Samantha M. West   *Virginia Beach, Virginia*

Max and Mary's Miracle

Our son Max was born on April 14, 2002. He became the light of our lives and the center of our world. With his mop of black hair and huge blue eyes, he captivated family, friends and even strangers in markets, restaurants and any other place we'd take him.

He amazed us with how much attention he paid to everything—babbling at lamps and lights and speaking to the television and any other colorful thing that he noticed. Max especially loved to talk to the stained glass windows at our church, St. Felicitas in San Leandro, California.

He soon began to recognize that I found it funny when he belched like a sailor on leave, and he began laughing himself. In other words, Max was like a little man, albeit with very bad manners.

My wife Leslie stayed home from work until Max was four months old, and then, on August 13th, 2002, we put him in day care with Leslie's Aunt Lupe. Max quickly became the center of attention at her day-care facility and the favorite of all of the older children entrusted to her.

On Tuesday August 27th, Leslie dropped Max off at about 7:30 a.m. and doubled back for the 35 minute drive to work. At about 9:30, she

received a call from Lupe's son, Noel, asking her to hurry back to Lupe's house because Max had stopped breathing.

Leslie left work, and on her way out asked her coworker to call me. She left instructions for me to be out by the curb in five minutes and she'd pick me up.

The drive to Lupe's house seemed surreal and endless. When we finally arrived, about 10 a.m., the police were there. They told us Max had already been taken to St. Rose Hospital. We were driven there and waited for news.

At about 11a.m., we received the most heartbreaking news we'd ever received. Max had never regained consciousness. He'd stopped breathing.

On Thursday, Aug 29, 2002, Fr. Wayne Campbell, a saint on Earth, said a Vigil for Max, in front of over 300 friends and family members, coworkers, and several people who didn't know us or Max.

The following day, Fr. Wayne performed the funeral rites for a child. This was very comforting to us, and very surprising, given the fact that we hadn't yet baptized Max. He explained that since we had planned it, and were following through on the required classes and attended Mass regularly, Max had received the Baptism of Desire.

Max was laid to rest that afternoon, and Leslie and I began the most difficult and painful period of our lives.

On Saturday Aug 31, 2002, we began what in our culture is called the "Novenario": nine days of rosaries asking for the repose of the deceased's soul and the forgiveness of his sins. In Max's case, however, we prayed for ourselves, because of the fact that he had no sins.

Once these nine days were over, we thought that it would be nice to somehow continue this beautiful gathering of family. We decided that once each month, my parents and siblings, as well as my wife's parents and siblings, would gather to have a meal, catch up and most importantly pray the rosary.

I didn't know it at the time, but it would come to make a great difference in our lives and would become the catalyst for some wonderful changes.

My oldest brother Manuel and I had not spoken to each other in five years, but when my son died, Manuel and I reconciled, and to my surprise, he has begun to attend our monthly gatherings and has brought his wife Diana, and their little girl, Brianna with him.

Needless to say, it makes us feel that Max's death wasn't in vain. The Blessed Mother has interceded for us with her son, and asked Him to help bring us some comfort.

I hope in sharing this story with at least one person in pain that it might allow that person to see that although living in our world can sometimes be painful, trying and at times seem unbearable, our Lord never abandons us. If we ask her, Mary will always be there to give Him a little nudge to send us even a little bit of joy out of pain.

Vicente O. Arias   *San Leandro, California*

Our Lady's School

I am a home-schooling mother of five children. Thirteen years ago, I had my third son, and, through peer pressure, had my tubes tied. Within a week, I knew I had done something very wrong, though I had never heard from any priest about sterilization.

I tried to speak to my husband about a reversal but he did not want to discuss it. I began praying the rosary and after five years, he suggested we have the reversal. I had the reversal and two more children. While I was pregnant with my fourth child, my oldest was 13-years-old and his seizures, that he had earlier suffered, returned.

At first they were mild and occurred occasionally. But soon he was having several each month. Within a year of my fourth child being born, he was having a seizure every day. When I became pregnant with my fifth child, he was having two or three severe seizures a day. He would turn blue, fall hard on the ground and often shake terribly in life-threatening seizures.

My husband would have to do mouth to mouth resuscitation to revive him. Our Blessed Lady protected all of us. These seizures only occurred when my husband was home, despite the fact that he traveled quite often and worked 60-hour weeks for IBM.

Soon after my fifth son was born, I was finding home schooling unbearable. I had two or three doctor appointments a week and was nursing a baby in addition to home schooling. All this, on top of the stress of never knowing when my son would have a seizure, was too much.

I prayed hard. I often awakened at 5 a.m. to take the dog for a walk and pray to our Lady of Victory (also known as our Lady of the Rosary), begging her to help me know what to do. One week in January, my husband had the opportunity to work out of the home. He decided that the home schooling was too much and the children would have to go back to school. I could not do that.

I prayed even harder to our Lady of Victory to help me find an answer. She knew that my husband wanted something, but I did not feel that public schooling was the answer. I begged her to lead me the way. Suddenly, home schooling mothers asked me if I was going to start a school. I said no. Having hosted a conference for home schoolers and a home school co-op in previous years, I knew how much work was involved and I could not see how I could possibly take that on given the circumstances.

Then teachers began to approach me asking if I was starting a school. Again, I said no. But now I was beginning to wonder. I continued to pray. In January, two years ago, my oldest son landed in the hospital. He had an 18-hour seizure. It was a nightmare, but many friends came out to pray for him and us.

When I was again approached by teachers and parents, I decided that this had to be an answer from our Lady. I had no idea how I, a mother of five with a baby and a son with severe seizures would start a school for home schoolers, but I figured that God would help me.

I began to let people know that I was considering starting a school. I asked who was interested and found a few. In March, my son ended up in the hospital with another severe seizure lasting four hours. Added to my other burdens was the financial burden of increasing medical bills totaling up to $17,000 out-of-pocket expenses in one year. Something we could not pay.

In May, my fellow home schoolers, held a Catholic home schooling conference dedicated to the Infant of Prague. Many poor financial decisions were made, looking as if the home schoolers would be saddled with a huge debt at the end of the conference. We had a good turnout with families from Georgia, Tennessee, Alabama, South Carolina, North Carolina, and Florida. Despite this, it was not enough to pay off the debt. Yet, when the dust settled, all debts were paid and we even made a small profit. I knew that this was not possible, yet it happened.

From this I understood that God could do anything. I was not to worry about money, He would take care of it. So I now earnestly began to find a location. I continued to pray to our Lady of Victory. I also decided to call the school Victory Academy, in honor of our Lady of Victory.

Since I wanted to begin a Catholic hybrid (combining home schooling and traditional schooling in which students met two times a week for instruction and home schooled three times a week.), I felt the best location would be at a Catholic church.

I had just left a church called St. Catherine's for personal reasons so I did not want to ask them. I tried several churches but was stalled. Finally there were two left, one of which was St. Catherine's, the other Transfiguration. At this point I stated, "Wouldn't it be ironic if I ended up back at St. Catherine's?" I attended meetings with the Transfiguration Church Board of Education. Despite, the pastor's support, I was turned down by the board. However, they asked me many legal questions that I was unaware that I needed to answer.

As I went about answering these questions, I returned to St. Catherine's to see what they would say. Since they knew I had left the church and went to a Latin Rite Church run by the Fraternity of St. Peter, I fully expected to be turned down. But I was informed that I could have the school for three months. Although it was more than I expected, I could not accept it. I could not hire teachers or set up classes not knowing where I would be in three months time.

I countered that I needed at least a semester. Two weeks went by and I heard nothing. We were now towards the end of July and we were supposed to open doors in mid August. I didn't know what to do.

Then, one morning, at the end of July, my husband tells me that this day was *the* day. If I did not receive the decision by that day, I would have to postpone the school to the following year. I went for my usual walk with the dog, and prayed the rosary to our Lady of Victory. Then I said, "You hear him, Mother, he said that if I don't hear today, it is over. Please, close the door if it is the Lord's will, if not let me know today."

I had to run some errands that day. Some were near the church, so I decided to drive by and see if I could find the administrator. He is never outside. Whenever I have come in the past, he is in his office that is behind a locked hallway. You needed to get an appointment with the secretary. I decided that if it was God's will, the administrator would be outside.

Much to my surprise, the administrator was outside, supervising a painting job for the all-purpose building. I did not want to seem imposing, but I needed to know today, so I got out of the car. On the way to the administrator, it occurred to me that if he said no, it would actually be a wonderful thing. I would not have to do the added work. I actually was looking forward to not having the school when, as I approached the administrator, he told me that I had it.

I was shaken because I was so sure that I would be turned down. I was confused and asked what he meant. He answered that I had the use of the building. He then told me that I had use of six classrooms, a nursery, the gym and the outside lawn as needed – free of cost. This was the biggest shocker, and he continued to explain that he wanted to see the school grow. I was speechless.

As I walked back to the car, I realized that I had received the answer from our Lady. I was elated to do her will, afraid that I couldn't do it, and in awe at how well she let me know. I was almost numb. Although I was asking her, somehow I was still shocked that I received the answer so quickly and decisively.

I began to get the school ready. It meant a lot of sleepless nights, and hard work. I decided to postpone the opening of the school to September. Two weeks before school opened, I received a call from a woman who was very upset. She told me she had permission to open the same type of school in September of the following year. I said I didn't know anything about it and suggested that maybe we could work together.

But when I spoke with her, I realized that she did not like the Catholic Curriculum I was using and felt that I did not need the accreditation since many Protestant schools did fine without them. She also said that the name would have to be changed. In short, she didn't like any of it, so I decided to continue with my plans.

For a month she made my life rather difficult, telling me that she received the permission again and I would have to leave the following year. She suggested that we could both have a school there and that she could have it on Monday and Wednesday, and I could have it on Tuesday and Thursday. I explained that there weren't enough Catholic home schoolers to warrant having two schools in the same location. Although she was persistent, she gave up after a month.

One week before we were to open doors, my husband and I found out that we needed to incorporate in order to protect ourselves from liability. The filing of the incorporation and the tax returns would cost $1,500, and we needed $600 up front. We did not have this. When I realized this, I felt defeated. My prayer was "Dear Mother, we do not have the money. You know our financial status. I thought you wanted this school. Is this what you want?"

No sooner did I finish this prayer that the phone rang. One of the parents of the students was calling to ask a question about billing. I told her that I was sorry but it looked as if the school would not be able to open. She asked me why. I explained the situation. She asked me how many students we had. I told her 20, and she said that was no problem. Each student had to pay an additional $30 to pay for the cost of the incorporation. Then we would do fund-raisers to defray the rest of the costs.

All of a sudden, the door was opened. What seemed so impossible just minutes before now seemed possible. I called an emergency meeting and asked the families if they would be willing to pay the extra $30. I lost two students. But on the first day of school, I gained three students.

We began with 20 students, meeting on Tuesdays and Thursdays. We offered grades 5-12. In the beginning it was chaos because no books had been ordered and the curriculum was not in, but we managed to do fairly well. In one month, we were pretty well settled into a routine.

In October, I went on retreat to the Sister Servants of the Eternal Word. It was what I needed. The day-to-day operations and the illness of my son and the demands of the baby were beginning to overwhelm me. I was thoroughly exhausted. I was able to not only get the rest I needed but also the spiritual uplifting and focusing that I also needed.

I was there during the feast of one of the apparitions of our Lady of Fatima. I also had a great devotion to our Lady of Fatima and was blessed to be able to visit her in Portugal two years earlier. I was ready to continue.

I had written a letter to the Archbishop asking if he would consider coming to the school to say the Mass. He did. He picked the Feast of the Miraculous Medal. Next to Our Lady of Victory and Our Lady of Guadalupe, Our Lady of the Miraculous Medal is my favorite. I also had just found out that St. Elizabeth Seton (which is the name of the correspondence school that we received our curriculum from) also had a devotion to Our Lady of the Miraculous Medal. I was thrilled to have him come.

On the day he arrived, I was nervously trying to get everything ready. I went to greet him when he arrived. Then I entered the church. There were maybe ten people inside. The sacristan approached me and said that surely there would be more people than this. I assured her there would be, although in reality I had no idea how many would come. I got on my knees and prayed. "Lord, I did this for You. I thought this is what You wanted. You heard the sacristan, I need more people than this." I heard in my heart: "Be still…and know that I am God." I felt at peace. I looked up and there were at least 100 people. Truly He is good. How unworthy I am.

We did our best to live the liturgical year in addition to the academics. We strove to have the students live the disciplined life of a good Catholic while celebrating and living the liturgical year and striving to better themselves in the areas of academics.

One of our classes was Professional Development. The students were taught interview skills, resume writing and speech writing. They were also taught college knowledge questions in which they had to answer a question in any field of academics, such as spelling, math, history, or science, within five minutes. We went to Regional Competitions in which we competed against four public schools who had done this for years. They practiced five days a week, we practiced one day a week—and we won regionals then took second in the state. (We lost to seniors—we were all freshman.)

In March, I received a free trip to Lourdes, France. I never receive anything for free but our Lady again provided. I was able to go to Lourdes with five other women and three very holy priests. What a blessing. When we arrived in Paris, we had a three-hour lay over. While we were waiting, one of the priests brought us to the Church of Our Lady of the Miraculous Medal. He did this even though he knew nothing about the abundant blessings we have already received from her.

Then we went to Lourdes and dipped ourselves in the ice-cold waters. We spent much of the time praying, although we also had some fun. On the second day, one of the priests and four of the women went on to Rome. Another woman and I stayed behind with two of the priests. Before they left, the priests received special permission to say Mass at 6 a.m. Through God's tremendous blessing, these three holy priests said Mass in the chapel of St. Joan of Arc and much to everyone's surprise, the intention for the Mass that day was for Victory Academy and myself.

It seems many months before, a good friend of mine wanted to thank me by having a Mass said for me. When the priest left for Lourdes, he took along the list of who he was to say the Masses for and on this day it was for me. No one had any idea but God who poured his blessings on me.

The school ended well, though I had learned a lot and had made many mistakes.

That summer, St. Catherine's was given permission by the Archbishop to start their own full time Catholic School. The administrator attempted to keep me there but as time went on, it became obvious that they needed more room then they realized. So I began to look for another place. I did not have to look long. My pastor, from the Fraternity of St. Peter, offered his building.

We now had 14 classrooms, a huge gym, a parish hall, a library and the complete support of the pastor. Again, it was offered to us for free for the first year. Truly the Lord was blessing this school.

There was a lot of work to be done. The school had to be painted, right down to the floors. We worked over two weeks for ten and 12 hours each day to fix up the facilities. Finally the day came, when the doors were opened. Because of the uncertainty of the location, we again were not able to register students until the first day. This meant initially we did not have books or enough teachers. But within a short time, everything was put together.

Despite the fact that now most people were driving on the average 45 minutes to the school, it was amazing to see that we again began with 20 students. Within a week, however, we added first, second, third and fourth grades. A month later we added kindergarten. By October we had 47 students. We would lose one student and gain two. God cannot be outdone in his generosity.

Some teachers volunteered their time teaching. Others volunteered their time in bookkeeping, filing and office work. Others donated copiers, supplies, file cabinets, desks, holy pictures and other items. It is truly a community affair. One generous soul donated a complete set of Thomas Aquinas.

Despite all of these miracles around me, the greatest personal miracle was that of my oldest son. He has now been seizure free for four months, is working and going to a technical school to learn to be a draftsman. Despite his learning disabilities and his hand shaking from the medication, he is able to do well in all of his classes, scoring in the 90s on his written tests. He now feels he has hope to be able to live an independent life after having had uncontrolled seizures for six years.

We are gearing up for the college knowledge competitions in January and hope to make it to state and national championships. But only if it is God's will.

So you can see that wherever our Lady and her rosaries are, God's will be done and He will not be outdone in His generosity or in His miracles. How blessed I am to be a part of it despite the difficulties. How unworthy I am to be chosen.

Annette B. Hew   *Acworth, Georgia*

The Sign of the Cross

My mom, Ann Fuschetto, was a devout Catholic who attended daily Mass and prayed the rosary every evening at bedtime. Once she told my daughter Michelle, who was in second grade, that she fell asleep sometimes before she finished praying it.

Michelle said, "That's okay Grandma, Sister Mary Raymond told us in class that the angels finish the rosary for you if you fall asleep before you finish it."

My mom liked that.

My mom had breast cancer that spread to her brain and eventually to her bones. She was very confused and in a lot of pain. I traveled from my home in Virginia, back and forth for many weeks, to take care of her in the home where I grew up on Staten Island, New York. The last few weeks of my mom's life, I prayed the rosary and the Divine Mercy Chaplet with her every night.

On the last night of her life, March 29, 2000, my brother Marc, my sister Susan, and I were praying the rosary around her bed while she was laboring to breathe. When we got to the end at about 10:50 p.m., we said the final prayer, and stood there and waiting for each breath.

My sister said, "Bless her like you do every night."

I made the sign of the cross on my mom…"In the name of the Father, and of the Son, and of the Holy Spirit…Amen."

As soon as I said "Amen," she took her last breath and died. This time she didn't fall asleep before the rosary was finished.

Paula F. Krewinghaus   *Yorktown, Virginia*

Spread the rosary…
The rosary puts all who have trust in it
into communication with Our Lady.

Pope Paul VI

I Knelt Broken Before Her

In 1988 I was four months pregnant with my first child when I had a test done to see how high the protein was. The results of this test came back positive, which meant there was a possibility of a birth defect that could range from spinal problems to deformities. This had to be the worst moment of my entire life.

The doctor sent me for other tests that included an amniocentesis that showed the baby's measurements were good, but it did not confirm any abnormalities. I had to wait four to six weeks for all of the test results, and they were the longest weeks of my life.

One day I was so desperately sad that I walked into a church hoping to speak to a priest for consolation. Until that day, I was not one to visit church often, and I was not one who prayed to the Blessed Mother, or prayed the rosary, even though I had gone to a Catholic school all my life.

As I walked into the empty church with tears in my eyes and the worst pain in my heart, I noticed an image I had never noticed until that day. For some reason, I looked to my left and there was an image of the Virgin Mary as she appeared in the grotto at Lourdes.

Not knowing anything about her or her miracles, I knelt in front of her to pray, asking only for the safety and well being of my baby. I stayed there a very long time, praying and crying at the same time. When I looked at her face, a sense of relief came over me and I knew that she would protect my baby.

From that moment, I have promised my devotion to her. I now have a statue of her in front of my house, which was one of my promises, along with teaching my children all about her and her miracles.

My life has changed in a very special way since then. I now know of her miracles, and I love her as much as I love our Lord. She is my inspiration, and there is not a day that goes by that I don't pray to her and thank her for her blessings.

Needless to say, my prayers were answered, and I had a beautiful, healthy baby girl! I can't begin to express my gratitude to our Lady of Lourdes for the hope and peace I found the day I knelt broken before her in that empty church. I know there is nothing—no pain or problem—too great that our prayers to our Blessed Mother and the rosary will not answer.

Niurka Del Valle   *Miami, Florida*

*I promise to assist at
the hour of death
with the graces necessary
for salvation all those
who on the first Saturday
of five consecutive months,
go to confession
and receive Holy Communion,
recite the rosary,
keep me company for a
quarter of an hour,
while meditating on the
Mysteries of the rosary,
with the intention
of making reparation.*

Our Lady of Fatima

A One Percent Chance

My story goes back to August 20, 2000, when my husband was awaiting a date for cardiac bypass surgery. He was in our driveway washing bugs from the front of our van wearing rubber boots and shorts when our next door neighbor came out to tease him about his attire. I was at the sink doing dishes with the window open catching the breeze, and smiling to myself at them joking about his new look. My husband Lorenzo said he was wearing his dancing shoes.

All of a sudden I heard my neighbor yell out, "Easy boy…easy boy." I quickly ran out the front door to see my husband half slumped on a milk crate. There were no vital signs, so our neighbor immediately started CPR as I called 911. When the paramedics arrived, there were still no vital signs, and they had to use the defibrillator three times before there were any signs of life. This happened again in the ambulance on our way to the hospital. In the emergency room, he could not breathe on his own.

I began praying the rosary and called the priest. He was celebrating Mass when his pager rang and said, "Whoever this call is for, I offer this Body of Christ." When he reached the hospital, they told him my husband had only a one percent chance to survive. They did not expect him to live.

My husband was in the hospital for two months, had bypass surgery, a pacemaker and defibrillator implant, and continues to live one day at a time. We celebrated our 45th wedding anniversary this year, and I am thankful that our Blessed Mother answered my prayers.

Rose Marie Ladouceur   *Pickering, Ontario, Canada*

Christ's Mother helps me,
else I were too weak.

St. Joan of Arc

The Rosary Brings Peace

A young woman in my cousin's neighborhood recently suffered a heart attack. Being a close knit neighborhood, the folks gathered at their parish church at 7:00 every evening for many weeks to pray the rosary for the young woman. Many of those people were in their 30s and had not prayed the rosary in years, so they asked my cousin for instructions on how to pray it.

The rosary united this neighborhood even more as they prayed faithfully for the recovery of their beloved friend. Unfortunately, the young woman died after many weeks, but having come together to pray the rosary faithfully for her gave everyone a sense of peace.

Audrey R. Zinsser   *Florissant, Missouri*

Scent of Roses

I am Lutheran, and due to my job as a Hospice & Hospital Chaplain, I come in frequent contact with Catholic patients and family members. I am still going to school for my degree, and have been trying to learn all about the different saints, as well as learn how to pray the rosary. For the past couple of months I had been praying the rosary, although it often felt more like I was butchering it, because I kept mixing up what to say, and when to say it. I knew I was a sad case for attempting this Catholic devotion, so I apologized to Mary for this.

During those months, I had been purchasing different types of rosaries, and one in particular was made of rose petals. Nuns in a convent in

Spain crush the petals and turn them into beads. I thought I would hang this in my car as an air freshener, and use it to pray with. Soon I discovered that the smell of this rosary was overwhelming to me. Also, when my son borrowed the car, he complained about how strong the rose smell was. After a month of hoping the scent of roses would die down, I decided to leave it in a little Catholic church, knowing someone would use the rosary and maybe like the smell more than I did.

I purchased another rosary; one that was made out of cocoa beans, and bought a rosary case for it. This rosary was my favorite, and I wanted to keep it in my purse. Just yesterday I was surprised when I pulled this special rosary from its case, and immediately smelled roses!

Thinking I was going nuts, I called the company where I bought the case a week ago. They said that the description of the case didn't mention the lining being scented with roses, and that in all the years they have been selling it, they never knew it to be scented.

This rosary case was brand new, and neither the case nor the rosary had been in contact with any rose petal items. Also, there was no comparison between this heavenly rose scent and the smell of the rose petal rosary.

I feel that Mary, in her wonderful and loving way, has shown me that my attempt at the rosary was still acceptable. Today I am blessed to have the scent of heaven on my cocoa bean rosary, and in my rosary case. I thank the Blessed Virgin Mary for this gift to me.

Sara J. Smeenge   *McHenry, Illinois*

*Mary shines forth
on earth until
the day of the Lord
shall come,
as a sign of
sure hope and solace
for the pilgrim people
of God.*

Vatican II – Constitution on the Church #68

One Rosary at a Time

I was recently asked to be a director of the Newman Center at a small college campus in rural central Illinois. The college itself is associated with the Disciples of Christ Church, and when the local diocese first discussed starting a Catholic campus ministry, there were some reservations from the school. After working out some details, we began our ministry in the fall when the semester began.

I immediately realized that more prayers were needed for this than anything I had ever done before. Therefore, on the Feast of the Assumption I began a 54 rosary novena, which ended on the Feast of Our Lady of the Rosary. The first rosary I prayed was while I walked around the campus. At the end of it, I dropped a miraculous medal in a crack on the steps of the Protestant chapel on campus. After consecrating the campus to our Lady, the miracles came pouring in.

The Protestant college chaplain was very cordial to me and the Catholic ministry, and willing to help out in any way we needed. Students began stepping up and taking leadership positions in the Newman Club. Before one meeting when we were going to select officers for the student organization, I had asked our Lady to bring three students who would be willing to serve, and we ended up having five come wanting to help the Catholic ministry succeed on their campus.

After a few weeks into the semester, we noticed a large, old Federalist style house for sale across the street from campus. Until then, we had been working out of the local parish a few blocks from campus. I immediately dropped medals of Our Lady and St. Rita (patroness of impossible causes) into a crack in front of the front door. Within a week, the local diocese purchased the house and it became our Newman Center. We decided that since our Lady had done so much for us thus far, it would only be appropriate if we named it Salve Regina. After the doors opened at the Salve Regina Newman Center, student involvement increased tremendously.

My favorite story about our Lady's work with the students came one night when a group of students were hanging out at the Newman Center. I had made a rosary for one student and we were discussing his use of it. Another student, who was a Protestant, noticed the rosary and was asking her roommate, who was Catholic, what it was. The roommate began explaining the rosary to her and after I noticed their conversation, I gave the non-Catholic one of my rosaries and a pamphlet that explained how to pray it.

A few weeks later she shared how she was praying the rosary almost everyday, and that it was making a huge impact in her life. Since then she has come to almost every Sunday Mass, and often attends daily Mass as well. Whoever said college students do not have faith clearly do not understand the intercessory power of our Lady and her rosary.

Beth A McMurray   *Eureka, Illinois*

In Time of Need

I had just finished praying the rosary one evening several years ago when I got a telephone call. My brother's apartment house had burned down. Someone in the building had fallen asleep with a lit cigarette, and that man was burned to death, but my brother had miraculously been able to escape unharmed. He is a very sound sleeper and had he been asleep at that time, they might not have been able to awaken him.

I ask Jesus and Mary to bless my family when I pray, and know that my brother Dougie is alive today because of their protection, especially since I was praying the rosary at the time of the fire. My brother always faithfully wears our Lady's Miraculous Medal and has a love for the Blessed Mother, although he has not attended church for many years. I keep him enrolled and am hopeful that he will return to the sacraments one day through the intercession of our dear Blessed Mother.

Patricia A. McDermott   *Highland Lakes, New Jersey*

A Happy Death

I was blessed with six sisters and two brothers. When we were growing up, our dad would sometimes drink too much, and we worried about him getting home safely in his Model T Ford. If he was late getting home for supper, my mother would hike us all upstairs to the boys' bedroom where we would pray the rosary together. We prayed in that room because we could see the very top of the hill from the window, and when he came in sight, we would all rush downstairs to help get supper on the table.

I always prayed the rosary so he would have a happy death. On the day of his death, I sat beside him praying the rosary aloud as he lay unconscious. He opened his eyes and said, "I want communion." I still pray the rosary daily for a happy death for all those who have no one to pray for them.

Florence B. Marshall   *Louisville, Ohio*

My children,
help me to combat
the evils of the Church
and of society,
not with the sword
but with the Rosary.

Pope Pius IX

A New Baseball Glove

This year, with tears of joy streaming down my face, I wrapped a baseball glove to give as a Christmas present to our 20-year-old grandson Ryan. He needed a replacement for his old glove, because he is planning to tryout for his college's baseball team next spring. We call that a *miracle!* Our dictionary defines miracle as: "A wonderful happening, contrary to, or independent of, the laws of nature; something marvelous, a wonder." Given that definition, we consider our grandson's journey from the early morning hours of Feb. 24, 2002 till the present, a succession of miracles!

On that Sunday morning, Ryan, alone in the car, fell asleep at the wheel while traveling toward home via the N.Y. State Thruway. His car careened off the road, overturning, but coming to rest in an upright position. He awoke surrounded by the crushed metal and broken glass of his once treasured, now "totaled" car. Since he did not lose consciousness, he became aware of a man with a cell phone standing next to him, telling him to stay right where he was and not to move! The stranger then called 911 to report the accident, following that call by one to our son and daughter-in-law. He gave the phone to Ryan, allowing them to hear his voice, undoubtedly, with the intent to lessen somewhat their natural fear and apprehension over the extent of their son's injuries.

When his parents first saw Ryan in the ER, they said his face was almost beyond recognition. It was bloody, extremely swollen and bruised, one eye was swollen shut. One ear was torn and disfigured, requiring a plastic surgeon to repair it. There were also several large scalp lacerations that required suturing. When I told my daughter-in-law on the phone that we wanted so very much to be there, she replied, "No, you would not want to be here". Because he could move all extremities, and his neurological responses were essentially normal, the ER staff felt his neck pain was probably a whiplash. However, X-rays revealed he had a broken neck and a partially shattered fifth cervical vertebra. Now the man that called 911 and gave Ryan that life saving directive not to move, became a person that Ryan, his family and friends, will be forever indebted to. His presence at our grandson's side that Sunday morning probably saved his life, and most certainly saved him from permanent paralysis. That gentleman, that "Good Samaritan" remains unidentified as of this writing. Whoever he was, human or divine messenger from God, we call him an "angel" and we call his presence at our much loved grandson's side that Sunday a miracle! Also, as serious and alarming as this accident was, we thank God, that no other vehicles were involved and no other individuals were injured, and no lives were lost.

We spend the month of February in Florida and it was there we received the word of Ryan's accident, injuries and need for surgical intervention. The shattered vertebra necessitated an extremely delicate and serious operation called a disc and fusion. Ryan remembers well signing the permission slip for that surgery which contained the words that the operation he was about to undergo could cause permanent paralysis and even death. Words cannot explain what our hearts felt as we envisioned our strong, healthy, athletic grandson lying helpless in an ER in Syracuse, NY, facing life-threatening surgery. Since we were unable to fly home and be with him at this time, we knew Grandpa's and Grandma's role was to cover him with as much prayer as possible. We made a call up North to a best friend, a strong "prayer warrior" requesting that she call the prayer group, prayer line, and any other people she could think of, to storm the gates of heaven for our Ryan. We called some friends in Florida, also and then began our consoling, powerful, intercessory prayer of the rosary—a prayer that has always been an important part of our faith walk as converts to Catholicism. We were sleeping at the time of the accident when our grandson was sitting alone in the wreckage of the car we helped him buy, bleeding, dazed and with a broken neck. However, we have been praying for Ryan since he was born—even before he was born—seeking our Blessed Mother's intercession, also on his behalf. We know all those prayers, rosaries, and fasts, covered and protected him in that special time of need.

Among those people our friend Rose called up North for prayers were two special priests whom we know well and who know Ryan. Both went to the hospital after receiving the call. One arrived just as Ryan was leaving the ER for the operating room without the benefit of having seen a priest. Father was allowed time to administer the Anointing of the sick to him and accompany him with his parents to the OR entrance. After the Anointing, Father asked Ryan how he felt and he said "I feel OK". He definitely was OK! The other priest arrived too late to see Ryan and was in the waiting room when our son and daughter-in-law walked in alone. This special priest, obviously assigned to them by God, embraced them, shed a few tears with them, and administered the "anointing" of love, prayer, comfort and care. Our son said later that at that moment, they had almost as great a need for this priest as Ryan had for the one God sent to anoint him. A God—incident? Absolutely! A miracle? We think so.

Ryan came through the surgery with flying colors and was discharged three days later on Feb. 27. When I was able to fly home March 5th to be with him, I was eager but a bit apprehensive about seeing him for the first time. Truly, I saw what I perceived to be a "walking miracle." Aside from a cervical brace supporting and protecting his neck and a long incisional scar from the surgery, the Ryan that walked toward me looked just as handsome as ever, no swelling, no bruising, no remnants of facial trauma at all and the damaged ear looked perfect! His gait was slow, but he was walking. When he wrapped his arms around me in a hug all I could do was cry and thank God for those arms that could hug and those legs that could walk.

Our daughter-in-law had told us from the hospital that Ryan's recovery would be long—6 months physiotherapy and a whole year before he'd really be himself again. At home now, we asked a wonderful Marian prayer group, who pray the rosary every day after Mass at Immaculate Heart of Mary Church in Liverpool, N.Y. to include Ryan in their prayer intentions. We attend weekly Mass there at times, though it is not the parish we are registered in. Their prayer concern for our Ryan was a definite sign of the beauty and blessing of the Body of Christ. Mary is not only the Mother of God but the Mother of us all, given to us by her Son from the Cross. What a blessing that we, though not "official" parishioners, were accepted as family in this rosary group, simply because we are all "One Body," one family, sharing the same Father and Mother. We know that the prayers of that group, along with those of many others, played a significant role in Ryan's rapid and amazing recovery. He had six *weeks* of physiotherapy, not six *months* and probably was his "old self" again in about six to seven months, not *one year!*

Ryan's great love since he was old enough to swing a bat, was baseball and we attended most of his games from little league t-ball to the varsity high school team. He was an excellent player—not always "the best" but close to it! As he watched the pro games after his surgery, he would wonder doubtfully if he would ever be able to play baseball again. He joined a league softball team in Sept. (fall ball) and to everyone's amazement, batted .500 and that included a home run! There was a mighty vocal cheering crowd for him at that game. But that was softball. He next tried the fast ball batting cage and said with awesome reality, "I'm hitting better than I did before my surgery!" Whether he makes the college team or not remains to be seen but the Christmas gift of all time will be the baseball glove we gave our Ryan in Dec. 2002!

Jacqueline & Charles Butterfield   *Liverpool, New York*

Our Lady Inspires the Rosary

There is a little church on Lake Superior dedicated to Blessed Kateri Tekakwitha, a Mohawk woman who had a great devotion to the Cross and the rosary.

For several years, three little girls, Erica, Amber and Amy, have been walking to Mass every Saturday through rain sleet and snow. They are now 11 and 12 years old. Amber and Amy are twins, and Erica is the oldest. Their mother is deceased, and they love to have the time with women from the parish.

They were at my house preparing for first communion and one day found three rosaries on my window sill. They wanted to know all about them and wondered what do they do with them.

"Are they necklaces?" they asked.

I explained to them that our Lady had given us the rosary so we could pray and always remember her son and his great love for us. They wanted to know how to pray it. I told them they would have to learn the prayers, and so we began.

They knew the Our Father, and the Glory Be and the Sign of the Cross, and the Nicene Creed we say at church. Only Erica knew the Hail Mary. I told them the story of the angel coming to Mary, exclaiming, "Hail Mary, full of grace the Lord is with you."

I told them of Mary visiting her cousin Elizabeth and Elizabeth saying to her, "Blessed are you among women and blessed is the fruit of thy womb Jesus." I explained that Jesus was Mary's fruit, just like an apple is the fruit of an apple tree. They did not understand womb. I explained that it is a special place below a woman's heart where a baby grows and is loved by its mother.

They looked perplexed. I had them repeat the words after me, but they could not remember. I had them act out the story. They understood the words Hail Mary. They understood Jesus was the fruit of Mary's womb. I said the words and they repeated, but they still could not understand or remember. They were frustrated, and I was frustrated.

I thought, *Perhaps if I sing it, they will be able to remember more easily.*

So I began to sing the prayer. The girls looked at me like I was the strangest person. They rolled their eyes. I finished and asked them, "Was I very off key?"

They looked from one to another trying not to embarrass me, and said nothing. I asked "Would you like to try it with me?" I sang, they tried but still were not able. Finally I suggested that we do something else and leave the learning of the prayer to our Lady.

We went on to another activity and had a snack to eat, when all of a sudden, Amber said, "Mrs. Bertagnoli, sing that song again! I can't get it out of my head. I love that song."

So back to the living room and couch we went and began to sing again. They sang the Hail Mary for half an hour or more.

After that day, every time I saw them, they sang the Hail Mary spontaneously. Every time there is something to pray about or they are scared, a chorus of the Hail Mary starts spontaneously among the girls.

They have asked the organist to play it for them. Last week they watched a video on prayer, even though they complained that they would fall asleep if they watched a video. But it was a video on the rosary for children.

They did not sleep, they sang, and were intent on every part of the rosary. They told me they *loved* that video.

The teaching of these young girls is totally under the direction of our Mother. I can try my hardest to explain and encourage, and it does not work, but our Lady inspires their heart, turns around their direction first with just their desire, and then as they pray and pray she directs them and inspires them more and more. She makes prayer a joy for them.

Cindy A. Bertagnoli   *L'Anse, Michigan*

A Hail Mary Sky

My mother had a special grace about her.

I remember learning how to pray the rosary through her devotion to it and our Blessed Mother. Every time we were outside, and the sky was that beautiful sky blue color, my mother would say, "Look! A Hail Mary Sky!"

And I know she said an extra Hail Mary that day.

Now, when I see that blue sky above me, I think of my mother and say an extra Hail Mary, too.

Mother died peacefully at home with a sky blue rosary in her hand.

I told my older sister that I remember the "Hail Mary Sky" and that it means so much to me that I followed my mother's lead and started a tradition of my own. Now when the sky is that sky blue shade with some clouds here and there, I call it a "Hail Mary Sky with Lace."

May you see many "Hail Mary Skies" and, of course, some with "Lace."

Janet R. Millerschin   *Metamora, Michigan*

A Mother's Teaching

My mother came from a family of 12 children, and as they grew up, as soon as they learned to speak and grasp a rosary in their hands, they learned to recite the rosary.

They would all kneel down at an early age and pray the rosary together, reciting it out loud. My mother said that sometimes this was very hard for them to do at such a young age, but all the children managed to get through it and learn their prayers.

To this day, my mother, at the age of 89, still recites the rosary each and every morning before she gets started with her daily routine. The Blessed Mother has answered many of her prayers and requests when she has prayed so lovingly.

She has prayed for her family's health and for normal requests for her children and grandchildren. We all adore the Blessed Mother and continue to pray to her each and every day.

Now that I have children, on our way to school each morning, my children and I stop and say a prayer at the Blessed Mother. Sometimes my youngest child will take a flower for her. We do love to stop and see her, and she will always be such a big part of our lives!

Nancy A. Bourke   *Miami, Florida*

My Special Mary

I have a really special Mary. She is my youngest daughter. She is 28 years old and was born a week before Christmas. She is a special needs adult with a very big heart. She loves being with older people. Her best friend is 80.

We were away from the Church for a few years but came back over two years ago. Mary is happier then ever before. Right away she joined the Altar and Rosary Society and Ladies of Charity at St. Mary's.

She didn't know how to say the rosary, but now it is her best friend. She carries it with her at all times. The special part of this story—besides Mary—is she started making rosaries with the rosary makers at our parish.

She just made some glow-in-the-dark ones for her grandmother, great aunt and a "old" friend for Christmas. She is so proud she can do this, and everyone is proud of her. She is our *special* rosary maker…

Kathy J. Laird   *Frankfort, Indiana*

The Family Prayer

Growing up, I remember on Friday night after dinner, my family would say the rosary around the dinner table. Everyone had a part. I would say the "Our Father"—being very small it was the one prayer I knew very well.

As the family grew older and moved apart, the tradition stopped when I was the only one home. I am the youngest of seven. I soon forgot how important the rosary was to the family until I was in my late 30s. My second oldest sister was ill with lung cancer for a number of years. She lived with half my brothers and sisters in California.

I could only afford to see her once a year. My two sisters in Chicago and I planned to go see her in August, but my sisters in Chicago got a great deal on tickets in July at the last minute. I knew I couldn't leave work without notice, nor could I leave my two children, so they went without telling me, not wanting me to feel bad about not being able to go.

My sister was living with her son at the time and had suddenly taken a turn for the worse. The whole family that was in California went to see her that Monday night. My oldest sister said, "Let's say the rosary like we used to at home."

So everyone said the rosary around her bed that night, and two days later she died.

Of course, my other sisters had to call me about our sister's passing, and they had to tell me that they had gone to see her without me and how she had died.

At first I was upset that I was the only one not there, until I got the details. As it turned out, I was there. On Monday night, I had my Secular Franciscan meeting, and we said the rosary as the closing prayer, which we did only once a year. It was the same time my family was saying the rosary in California.

The rosary united us again and helped me deal better with her death. The rosary now always reminds me of how close my family is in God's loving care.

Anne T. Modrow   *Winston-Salem, North Carolina*

Love the Madonna
and pray the rosary,
for her rosary
is the weapon
against the evils
of the world today.

Saint Padre Pio

Friends Gather

During the past several years, our school secretary has gathered people together to pray our Lady's rosary. Every Wednesday during the months of May and October, we come together to pray. It is amazing how the numbers have grown from three or four to sometimes 20 people. Often dessert is served following, and many friendships have developed through our coming together.

In years past, my mother has said that there was a tradition of "block rosaries" said. All the Catholic neighbors would gather at someone's home every week and recite the rosary together. Perhaps this is a tradition in our age of uncertainty and turmoil to begin once more.

Barbara A. Colbeck   *Livonia, Michigan*

How Love Came Into My Life

Our Blessed Mother has been my example to follow throughout my life. My love for our Lady started at the young age of six or seven when I lived in a small town with my family. I am a twin to a brother and have a younger sister. For a long time in my life, I did not feel love from my mother.

When I was about six or seven years old, I was at Mass staring at a statue of Mary when I began to feel such peace and a sense of love that I remained in my seat after Mass was finished. My family noticed I had not returned home with them, so they came back looking for me.

176

I really didn't want to leave the church, afraid that I would never feel such a wonderful presence of peace, love and joy again.

However, Mary has been in my heart and life ever since. She has introduced me to her wonderful Son Jesus, and I do not go anywhere without my rosary.

As a young woman, I went to daily Mass to pray for a good man to come into my life. My prayers were answered, and I have a wonderful husband who also has a great devotion to Mary. We have been married 40 years, and have been blessed with three wonderful children, two great son-in-laws, and three beautiful grandchildren.

I have been in a prayer group with three other women for 27 years. Every Tuesday we gather together to praise Jesus, read the Bible, and pray the rosary. I credit all the blessings in my life to the day Mary touched me with her love when I was a young child.

Barbara Ann Morey   *Gatineau, Quebec, Canada*

Help in a Storm

In early October 2002, I was driving on a Canadian highway in a really bad rain. I could barely see, but I was headed for a spiritual direction session and was expected by a certain time.

I had not been one who said the rosary on a regular basis. As a matter of fact, I used to leave after Mass when the rosary began. However, this day I noticed my rosary in the car and I picked it up. I began praying the new Mysteries of Light (I was in touch enough to know of them). I truly believe that I weathered that storm through the intercession of the Blessed Mother.

After I reached a point where it was no longer raining, I saw this beautiful rainbow, actually a double rainbow. I drove off the highway in order to take a picture of it. It came out slightly distant but the rainbow was there.

Since that incident I have prayed the rosary more frequently, in my car quite freely and not just in a time of trouble.

Sharon E. Leroux   *Sunderland, Massachusetts*

A Special Gift

I was visiting my father at the nursing home one Sunday afternoon. He had been there for a few weeks. He was there because he developed a blood clot after his surgery and was without oxygen for four or five minutes. Needless to say, he never came back to us mentally.

One of the habits he developed after his surgery was the clearing of his throat to get rid of the mucus in it. This occurred almost every two to three minutes, all day long.

That afternoon I took dad's rosary and began saying it aloud at his bedside. As I said it, I noticed that he started to relax more and more. By the time I was finished, he was no longer clearing his throat. He was relaxed and resting comfortably.

I truly believe that Mary helped my father that Sunday afternoon. He lived another three months and he never had to clear his throat again. Thank you, Mary.

Kathy Townsend   *Bellevue, Nebraska*

*In heaven, the Virgin Mary
is always next to God,
and there she never stops
praying for us.*

                              -St. Philip Neri

My Beginnings as a Rosary Lady

February 2003 marked the sixth year since my conversion to Catholicism. Joining the Catholic faith was a decision I had wrestled with for several years. Being a former Lutheran, and originally Baptist. I struggled with the idolatry issue, especially concerning the Blessed Virgin. Then, when my stepsons started coming home from their Catholic school with questions about their faith that I could not answer, for their sake, I began Catechism lessons.

As I studied the Catechism, I came to understand idolatry differently. One of the students in my Bible study group made this comment: "What better way to get to the heart of a man, than through his mother?"

I really wanted our family to be unified in our religious beliefs, especially since my own sons were now attending preschool at our parish, and felt a great urge to be married within the church.

Shortly before my confirmation, I bought myself a lovely rosary made from crystal aurora borealis beads. I didn't know how to pray the rosary yet, but I was going to learn. After my Confirmation Mass, Father Byrnes presented me with another rosary, one made of Job's-tears.

My oldest son fawned over the gift and said he would like to have one on his confirmation. After searching several shops, I gave up on the idea of locally finding a Job's-tears rosary for him, and I still had some time until his confirmation.

In the meantime, I contacted Our Lady's Rosary Makers, hoping they would have a lead on where I could find a Job's-tears rosary for my son. They didn't, and I ended up ordering kits to make cord and wire rosaries for the missions.

In no time at all, I was making rosaries, and was quite pleased with the feeling of stewardship it gave me.

Then, a grandmother who attended daily Mass with my youngest son and I asked me to make single decade rosaries for her prison ministry. I gladly obliged. After that, my first grader asked if I could teach his classmates how to make the rosary. I solicited the help of another mother who attended Mass with me, and we were on a roll. I began to think of us as the "Rosary Ladies."

After first grade, we went to the kindergarten classes. When the new school year started, the second graders made rosaries for the missions in Fiji. We received a wonderful letter from the priest, stating that the rosaries arrived a few days before the students' first communion, and they were able to give each of them a new rosary. They even sent a picture of all of them proudly displaying their rosaries.

Now, each school year we visit the classrooms, and continue to make rosaries to donate to various missions and pro-life groups. After the September 11th tragedy, the second graders made rosaries to send to a Catholic parish near the World Trade Center. The children were so pleased to be helping others. This year the kids are making a personalized rosary to keep for themselves.

In order to help fund my mission rosary project, I began selling the wire rosaries at my son's school for first communion and confirmation gifts. Soon I was selling on eBay (momof 5boys1), and began my own massive collection of unusual rosaries. All of my sons and I have a Job's-tears rosary now. A local Catholic store buys my rosaries and sells them in their store and on their web site.

Aside from raising funds for the mission projects, I pray that my efforts will further the devotion to the rosary, and the Blessed Mother. It gives me great joy to know that my creations are in the hands of people all over the world, and are being used to strengthen their commitment to their faith, our Lord Jesus Christ and His mother. May the Holy Spirit come down upon me and continue to bless me with this gift for years to come, and may our Heavenly Father find pleasure in my works.

Shannon S. Naughton   *Aurora, Colorado*

The Rosary is the scourge of the devil!
Pope Adrian VI

My Journey Back Home

I was born, baptized, and raised a Catholic. My mother's death and an unfortunate situation involving insensitive words spoken by my pastor at the time drove me away from my church in 1987. Although I never abandoned the faith, I was no longer a practicing Catholic. Years later, after marriage, two children, a new home, and being downsized from my job, I came back to my church.

One day, I found myself in the religious section of my neighborhood bookstore. I chose to read inspirational books. I wasn't even a reader. I felt as if I was drawn to this moment. I chose books on angels, miracles and devotion to Mary.

And so it began. Where doors were closed, windows were now being opened. I learned for the first time in my life, on my own, to pray the rosary.

One Tuesday night, I sobbed and sobbed uncontrollably during a meditation of the sorrowful mysteries. I felt the weight of the world being lifted from my shoulders. I prayed to St. Joseph for employment daily. I was offered three jobs in 60 days, the last day extended to me my previous employer.

My fascination with the devotion to Mary grew. I did a lot of research about her apparitions. My family and I began to attend church religiously in my new community.

With the help of books, tapes, and numerous Catholic on-line resources, I developed a whole new knowledge, understanding and appreciation of my Catholic faith. I have joined prayer groups on-line and attend Marian conferences yearly. I have found and made many new friends as a result.

Almost ten years later, both my husband and I have quit unhealthy habits. Our children are thriving in their academics and in their faith. Our family is one that serves the Church and the community on an ongoing basis.

We have been blessed with many graces. I like to believe I owe it to intercession of our Blessed Mother Mary, and the power of the rosary for peace. This peace I have felt internally and share with my family, friends, neighbors, church and community. She has also brought me closer than I have ever been to her Son, my Lord Jesus Christ, despite other trials in my life since then.

Jennifer L. Garrity   *Chicago, Illinois*

A Special Grace From Mary

I had been out of the Church for over 30 years, but I did pray the rosary a little. Then I lost my youngest son, at the age of 19, to suicide. I am really glad I had my faith to fall back on.

I was worried whether or not he had gone to heaven. I started praying the rosary in earnest for a sign he went to heaven. The first promise of Mary to those who recite the rosary is they shall receive signal graces.

After three months my uncle called and asked if I would like to go to a Marian conference with him, and to bring my Wayne Wible book, that he would be there, and I could get him to autograph it for me.

I went to the conference, and it was excellent. I also went to confession, and I received Holy Communion. Then I told Jesus that I would never leave him again.

After the conference, I waited in a line of one hundred people, to get Wayne to sign my book. We all had name tags, so when I got up to him, he looked up and said, "Hi, Roy."

He held out his hand, and we shook hands, and as he started to release my hand, he gripped my hand really tight and looked me straight in the eyes for a few seconds, and then said, "I know your story. I have something for you."

Then he let my hand go and reached into his coat pocket and brought out this Miraculous Medal. As he handed me the medal, he said, "Here, Mary told me to give you this and that she blessed it in Medjugorje."

Thank you, Wayne. Thank you, Mary.

Roy P. Proctor   *Friday Harbor, Washington*

Mary's Healing Intercession

My husband Tom was healed as the result of many rosaries.

Tom had stomach problems, causing his stomach to hurt him so much he couldn't button his pants. He went to the doctor who said he would run some tests to see what the problem was.

In the meantime, Tom and I went to a Eucharistic Marian Conference in Spokane, Washington. We had the privilege and honor of seeing the image of our Lady of Guadalupe that has traveled all over the world: to conferences, abortion clinics—wherever they need our Lady's intercession.

Tom had been praying the rosary to our Lady for healing. He touched his rosary to the image and was healed instantly. No more pain and no need to return to the doctor.

Our Lady, through her intercession to our Lord did it, and he is healed to this day.

Also I know that our daughter's vocation to the Poor Clare Nuns is the result of many rosaries, family and private.

Lillian Byrne   *Denton, Montana*

All generations will call me blessed.

Luke 1:48

Revisiting the Rosary

My story is about the experiences I had teaching students about the rosary during the years I taught CCD classes in Columbus, Ohio. I had the opportunity to teach fourth grade for three years at St. James the Less Church and fifth grade at Our Lady of Peace.

During the month of October, I invited the students to bring in their rosaries from first communion. They could also bring a special rosary from home if they chose to, and I would also bring in "special" rosaries and tell stories about them.

One was a rosary that my father had purchased in Rome in the mid 1950s. Another was my grandmother's handed down to my mother, which now belonged to me. The last rosary was my first communion rosary.

Without my direction one child would ask permission to handle the rosary. As each student picked the rosaries with sincere appreciation, I explained what each rosary was special for and what they represented, such as how my mother taught me the rosary and her love of the Blessed Mary.

Soon the students would open up and tell about their experiences with rosaries. How they prayed as a family, with one parent, or with another family member. How it brought them closer together.

Many would be unfamiliar of how to say the rosary. It was always a wonderful experience watching the expressions on their faces as they learned to hold and say the prayers on the rosary. Each student had their own way, but all revered it as something special and holy.

We would say a decade of the rosary each week for opening prayer of class. We talked about the mysteries, and the children realized how it told the story of Jesus and Mary. At the end of the month when I told them we would go back to our usual opening prayer ritual there was always a sadness in the class of saying good-bye to a friend. I would occasionally use the rosary in the classroom for prayer, but it was not the same as our special time in October.

At the end of the year I asked the children what their favorite times in class had been. Learning about the rosary and how to use it was always one of their top things to do. I even learned from parents how the children would want family time saying the rosary together.

From teaching the rosary, I began to say the rosary more often. I would ask Mary to intercede and help a student, help the other classes preparing for sacraments or to help me prepare my class work. I had the opportunity to look at the rosary through a child's eye and found again the holiness that my mother taught me over forty years ago.

Loretta A. Horton   *Columbus, Ohio*

The Death of Robert James Collins

Robert James Collins is my brother. A product of our mother and father's faith that took root and blossomed into a wonderful family. His life was full of adversity and disappointments, but he managed to marry a wonderful wife who was full of the same faith strength as his own. Together they had a great devotion to Mary the Mother of Jesus.

Daily recitation of the rosary was part of their daily life from the day they were married. All of his children who were present at the time were absorbed into the tradition. It is no wonder then, that I tell you of his death, for this is his glory.

Bob's death came as a result of a bout with cancer of the esophagus, complicated by diabetes. He submitted to the usual attempts to be cured but all attempts failed. Through his powerful will, he managed to survive for two years.

He realized the eventual outcome was coming near, so he prayed for forbearance. As the end approached, he fell into a semiconscious state. His eyesight failed, and he was unable to talk for several days.

On the day Bob died, November 26, 2002, he was surrounded by his family: his wife, sons and daughters, and some grandchildren.

Several months before, one of his sons audiotaped his father leading the family rosary—the Glorious Mysteries. Now, at his bedside the family began to pray the rosary, and his son played the tape of his father leading the rosary. Even though he could not speak, Bob was moving his lips with the prayers on the tape. It was the Glorious Mysteries that he loved!

At the conclusion of the Fifth Mystery he smiled and took his last breath and died. It was 2:10 p.m., the exact moment that his mother had died many years before. The Blessed Mother, I am sure, was there to take him by the hand to meet the Lord. The Lord blessed him with a most peaceful death.

Good and faithful servant, as your family continues to pray the rosary, intercede with the Most High for their continuing love of the rosary and the grace of a peaceful death!

Martha Collins   *Madison, New York*

The Guardian Cowboy

I always take my rosary with me and pray it when I'm riding. This one particular time we were gathering cows, and it had been a long day. We were trying to move them into a little meadow. They didn't want to cooperate. So I said a little prayer to my guardian angel: "Please help me!" You know, those cows went right through that gate!

Tom Byrne   *Denton, Montana*

The beads are there for the sake of the prayers,
and the prayers are there for the sake of the mysteries.

Maisie Ward

Answers From Mary

We are a group of 20 women in Buenos Aires, Argentina. We meet the last Friday of each month to pray the rosary. Our image is the Virgin of Schoenstatt. We also read messages from our mother the "Virgin Del Rosario de San Nicolas."

Every time that somebody has a problem, we open the message book at any page, at random, and there is the answer.

Our prayers are so strong that one of our friends, after seven years, was able to get pregnant, and now she has a beautiful son. Another friend had a physical problem, and now she is perfect.

Mónica Mendez   *Buenos Aires, Argentina*

The Water in our Cellar

My rosary story happened in the middle 1970s, while I was still living at home with my father, mother and brother. It was a Saturday night, and we were experiencing a heavy rainstorm.

Our cellar had an opening in the floor where the water was gushing in and flooding the cellar floor. My dad and brother had on boots, and with mops and brooms were working very hard to get as much water into the pails as possible. My dad had found a plumber who agreed to come with the stipulation that the house call alone—starting from when he left his house to come to our house—would be $60.00. And that would be before he started work.

My mom was upstairs on the first floor, and I was in my bedroom praying the rosary about this emergency. I was either at the end or towards the end of the rosary when I heard my dad and brother talking, as if something else had happened. I picked up on this and went downstairs.

My dad was staring at the opening where the water was coming from. I asked what had happened.

My dad went to Mass on Sunday, sent us to Catholic school and believed in God, but beyond that, he was not a spiritually inclined person. I never told them I'd pray the rosary, and my family did not know I was praying about our flooding cellar.

But just then, my dad turned to me and asked, "Were you praying?"

Considering my father's faith, this was a Holy Spirit statement coming from my dad.

I said, "Yes," and I knew that he knew that the prayers definitely had a connection to the water suddenly stopping.

The plumber, who had already arrived and had started his "house call," said he would charge us nothing.

So it was a big miracle and a little miracle. It was stilling raining outside, so I hadn't stopped the entire rain, but the rain had stopped pouring into our cellar. Our Lady will never let us down if we have faith.

She is truly a loving mother.

Elisabeth M. Crupi   *Scardale, New York*

My Rosary On the Rearview Mirror

It was about one o'clock in the morning in September, 1989. I was driving from Coeur d'Alene, Idaho, back to Spokane, Washington, after watching my then boyfriend playing in his band at a resort. I was tired and had to work in the morning.

I had four jobs at that time: at a radio station, a retail store, a weightloss clinic and a company that provided security for events.

When my boyfriend walked me to my car that night, he made a comment how worried he was because I looked tired. A bad feeling came over him, but I reassured him that I was fine and that I would hurry home to bed.

I never made it home that night. As I drove home I felt very tired and made it as far as the Spokane Valley. I never knew I fell asleep. (I now caution anyone who is tired and behind a wheel, don't be too over confident because you never realize that you are falling asleep—just pull over!)

I woke up, slumped over, just in time to see that I was driving on the shoulder hitting reflectors. I had no control of the car. The last memory I had was the car starting to roll.

I am not sure how long I was unconscious, but I thank the Lord I awoke—a true blessing. Otherwise, I would have smothered. This was all part of His plan. When I awoke, I was face down, not being able to turn my head because the car was on top of me. I was able to turn my mouth just enough to spit out the dirt in order to breathe. Since my body was twisted somehow I was only able to move my left arm and my feet from the ankles down.

It was a complete shock to my system. My first thought was, *Oh well, when I get this car off of me, I'll just hitch a ride home.* Normally I would never consider hitchhiking, but I was not thinking rationally or logically.

The only pain I had felt thus far was the intense pressure placed on my head. Glass was all over my arms and face. I was covered in cuts, and after struggling to breathe and to move, blood started running down my face from my head. Was my head cracked open? What was the extent of my injuries?

Where am I? I wondered. *Will anyone find me? How long do I have to live?*

At this point it became real! This was truly happening! I honestly thought I was dying. What an indescribable feeling this was. All I could do was pray. I prayed the Our Father and Hail Mary over and over again. I prayed that if I should die that I wouldn't be lying here too long without my family knowing.

Time was not apparent to me, but I finally heard a car slow down, then voices. By this time I was hyperventilating and shaking uncontrollably. I heard footsteps come toward me. It was a band returning from playing in Coeur d'Alene.

They picked up the car off me, rolling it aside. I later learned that they almost never stopped to help after seeing my feet from under the car because they believed I was a dead body. They were just going to call 911 and wait at a distance. Seeing my feet move changed their minds.

Now that the car was off me they debated whether to wait for the ambulance or take me themselves after they saw my physical injuries. They decided to take me to the hospital and along the way, they asked me things such as my name and what year it was.

After we arrived at the hospital emergency room, as I was being cleaned and having my wounds attended to, I remember the paramedics rushing in and looking at me in shock, amazed that I was not more badly injured. Not demeaning my injuries, but the paramedics, who had already seen the crash sight and my damaged, empty car, expected to see a paralyzed vegetable. When my boyfriend passed my car on the way to the hospital, he expected the worst as well. The Blessed Virgin Mary was definitely taking care of me!

I wasn't going to run any marathons anytime soon. It was as if a freight train hit me. I had cuts and bruises all over my body. My face was swollen and puffy and my eyes were almost shut. My hair was torn out on the right side of my head with my ear looking as if a dog chewed on it. With a neck brace, back brace, sling for my broken collarbone, bandage on the side of my head, blood clot in my right leg, one might have imagined that I had fought in a war.

My memory was nothing to brag about either. I forgot things as soon as I was told them. I forgot how old I was at one point. Most of my speech was slow and slurred. I figured that no one would want me back at my job on the radio for while.

I could not take care of myself at my apartment. My mother and father took very good care of me at their house for some weeks, assisting me in eating, bathing and getting dressed. I was off work for about a month and a half. Bless my parents' hearts, true saints for putting up with me!

My father went to the crash sight and to the wrecking yard to see if I left any belongings behind. When he returned, he gave me my Lady of Guadalupe rosary that he and my mother had brought back from Mexico for me, which I had kept wrapped around my rearview mirror. I asked him where he found it, he told me it was right where I had always kept it.

How could it have still been where I kept it? The mirror was even gone, nowhere to be found! My rosary was still in the hole where the mirror used to be. The car rolled about three times, cracking the windshield everywhere with pieces missing. The rosary, wrapped around the mirror, should have disappeared with the mirror. It wasn't logical that it would be wedged in the small hole in the glass where the mirror used to be.

The Blessed Mother was telling me, that through everything, she never ever left my side. She remained exactly where I placed her. An accident that should have resulted in much worse injuries, or that should have been fatal, was not. And to make matters worse, which should have surely complicated my injuries, I was not wearing my seat belt.

As I look back at all the events that took place—the astounded paramedics, the critical damage to the car and my rosary still remaining—this was definitely a miracle from our Blessed Mother.

It's the year 2002 now, I'm married to a wonderful man and we have a beautiful one-year-old daughter. To this day I still never drive without a rosary hanging from my rearview mirror. I say the rosary daily. I have never forgotten the protection and blessings our Lady has bestowed on my family and me. She is so precious to me! My daughter will also learn about her, just as my mother and father have taught me. Thank you, Blessed Mother!

Diana Affonso (Sattler)   *Orting, Washington*

*Hail, full of grace,
the Lord is with you;
through you salvation
was brought to the world.*

Saint Bonaventure

Unconditional Love in My Marriage

I always felt a closeness with our Lord since the days of my youth. I would get feelings of what to do and what not to do, more like a voice steering me in the right direction. There were days of happiness and days of sadness, but they always brought me to the Lord, even when I strayed. I prayed the rosary, but not often—until I was led to pray the rosary.

I am a mother of three children in a marriage lasting close to four years. About three months ago, our marriage took a turn for the worst. I had a strange feeling we were growing apart. The intimacy in our marriage had lost ground, and our only conversations revolved around the children. I was a stay-at-home mom while my husband worked. We were tight on funds and lived with my parents. This was his excuse to party with his friends and come home the next morning.

One day, I got a call from a friend with devastating news about my husband being with another woman. My heart was shattered. I had confronted him, and I was thankful he confessed. My first human reaction was to consult with my close friends hoping it would help me deal with the pain. It helped, somewhat, but I still felt an emptiness within. I started to pray even more.

After nights of crying in my pillow, I asked the Lord to give me wisdom, understanding and strength to do His will, not mine. At this point in my life, I felt if anything could be better, I needed to humble myself and wait for Jesus' cue, although I just wanted to pack up luggage and tell my husband to leave.

Then, I felt my spirit experiencing drastic changes that had to be from a higher power. I was led to pray the rosary, and at times with my children during lonely nights and in Catholic e-chats with others praying, Mother Mary would intercede. I felt so close to our Lady. She was leading me to the Lord with all the prayers of the Most Holy Rosary.

What a gift the Lord sent, a Blessed Mother to pray for us. Everything was possible with our Holy Family up in heaven, our Father, our Lord, the

Holy Spirit, our Blessed Mother, and our Holy Saints. I felt I knew them on a personal basis. Nothing in this world meant a thing to me, but the relationship I shared in spirit.

This special relationship gave me a better outlook with the relationships that I had here on Earth, even with strangers and enemies. There were still days of confusion with my husband, but it didn't matter to me because I knew the Lord loved me with an unconditional love. I still prayed the Most Holy Rosary.

Through all the days, I felt the Lord dealing with me. I was led to go back to college, I found peace within myself after being cheated on, and I knew that I was in the process of forgiveness with my husband.

Today, I don't how I could have been so strong without my Heavenly Family. The Lord showed me so much during this trial. I now look at hard times knowing Our Lord is there by my side wanting the best for me, a sinner. Thank you, Lord, for our Blessed Mother, and thank you, Blessed Mother, for the Most Holy Rosary. I pray for all the marriages out there going through trials. Remember, our Lord's love is the greatest. May our Blessed Mother and Holy Saints pray for you and your families.

Angela M. Bilan   *Kapolei, Hawaii*

Brian's Rosary

It was September 8, the day the Church celebrates our Lady's birthday. I had no sooner arrived home from an out-of-town retreat, when I received a phone call from my husband Tom requesting that I come down to the hospital right away. Upon arrival at the hospital, Tom broke the news to me that our son Brian was in surgery to repair damage he had done when he accidentally shot himself in the leg and severed a major artery.

Tom was there when they brought Brian into the hospital, and his description of Brian was that he looked like a casualty victim from Vietnam. Then he handed me a bank envelope and said, "Here is Brian's rosary. It is covered with mud, and Brian wants to leave it that way."

I went to the chapel in the hospital and knelt in front of the tabernacle and prayed countless rosaries until I thought it was time for Brian to come out of surgery. When it was time for us to see Brian, I could not believe my eyes. After Tom's description, I expected the worst. Instead, I found Brian sitting up in bed, talking and joking with the nurses. He even requested to watch the video *Young Guns*.

During the days that followed, Brian related his experience to me. He told me that early on the morning of September 8, he had a strange premonition that something was going to happen to him that day. Since it was a beautiful day, he decided to spend some time in the woods nearby. As he headed towards the woods though, he felt the urge to turn around and go back home to get the wooden rosary he had brought from Medjugorje last summer.

When Brian got to the woods, he did some target shooting, and as he was putting his gun into his holster, his gun accidentally went off and hit him in the upper right thigh. Brian immediately blacked out, and when he came to, he could not hear or see anything for a time. When he realized what had happened, he yelled for help although he could not recall having seen anyone else in the woods that day though.

Brian realized very quickly that he could not walk, so he tried to hop on his other leg. Each time he would try to stand up, though, he would fall down again. Weakened from the loss of blood, he fell to the ground and began crawling on his belly.

It was not long before he noticed he was bleeding so profusely that his jeans looked like they could be used for a Santa Claus suit. They weighed him down so much from the blood and the mud he was crawling through that he eventually removed them so he could continue to move.

Brian then removed his shirt and tried to make a tourniquet with it, but it was not successful because his leg had become so swollen. He became dehydrated, so he crawled to the mud puddles and sipped the water out of them. Brian said he had to stick his lips down into the puddles because of

194

the layers of gas and oil from all-terrain-vehicles (ATVs) that formed a film on top of the puddles. He said that by that point, even the stagnant mosquito-infested water in the mud puddles tasted good.

During this time Brian's hearing began to fade in and out, and his breathing became labored. As he continued to crawl from mud puddle to mud puddle, he screamed for help, but there seemed not to be another soul in the woods that day. This went on for two and a half or three hours.

Before Brian had discarded his jeans, he took his wooden rosary from Medjugorje out of the pocket. He wrapped it around the fingers of his left hand, and crawled to the next puddle. As he lay on his back in the puddle he relaxed and began to pray the rosary. Brian said that before he found his rosary he was very angry, but as he began to pray the rosary he relaxed and came to terms with the idea that he might not make it out of the woods.

Dragging himself from puddle to puddle, he continued to pray the rosary. Finally Brian reached what looked to be the last puddle. In front of him was a big hill. He made himself as comfortable as possible, and prepared to die.

He closed his eyes as he prayed in his rosary for God to send him an angel to rescue him, or, if that was not God's plan, then to let him die peacefully.

Then he heard the noise of motors! With what little strength he had left after having crawled approximately 500 yards, Brian yelled for help. Two men on ATVs heard his cries and came over and asked him what was wrong. By this point, he was not bleeding any more because he was virtually out of blood.

Brian told them that he had been shot. Then they asked what was in his hand.

Barely able to breathe, much less speak, he answered, "My rosary."

The men helped him onto one of the ATVs for the half-hour ride to the nearest house, where they called 911.

Brian's surgery was successful. Amazingly, the bullet had exited the leg through the back and had not done any damage to the bone, surrounding muscle or major nerve. The next day a policeman came to the hospital and told us how very lucky Brian was. He said that if the men on the ATVs had not picked Brian up when they did, he would not have survived. If they had gone for help and then come back, it would have been too late. He had not much more than 20 minutes left.

When the policeman gave us the names of the men on the ATVs, we called them right away to thank them. Eric Swindlehurst and Christopher Firment both humbly admitted that it was God who saved Brian and that they had just been in the right place at the right time.

Both men told us that they had not been planning on going riding that day—it was a spur of the moment decision. They also told us that they almost never go to that part of the woods, and had not been there in months. What is even more amazing is that even with their helmets on they were able to hear Brian's cries for help over their loud motors. And where they found Brian was the exact opposite direction of the way Brian had intended to go.

Brian had been so disoriented, as he faded in and out of consciousness, that he headed the wrong direction in the woods he had been so familiar with since he was a child. Brian was also surprised that the men were able to see him at all because his whole body except for his head was immersed in the deep puddle.

Several months later, as I was telling this story, a nurse asked me how much damage Brian sustained. She was surprised when I told her that he had no damage at all. She said that because of the large loss of blood over a long period of time he should have had kidney, liver or brain damage.

Our son could have lost his leg, or he could have gotten a terrible infection from the stagnant water. Other medical personnel I have spoken with agreed. Brian was back at his college classes a week and a half later and began jogging again the following month. Brian even made the dean's list that semester, for the first time! Our Lady of Medjugorje said, "The rosary alone can already work miracles in the world and in your lives."

June A. Klins   Erie, Pennsylvania

We do not hesitate to affirm publicly that we put great confidence in the Holy Rosary for the healing of evils which afflict our times.

Pope Pius XII

58th Year of Our Honeymoon

Claire and I are in the 58th year of our honeymoon. We have five married children with their own families, which so far adds up to 14 grandchildren and 12 great-grandchildren.

Years ago, when we walked to St. Paul's Church to speak to a priest about marriage, my wife was only 19 years old, and I was 18. Father Jameson, who is now deceased, said, "You kids are awfully young to get married. I'll do it, but I hate these wartime weddings. They never last."

Claire worked for the Federal Bureau of Investigation at that time. I was in the United States Navy, stationed at the Naval Magazine in Baltimore, Maryland. Our prayer was that we would never be separated for more than a week, and it was soon put to the test. In July of 1945, I was transferred to Boston and put on a brand new ship. It was preparing for its "shakedown" cruise and was scheduled to go to the Pacific Ocean. I left Claire at a hotel in Boston. She went home to Bangor, Maine and the ship left port.

Father Kilek, the Chaplain, had Holy Mass every morning in his cabin. I was the only one of 2,600 men to take advantage of this grace. He said, "I hate to tell you this, but you will be away from your wife for about three months."

I said, "I don't think so, Father. We have been praying that we would never be apart for more than a week."

On the third morning, Father Kolek and I stood at the rear of the ship watching the wake disappear into the horizon. Suddenly, we felt a vibration and the wake started curving to the east. Father Kilek, being an officer, was able to learn that one of the ship's four diesel engines had broken down. We were on our way back to Boston.

I telephoned Claire and she came back to Boston on the seventh day of our separation. The war ended, I got off the ship, and we went to live in Bangor where Claire had our first baby. To this day, I am convinced that the power of prayer changed the course of that monstrous warship.

Robert Kieckhefer   *Fairfield, Pennsylvania*

Impossible Miracle

"Did you ever have a miraculous answer due to your devotion to the rosary?" Well, there are miracles, and then there are miracles. I consider myself a rosary miracle!

The family rosary was my introduction to prayer. As a little tyke, when we all knelt down after supper to pray the rosary, I'm told that I would go from chair to chair saying, "Amen!" Such was my introduction to our Blessed Lady and her rosary.

Throughout my childhood years, my mother had a better way for us to get to sleep than by using Tylenol PM—she would tell us to get in bed and pray the rosary. Most of the time, I fell asleep before I finished.

When I was in my last year of high school, my buddies and I had long talks on what we wanted to do after graduation. We knew we had to go to college, and had taken and passed the entrance exam into Loyola University. This told me that I had the intelligence necessary for studies for the priesthood. Knowing that, I turned to God for guidance, and made a novena of nine days of Mass and the rosary, asking to know His will.

When I left for the seminary, one of my sisters expected me to return home in six weeks. She said, "He'll be back! He went on dates and to all the school dances and enjoyed them all. He'll be back!"

Our Blessed Lady had other ideas. There were, of course, some tough times during my seminary years, as well as after I was ordained a priest. However, I was always determined to stick around until they kicked me out. That was over 50 years ago and I'm still waiting!

I continue to pray the rosary daily, and am still Mary's miracle of simple trust, love and daily living. Thank you, my dear Blessed Mother. Please continue to keep me under your loving care, because I am your "impossible miracle!"

Fr. Maurus Kelly, OFM　　　　　　　　　　　　　*Santa Barbara, California*

Angels Dancing on the Chuppah

My sister Christine and I had a wonderful (and beautiful) floral business in lower Manhattan for ten years. Our clientele consisted of many famous celebrities, as well as others who called on us to create floral arrangements for special events and weddings.

While it was a very exciting time in our lives, it was also very stressful. Long hours, and working with a perishable product in a demanding city took its toll on us.

Like all businesses, we would have our times of crisis, but whenever those times occurred, we responded in the same way. I would get on the phone with our mother, Geraldine, tell her the crisis, and she would say what she had said all our lives when we were upset about something: "Don't worry, I'll pray the rosary right now. The Blessed Mother will take care of it. She never lets me down."

One day we were working on a beautiful and detailed wedding in an exclusive club off Fifth Avenue in New York City. In the grand entrance, which was really a large marble room, was a huge decorative fireplace, at least ten feet high and ten feet wide. Since the club no longer used it as a working fireplace, it was a wonderful focal point, and where we decided to create a chuppah (a little house) for the wedding, as this was a Jewish wedding.

We hung glimmering organza curtains across the front of the fireplace to disguise where the fire would have been and arranged white flowers such as roses, orchids, snapdragon, hydrangea, and stock across the mantle. Then, to create the "little house" that the couple, the rabbi, and the families stand under, we placed two, eight-feet tall columns in front of the fireplace at each side.

The two gentlemen who worked for us that day were to crisscross more of the organza from the ends of the mantle to these columns, draping the excess fabric down the columns and putting large arrangements of more white flowers on top of the columns to anchor the fabric in place. I explained to them that the crisscross was to be soft and gentle, but not too low, as people would be standing underneath it. When it was done, it was truly beautiful, soft, white and fragrant—a special and romantic place for this couple to make their vows.

After we finished decorating this area we moved on to the other areas of the club, hanging garlands down the staircase, decorating the cocktail area and dining room, and finally presenting the personal flowers to everyone in the bridal party. For a wedding such as this, we would stay for the ceremony, and then leave.

As my sister and I sat in the background and watched people begin to arrive, I got a very sick feeling in my stomach. Somehow the crisscross of organza was sinking and getting much lower than I remembered it hanging. I asked one of the workers who was still there to go and stand underneath it, and sure enough, the fabric was touching his face. When we had set it up, it was above his head. What was wrong? I was in a panic, imagining that this was the end of our careers, and that we would be sued, or at least not paid for all of our hard work and efforts. Not to mention the bride would have her special day ruined.

I got on the telephone with the gentleman who set it up and told him to tell me exactly what they had done.

"Well, we wanted to fluff up the organza, so we stuffed it with some extra fabric," he explained.

"Did you pin it in place?" I asked.

"No," came his reply.

"No?!" I screeched back. "It's sliding into the center of the fabric and stretching it. It's too late for me to do anything. The musicians and guests are arriving."

"Sorry," he said quietly.

I hung up the phone. What was I going to do? I did what I have done all my life. I called my mother who was at home on Long Island, and started crying, telling her what was happening. She said what she always said: "Don't worry, I'll pray the rosary right now and the Blessed Mother will take care of it. She never lets me down."

"How could she possibly take care of this?" I cried.

I wiped the tears from my face, tried to compose myself, and went back to where the chuppah was.

Now the area was filled with the 200 invited guests and I put my head down, waiting for my shame, which I was sure would come. The music began, and I heard the gasp you usually hear when the bride comes down the aisle. I was used to people reacting with pleasure and delight at how beautiful the bride looked, but today I knew the murmurs must be about the rapidly sinking chuppah.

My sister poked me in the side and said, "Look at them." I looked up and saw the family members from both sides of the family standing underneath the chuppah, and they were the shortest people I had ever seen!

I had met the bride and her mother before the wedding, and knew they were quite petite, but amazingly, so was everyone else. And the rabbi was the shortest of them all, maybe five feet tall at the most. I couldn't believe it!

I kept praying, "Please let the ceremony end before the chuppah comes down any further."

At that point the rabbi said in his very touching talk to the couple, "This is a day of such joy, that even the angels in Heaven are rejoicing." He raised his hands very dramatically, and proclaimed, "The angels are dancing on this beautiful chuppah!"

"Oh no," I thought, "Please, not on the chuppah!"

My sister started to giggle, and so did I.

The ceremony ended right after that, and I did what I always did at the time of a crisis. I ran to the phone and called my mother. She was right again. The Blessed Mother had taken care of it. She never let my mother down.

Six years ago, my sister and I closed our business and went home to take care of our mother who was diagnosed with Alzheimer's disease. She passed away January 2002 having prayed her last rosary before she slipped into a coma. Her legacy to me was her faith in the Blessed Mother, and the power of the rosary. Now when there is a crisis, I pray the rosary, and know that I am praying it with my mother. The Blessed Mother never lets us down.

Elizabeth M. Keihm   *Seaford, New York*

A Safe Return

I have always had a great love for the Blessed Mother. I remember as a child (one of nine children) in my family, we would gather around a statue of the Blessed Mother to say the rosary every night. I grew up having a great love for the Blessed Mother and the rosary. When my husband was diagnosed with Lymphoma, I naturally turned to our Lady. I am most thankful to report that he has been cancer free for 11 years. I owe it all to the Blessed Mother.

Another story told to me by my mother: It was during World War II. I had two brothers in the army, and one day while in church my mother was praying to Mary, and asked her if her boys would be coming home from the fighting. She said that Mary moved her head yes. Both of my brothers came home without a scratch. Thanks again to our Lady.

Georgianna M. Trussell   *Mt. Vernon, Ohio*

Healing Love

It was a Friday night some years ago. I had just settled down to watch a movie when the phone rang. This was unusual as no one calls me at nine o'clock in the evening unless it's an emergency. I answered the phone and a sweet young voice introduced herself to me as Mary, from my church. She asked me to lead the rosary the next afternoon at 3 p.m. at our church for Respect Life. I told her I had never done that and I had no idea what to do as I have always prayed my rosary in private. But Mary was very insistent and kept telling me there was no one else available. She said she would be there and stay with me to give me some moral support.

Saturday arrived, beautiful and clear. I got to the church a few minutes early and a couple I knew came in and asked who was going to lead the rosary. I said I was. They came over and gave me, because I was willing to lead, the most beautiful picture of Our Lady of Medjugorje and told me it had been taken by a priest from Rome who had gone there to be with the children for the apparition of our Lady. The priest had not seen Mary but when the children's heads went back he pointed his camera to where he thought they were staring and he snapped. The result is incredible and gives me Jesus bumps every time I look at it, even today.

There were seven people present and I asked them to think of this as a beautiful bouquet for our Lady. Think of each Our Father and Glory bead as a white orchid and each Hail Mary bead as a pale blue rose. We began and it was going along just fine. Around the third decade, Mary started sniffling and I sensed something was wrong. By the fourth decade, she put her head on my shoulder and began to weep quietly. I did not know what to do but to ask our Blessed Mother to comfort her as I knew I had to go on.

When the rosary was finished I was able to hold Mary as she sobbed and told her story. She had had two abortions and until the middle of the third decade of the rosary that day she had never felt it was wrong. It was like a curtain rose from her heart and all of a sudden she was almost out of her mind with grief for her two babies and what she had done to them. I held her for a long time until she was able to stop crying.

Father celebrated the 4:00 p.m. Mass and Mary went to the altar and told the congregation of what had happened to her. Father then had a healing service after Mass and everyone stayed to help Mary and pray with her and for her and to comfort her. It was an incredibly moving experience. God allowed me to share in it all because I said "YES!" Thank you my Lord!

Mary did go on with her life and now is the mother of a beautiful young girl! May God be praised!

Sister Katherine   *Victoria, Texas*

On A Dark Night

I had heard that even if one could not find the time or inclination to pray the rosary, simply to carry a blessed rosary was a prayer and a protection itself. One day I experienced actual proof of this statement.

Since the time I was a teenager drugs were often a main part of my life. No matter the resolutions or the good intentions, time after time I would be swallowed up by them. The drugs had a hold and I was their captive prisoner. One night I got into a particularly bad situation. I did not have any money but I wanted drugs. Bad enough in fact that I did not use my head and placed my self in an extremely foolish and dangerous situation.

I walked the streets until I found some people who could supply the drugs I needed. They took me up into a dark deserted room. I am not sure how many were there, perhaps four or five. I asked for the dope but they wanted my money first. I didn't have any. These were tough street people and they didn't like being taken for a ride. I didn't know what to do. They were getting upset and one tough lady in particular was pressing me for the cash. She was inches away from my face as I pushed my hand into my front pocket and pretended to find some money. As I reached my hand into my pocket to pull out whatever was there. The only thing I came out with was my rosary.

All of a sudden that tough woman of the streets paled and backed away. She said to the rest of them in a firm voice that meant she was not going to be messed with. "You leave him alone!" One dude was ready to come in for a kill, but her voice came out again like cold steel and she said coldly, "I said, you leave him alone." Then she turned to the rest of them, "Come on, let's get out of here." In seconds they were gone and I was left alone in the dark, the rosary still in my hand and my mouth open in disbelief. The power of Mary and that rosary has left an impression I will never forget.

Scott Robinson   *Spokane, Washington*

The Fruits of a Mother's Love

My twin sister Wendy and I were born three months premature on March 7, 1980. As a result of our coming into the world so soon, Wendy suffered a cerebral hemorrhage, which claimed her little life just a day and a half later. The doctors said there was no chance that I could possibly survive, but I did, thanks in no small part to the fact that my sister had transfused virtually all of her blood into me while we were still in our mother's womb.

I was so weak and sick as a newborn that I remained hospitalized for two and a half months. Then, shortly after they allowed my mother to bring me home, I was diagnosed with Cerebral Palsy. This is a neurological disorder that makes me unable to walk, and with which I've now been living for nearly 23 years.

In 1994, I made the decision to undergo major surgery in which a steel rod would be fused along my backbone to correct severe scoliosis. The night before the procedure, my mom, who has had a special love for the Mother of God all her life, suggested I attempt to pray the rosary all the way through and ask God for help. Having never really prayed the rosary before, the mere idea of it intimidated me. I tried in sincere earnest to pray it correctly, but my mind was so filled with fear and confusion, I kept getting off track. I never succeeded in praying an entire five-decade rosary that night, and by the time I gave up I was thinking, "That was recited so lamely, it probably doesn't even count."

By God's grace, the surgery went extremely well, and I woke up breathing on my own, without the aid of a respirator. This was a considerable feat for a young woman like myself who was born with underdeveloped lungs. Some time later, while I was still in the hospital, my mom told me that she had paced back and forth and prayed five separate five-decade rosaries while I was undergoing surgery. She also said she would have kept on praying, had my wonderful surgeon not approached my parents and told them that the operation was complete, had gone smoothly, and that I was being taken to recovery. She added that one of the things she had specifically asked for in her prayers was that I wouldn't have to bear the added cross of waking up with a respirator lodged down my throat. She knew more than I all the incomprehensible pain and suffering I would endure on the long and daunting road to recovery.

When I was released from the hospital just ten days later, I learned of something that my entire family and I found quite unbelievable. Thankfully, while I was in the hospital I had to spend only one night in ICU. During that time I recall many of my visitors commenting that there was an able-bodied girl the same age as me in the next room who had also just undergone spinal fusion surgery. Apparently her doctors not only had to keep her respirator inserted for a while, but she was still in ICU the very day I was being sent home.

Clearly, it was the Holy Spirit who revealed to my mom beforehand the immense magnitude of suffering I would face as the result of having my back operated on. Prior to going through the surgery, I had some idea of what the recovery would be like, but was totally ignorant of the intensity and duration of the whole ordeal. Looking back though, I wouldn't change a thing.

All the trials I went through were very difficult, but they also enabled me to become closer to God than I had ever been before. I pray the rosary often now, and in doing so, have fostered fervent devotion to the Most Blessed Virgin Mary. Because of my spiritual growth, I now realize without question that things surely could have turned out very differently for me in the absence of humble, ardent prayer on the part of my loved ones. Most especially, the outcome could have been very different without the constant stream of rosaries offered up on my behalf to the Virgin Mary from the lips of my ever faithful and loving mother.

Dawn Pell   *Clinton, Maryland*

I have called upon Mary
when my soul was troubled,
and in her kindness she has heard me.

St Bonaventure

No One Could Throw It Away

This is a small but beautiful story of how one man with a dream made a difference. Ernie Haase, a member of the Knights of Columbus in Richfield, Minnesota began making rosaries in the 70s. Then he had a disturbing dream in which he dreamt that people were not treating the rosary rightly, that they were just being thrown out in the garbage. He resolved to build a rosary that not one could throw away!

He decided he would build the largest rosary shrine in the world. He put much of his funds into the project and made many sacrifices. Others joined in with him and finally he was able to make it a reality. However, where he lived there was no land available. But the Blessed Mother came through. One of Ernie's friend belonged to the parish of Saint Elizabeth that had enough land to build the Shrine. The idea was presented to the parish council and they approved it!

On May 18, 1983 Bishop George Speltz of St. Cloud, Minnesota dedicated the Shrine of the Most Holy Rosary.

Ivetta J. Watercott   *Isanti, Minnesota*

The Blessed Mother Finds a Job

In 1997, my husband was transferred from Montreal to Toronto with Canadian National Railways. The move was a blessing for him and for the family in many ways, but the adjustment was difficult for me. I left a comfortable job as departmental secretary in biology at Concordia University in Montreal, only to find myself in a strange, cold city with three children. We also learned that the cost of living in Toronto was much higher than in Montreal, so I also needed to get a job to supplement my husband's income.

By 1999, I had been through a series of unsuccessful jobs that created much inner anguish and frustration within me. Then one day, as I sat on a bus stop bench at the edge of a highway in Brampton, I began to silently pray and finger the rosary that was in my jacket pocket.

Instantly my feelings were released and I sat there crying like a baby. As you know, our Lady is our mother, and I sensed she was very close to me at that moment. I could see in my mind's eye a hospital setting wherein I was part of the team. I smiled to myself, knowing confidently at that moment our Lady had a job lined up for me.

I continued through the motions of applying for jobs and going for interviews, and within a couple of weeks an agency associated with the University of Toronto placed me as a temporary medical secretary at the Portuguese Mental Health and Addictions Clinic at Toronto Western Hospital.

I met some wonderful people there, many of whom had grown up in Portugal. I loved the job and grew close to the patients, some of whom suffered incredibly as immigrants to this large, fast-paced city.

I also gained valuable experience as a medical secretary. Subsequently, a supervisor from a law firm where I had worked for a few weeks called me when she heard that I was gaining medical terminology experience. She had a spot open in her litigation department for a medical secretary to type documents for the medical defense litigators. That was three years ago, and I'm still there.

I am truly amazed and grateful for our Lady's intercession and love. We often attend Mass at a downtown Redemptorist parish where the icon of Our Lady of Perpetual Help is displayed in a chapel. This icon is a powerful reminder to me that our Lady has always been, and continues to be, there with me.

I have worked in four cities, and in each one I have managed to find a Redemptorist Parish where devotions to Our Lady of Perpetual Help call me home to find solace for my soul under her watchful gaze. Recalling these events brings tears to my eyes even now, knowing the love and power that our Lady has in my life. Our Blessed Mother has interceded on my behalf so many times that I feel I could write an entire book myself.

Mrs. Dale Bisanti   *Bramalea, Ontario, Canada*

The Cat Saved Our Marriage

One of the most curious experiences of my veterinary career happened through Diane…she of the prayer-cured cow from the experimental farm. Diane is friends with a semiretired priest from Comox, Father Joe. She asks Father Joe to bless *everything* that isn't normal and healthy. This is a regular part of farming in Europe, but a forgotten practice in North America. Father, on the other hand, a shy and humble man who doesn't appreciate publicity, is definitely not into miracles. Diane has a way of asking that makes it difficult to refuse, so Father Joe prays whenever she asks, even if it hurts. If the fruit trees aren't bearing the way they should, then Father Joe is summoned to bring down the full force of God's mercy.

At one point, the herd of cows at the experimental farm was beset with various complications to their health. Father Joe was sweet-talked into blessing the entire herd. Diane asked Carole, my mother, and me to be on hand to lend support. Apparently, Father felt that if the veterinarian were involved, it wouldn't look quite so weird.

Father arranged the blessing for the noon hour to reduce the chance of "pagans" being present. The four of us then accompanied Father to the barnyard for the blessing. That blessing proceeded with great haste; some seventy cows were covered in a period just short of ten minutes. Diane reported that the herd's health seemed to improve.

Sometime after this, I was in my office feverishly trying to revive a semicomatose Siamese cat. This cat was in serious condition from a disease known as feline urinary syndrome or FUS. This condition is essentially due to a plugged urinary bladder resulting in uremic poisoning. Once the animal becomes comatose, the prognosis is poor. If the condition is not relieved, usually within 24 hours of complete blockage, the cat proceeds to sustain irreversible damage to heart, kidney and other vital organs. This was the case with Elsie and Bob's cat. It was comatose. I had managed to free the crystals from the uretha and was proceeding with intravenous fluids in an attempt to flush the cats system of the toxic chemicals in its body. With large volumes of intravenous fluid-flushing and rigorous therapy, some animals, even though comatose, will respond after a period of several days. At that moment, who should arrive on the scene but Diane and Father Joe, just popping in to say a hello. Diane is an animal husbandry major and ever curious of medical theory. After explaining to her the physiological basis of FUS, she hurried into the next room to collar Father Joe.

"You've got to come help Jim. He has a serious problem with a patient," Diane pleaded. Poor Father Joe. You could see the agonized expression on his face that clearly betrayed his thoughts…"All those nurses present are probably nonbelievers; what will they think?"

If only there had been a video camera available to capture the moment. Father Joe glanced over both shoulders, hoping against hope that none of the unbelievers would notice. I watched as I witnessed what possibly may have been the smallest and speediest sign of the cross ever in the history of Christianity. Less than three seconds elapsed during the blessing of the recumbent cat. Father Joe then did an abrupt about face, marched quickly out of the door, retreated to the car, and sat waiting the return of Diane.

Diane sighed, "Well, I guess I better go," and followed him to the car.

Now the strangest of all, the cat which lay flat out on his side, immediately rolled over on its chest, stood up, arched his back, stretched, and began to purr. He then meandered over to my side of the table and proceeded to bestow on me an affectionate rub. For my part, I just stood there rather dazed. What is going on here? Never had I witnessed anything quite like that. Then a perplexing question came to me. If this sort of thing is real, and if supernatural things do happen, why on Earth would God ever use one of his most humble priests to save the life of a cat?

The next day, the cat remained in a normal, healthy condition, eating and being a typical nose-in-the-air Siamese. I contacted Elsie, the owner, to inform her that her cat had recovered and could be discharged. I felt a little awkward after explaining earlier how serious the cat's condition was, the guarded prognosis, and the long recovery expected. Elsie and her husband, Bob, came to retrieve the patient. Since she was a fellow parishioner at St. Patrick's Church, I couldn't help but let it all out; what had taken place. Bob managed to look off into space as if I weren't talking. What I didn't know then was that Bob didn't believe in anything. Nor did I know that their marriage was in the process of coming apart at the seams with a permanent separation. For my part, I was exuberant over the cat's remarkable recovery.

Diane giggled with delight when I explained the scenario to her over the phone and she relayed the story to Father Joe. He made it clear that he wanted to hear nothing more of the event. Curiosity, though, doesn't only catch the cat; it sometimes catches up with the odd priest. Two month later, Father Joe phoned to inquire, "Did that cat really get well the way Diane described?" "Yes," I said. "I have never seen anything like it. Would you mind coming to work full time in this office, Father Joe?" He laughed and good naturedly declined. "But I wouldn't mind seeing that cat again," he ventured, "just to relieve my curiosity." "Okay," I agreed. "I'll line up a visit for you with the owners. They are extremely anxious to meet you."

I contacted Elsie and arranged a meeting. The three of them enjoyed a long, friendly visit. They discovered that they had mutual acquaintances in Edmonton, Alberta, where Bob had formerly been in the oil drilling business. Father Joe had been a math teacher in Edmonton for several years. They struck up a lasting friendship and over time, Father was able to convince the couple that divorce was not a good or necessary answer to their problems. From then on, the marriage, with counseling, improved each day.

A few months passed and it was announced that a Marriage Encounter would be held in Campbell River. Now a Marriage Encounter is a weekend event which is a further development of the Cursillo. It is not meant for marriages in trouble, but is a movement to make good marriages better and to prevent future difficulties. One of the objectives is the development of communication between a couple. The lack of communication is often the start of the disastrous road to divorce.

Elsie intercepted me leaving Mass one morning, "Jim, you have made a Marriage Encounter before; could you come to our home and convince Bob to attend a Marriage Encounter with me?" "Sure, no problem," I assured her with unbridled confidence. However, I quickly discovered Bob was no pushover. He was like my kids. One word about spiritual things and the door slams shut. To reduce the clumsiness of the visit, we switched the conversation to the more acceptable level of well drilling and Bob's occupation of game fishing guide.

Having achieved a colossal failure, I rose to leave. Elsie groped in desperation, "Jim, didn't you make a Marriage Encounter once?" With obvious uneasiness in my voice, all I could think to say was, "Yes. I did, but if you guys are thinking about it, be careful, you might fall in love all over again."

I departed from their home depressed. I felt I had let Elsie down. The Marriage Encounter could have been a real boost to their recovering marriage. I had not yet discovered that prayer is the best solution to every problem. I prayed only at the brink of disaster or impending death. Directly without reasoning why, I went home and knelt down next to our bed. Dejected, I prayed for Elsie and Bob what could have been the most sincere pleading rosary of my career. Just as I finished the last Glory Be, the phone rang, Carole answered. It was Elsie, elated, calling to tell us Bob had invited her to attend the Marriage Encounter with him! I knew that cowboys shouldn't cry, but this cowboy turned into mush.

Elsie and Bob enjoyed the next four years in marital bliss. Then suddenly, without warning, Bob suffered a heart attack during a playful moment at home. He was chasing Elsie around the patio when he slipped into eternity. On the surface it seemed tragic, but we realized everyone eventually dies. How sad it would have been had not that old Siamese cat led them to stumble into a loving reunion, and Bob had not discovered that true love surpasses any other kind of joy.

After Bob's death, Elsie moved away. I received a letter from a veterinary hospital requesting their cat's medical history. More out of mischief than from proper medical practice, I detailed the entire account, using medical jargon, of the blessing by Father Joe in my reply. I would imagine those veterinarians figured there are some pretty kooky veterinarians residing in British Columbia.

Elsie and the Siamese encountered another adventure before the move to Alberta.

She told of a day driving in downtown Campbell River when she thought, "Gee, people in Campbell River are certainly friendly; everyone is waving to me." When the waving continued, she thought "some of those bystanders look pretty serious." She decided to stop and see if the car had a problem. There on top of the car was the cat, spread-eagle with all four sets of claws dug securely into the roof of the hardtop convertible, hanging on for dear life. The cat's name, by the way, is "Lucky."

Jim d'Urfe Proctor, DMV   *Campbell River, British Columbia, Canada*
Author: Sailing Beyond the Sea, ISBN:1-882972-86-4

Finding a God Loving Spouse

My name is Mario. As I was growing up, I had originally thought God was calling me to become a priest. Following the suggestion of a deacon, I left the idea in abeyance and attended a secular college after twelve years of a Catholic school education. Then I realized perhaps God was calling me to the married vocation.

In college, I became a member of the Newman Club in the hopes that I would meet a young Catholic lady, whom, if it were God's will, I might eventually marry. I wasn't having too much in the way of luck on my own. Anyone in whom I was possibly interested saw me as a friend. I decided I needed some heavenly assistance and guidance.

I found a rosary novena booklet. The novena would be prayed in the following manner: twenty-seven days of petition followed by twenty-seven days of thanksgiving. I prayed the novena as specified and Mary led me to meet a young lady.

An interesting sideline is that at the first meeting neither one of us saw the other person as a good dating partner, let alone a possible future spouse. She viewed me as entirely too serious and I viewed her as entirely too much of a joker. As the heavenly plan went, we eventually saw beyond the surface personalities and began to know the true person. We found we shared similar religious convictions, we started dating and soon we knew we had met our future spouses.

Then and only then did we discover that both of us, unknown to the other, had been praying the same exact rosary novena. In thanksgiving to Our Lady, Queen of the Rosary, we celebrated our twenty-sixth anniversary December 2002. The final interesting point is my wife's name; everyone knows her as Ro; her real name is Roseria in honor of Our Lady of the Rosary.

Mario A. Lipari   *Ocala, Florida*

Dear Sweet Grandma Bloom

Growing up in a loving family I was so lucky to be around many good people. One of the best was my dear sweet grandma Bloom, my father's mother. By the time I knew her she was an elderly woman with arthritic knees, requiring my assistance to get up and down from chairs or take a walk. I loved that she needed me and I could help. Then she would give me that loving smile only a grandma can give.

She guided me spiritually, emotionally and I guided her physically; we made a perfect match. This loving woman was usually wearing her favorite color of lavender and always a large apron with pockets. The pockets always had a rosary in them and her end table had holy cards and prayer books. She touched the rosaries inside the pocket as she talked, dozed or read her prayer book.

She taught me to love the touch of the rosary. Many a time as we sat in her back yard she would say, "Lets pray a decade of the rosary for this wonderful day." The joy of saying the rosary with my grandma on a beautiful day still lingers in my heart and makes me smile.

My grandma always said that saying the rosary was a way of connecting with the women of our past. They said rosaries for us and now we say rosaries for those to follow us.

Often she said if you can not find the time or your heart is breaking so bad you can not say a prayer, touch that rosary you are carrying, feel the crucifix, feel the love in the beads, think of the Blessed Mother and help will come to you. I have found those words so comforting through the trials of my life.

Cathy Bloom   *Brownsburg, Indiana*

Mysteries—Ancient and New

Revisiting the Rosary

Richard N. Fragomeni, Ph.D.

On October 16, 2002, John Paul II issued an apostolic letter entitled *"Rosarium Virginis Mariae"* ("The Rosary of the Virgin Mary"). In this letter, addressed to the bishops, clergy, and faithful of the Church, the Pope proclaims the period from October 2002 to October 2003 the Year of the Rosary. Along with the proclamation, John Paul II offers an inspiring catechesis on the meaning of the rosary in the devotional life of Catholics. This catechesis is placed within an extended meditation on Mary and her role to lead all believers to her Son, Jesus. In fact, the Holy Father calls the rosary "Mary's school," in which she invites her children to learn the lessons of Christ by contemplating the fifteen joyful, sorrowful, and glorious mysteries of her Son's life.

These threefold mysteries are certainly familiar to those who pray the rosary as part of their devotional life. The traditional mysteries are a way of keeping the memory of Christ alive and fresh in the minds and hearts of those who seek a deeper relationship with the Lord. In a real sense, the Pope reminds us, the mysteries of the rosary are also a way of coming into contact with Mary and her vision of Christ. "In the recitation of the rosary, the Christian community enters into contact with the memories and the contemplative gaze of Mary." (RVM, 11). In other words, the mysteries are a compendium of gospel stories. They lead us step by step into the plot of salvation, causing the one who prays to enter more deeply into mysteries of grace. We enter not alone, however, but with Mary as our guide.

The joyful mysteries begin with the Annunciation of the Lord, the great moment when Mary is invited by the divine messenger to be the Mother of the Savior. This joy continues to sparkle in Mary's visit to her cousin Elizabeth and reaches a unique brilliance in the birth of Jesus. The fourth joyful mystery leads us to contemplate the fulfillment of the Law in the presentation of the firstborn male child in the Temple. The finding of the twelve-year-old Jesus in the Temple marks the fifth mystery of joy, which is mixed with anxiety and drama.

The sorrowful mysteries continue the meditation by recalling the passion and death of the Lord. The heart of the gospel is the proclamation of these mysteries. They bring to a powerful focus the magnitude of pain that demonstrates God's self-emptying love for us and for all creation. From the agony in the garden to the scourging and crowning with thorns, the rosary, prayed in reverent contemplation, leads us to Calvary with Mary and the beloved disciple so that we may gaze with them upon the Lamb of God, who takes away the sins of the world.

Beginning with the Resurrection, the third set of mysteries is a glorious incantation of the power of God over sin and death. The rosary unfolds the exuberant glory of the Ascension of Christ and the descent of the Holy Spirit. Finally, at the close of these mysteries, we turn again to Mary and celebrate her death in the hope of her Son, proclaiming her glorious Assumption and her coronation as Regina, Queen of the heavens.

While these fifteen mysteries have served the devotional prayer of the Church for nearly a thousand years, John Paul II introduces five new ones in his anniversary letter on the rosary. The Pope cites two reasons for introducing these mysteries, which he calls the mysteries of light. First, he believes that the traditional mysteries, while laudable and rich in significance, leave out important moments of Jesus' life. These moments, if contemplated in the manner of praying the rosary, would offer the Christian community the opportunity to mediate more fully on the manifestation of Christ in his public ministry. Thus, John Paul II feels that the mysteries of light will enhance the depth of prayer and appreciation for the wonders of God in the life of Jesus.

Second, the Pope hopes that these new mysteries will offer "fresh life" and "enkindle renewed interest in the rosary's place within Christian spirituality as a true doorway to the depths of the Heart of Christ, ocean of joy and of light, of suffering and of glory" (RVM, 19). In fact, the aim of the entire apostolic letter seems to be to awaken among Catholics deep appreciation for praying the rosary. The Pope lauds it as a prayer for peace, a prayer for families, a prayer for children, and a prayer for a new millennium.

The entire life of Jesus is a proclamation of light in the midst of darkness. The Pope, therefore, has chosen five moments in which the light of Christ burst forth, bringing a radiance to the faces of all who encountered him. "Each of these mysteries is a *revelation of the Kingdom now present in the very person of Jesus*" (RVM, 21). In a sense, the mysteries of light are five epiphanies upon which we meditate with Mary, who invites us to listen to her Son and follow his teachings.

1. The Baptism of the Lord

The first mystery of light is the Baptism of the Lord. It is here that we recall how Christ, the innocent one who became "sin" for our sake, descended into the waters of the Jordan. It was at this time that the Spirit descended upon him while the Father declared him the beloved Son, pleasing in the sight of God and all people of good will.

2. The Wedding Feast at Cana

The second mystery of light takes us to a wedding feast. Wedding celebrations are signs of hope, love and the faithfulness of persons in a covenant. It was at Cana, the recent apostolic letter reminds us, that Jesus performed his first sign; changing water into wine. Thanks to the intervention of His mother, the first believer, the hearts of the disciples were opened and people began to believe in Him. He brings to pass the ancient hopes of a covenant, which will be a rich marriage communion between God and the people. It will come to pass on a holy mountain, where all will feast on rich wines and choice foods. On that mountain there will be no more weeping or mourning. The best has been saved for last.

3. The Preaching of the Kingdom of God; the Call to Conversion

For three years Jesus revealed his glory in his ministry of preaching and healing. He preached with words and with mighty deeds. He healed the sick, forgave sinners, associated with tax collectors and prostitutes. He inaugurated a ministry of mercy by calling sinners to conversion. The miracle was that sinners responded. Throughout his work, Jesus showed what God was really like: a humble servant, self-emptying and willing to lay down his life for the sake of others. This same kind of compassionate ministry is committed to us, the Church, so that all may hear the preaching of Christ and know that all are welcome in the kingdom of God. We pray for all sinners, now and at the hour of death. We pray that all will come to the conversion to which Christ invites us.

4. The Transfiguration of the Lord

Our Holy Father calls this mystery "the mystery of light *par excellence*." The Transfiguration of the Lord, traditionally believed to have taken place on Mount Tabor, is an epiphany of glory. While in prayer with Peter, James, and John, Jesus was taken into the company of Moses and Elijah. The heavens opened, and the glory of God shone in the face and garments of Christ as the Father said, "This is my Son, the Beloved; listen to Him!" (MK 9:7) The experience served as a moment of preparation for Christ's passion and death, offering the apostles a moment of light that would help sustain their hope after Jesus died in darkness. The Transfiguration of the Lord is a declaration that we, too, can share in Chris's glory by having our lives transfigured by the Holy Spirit.

5. The Institution of the Eucharist

On the night before he died, Jesus celebrated the paschal feast in the company of his disciples. This final mystery of light takes us to the upper room in Jerusalem. We remember how Jesus took a basin of water and washed the feet of His friends, asking them to "love one another as I have loved you." In the same spirit of service, He took bread, handed it to His companions, and said, "This is my body, which is given for you. Do this in remembrance of me." He did the same with the cup, saying, "This cup that is poured out for you is the new covenant in my blood" (LK 22:19, 20). In this testament, Jesus demonstrated that He loves those who are His own; He loves us to the end. As a living memorial of His death and resurrection, we continue to eat this bread and drink this cup until He comes again in glory. The light of Christ's Eucharistic gift continues to shine in the Church, showing us the way of service for one another.

The third chapter of "The Rosary of the Virgin Mary" outlines the essential method the Pope recommends for praying the rosary. He begins by acknowledging that the rosary is based on the method of repetition. The Pope likens this method to the dynamics of love. Those who are in love never tire of repeating the words "I love you" over and over. In this sense, the rosary moves us into an intimate place wherein the mysteries of Christ can be contemplated with Mary.

The letter continues by suggesting ways in which the rosary can be prayed more contemplatively. For example, the Pope suggests that icons of the mysteries could be used to increase devotion by concentrating the mind and eye on rich images. A short passage of Scripture could be read following the announcement of each mystery. Silence is encouraged after the Scripture text and before the recitation of the Lord's Prayer and the ten *Aves*.

The Pope also recommends that a short prayer be said after the Glory Be to conclude each mystery. While John Paul II acknowledges that such devotional prayers already exist in many places, "the contemplation of the mysteries could better express their full spiritual fruitfulness if an effort were made to conclude each mystery with *a prayer for the fruits specific to that particular mystery*" (RVM, 35).

Finally, the Pope offers a pattern for the distribution of the mysteries over the course of a week. He explains that "this weekly distribution has the effect of giving the different days of the week a certain spiritual 'color,' by analogy with the way in which the Liturgy colors the different seasons of the liturgical year" (RVM, 38). Therefore, he suggests that the joyful mysteries be prayed on Monday and Saturday, the sorrowful mysteries on Tuesday and Friday, and the glorious mysteries on Wednesday and Sunday. Thursday would then be free for meditation on the mysteries of light.

The rosary is Mary's way to Christ. It is her school, where she still forms her children as she formed her Son. The apostolic letter of John Paul II begins a new era for this prayer. May this Year of the Rosary be a time when we find in Mary's lessons a deeper communion with Christ.

APOSTOLIC LETTER
ROSARIUM VIRGINIS MARIAE
OF THE SUPREME PONTIFF
JOHN PAUL II
TO THE BISHOPS, CLERGY
AND FAITHFUL
ON THE MOST HOLY ROSARY

INTRODUCTION

1. The Rosary of the Virgin Mary, which gradually took form in the second millennium under the guidance of the Spirit of God, is a prayer loved by countless Saints and encouraged by the Magisterium. Simple yet profound, it still remains, at the dawn of this third millennium, a prayer of great significance, destined to bring forth a harvest of holiness. It blends easily into the spiritual journey of the Christian life, which, after two thousand years, has lost none of the freshness of its beginnings and feels drawn by the Spirit of God to "set out into the deep" (*duc in altum!*) in order once more to proclaim, and even cry out, before the world that Jesus Christ is Lord and Saviour, "the way, and the truth and the life" (*Jn* 14:6), "the goal of human history and the point on which the desires of history and civilization turn".[1]

The Rosary, though clearly Marian in character, is at heart a Christocentric prayer. In the sobriety of its elements, it has all the *depth of the Gospel message in its entirety*, of which it can be said to be a compendium.[2] It is an echo of the prayer of Mary, her perennial *Magnificat* for the work of the redemptive Incarnation which began in her virginal womb. With the Rosary, the Christian people *sits at the school of Mary* and is led to contemplate the beauty on the face of Christ and to experience the depths

---

[1]   Pastoral Constitution on the Church in the Modern World *Gaudium et Spes*, 45.

[2]   Pope Paul VI, Apostolic Exhortation *Marialis Cultus* (2 February 1974), 42: AAS 66 (1974), 153.

of his love. Through the Rosary the faithful receive abundant grace, as though from the very hands of the Mother of the Redeemer.

The Popes and the Rosary

2. Numerous predecessors of mine attributed great importance to this prayer. Worthy of special note in this regard is Pope Leo XIII who on 1 September 1883 promulgated the Encyclical *Supremi Apostolatus Officio*,[3] a document of great worth, the first of his many statements about this prayer, in which he proposed the Rosary as an effective spiritual weapon against the evils afflicting society. Among the more recent Popes who, from the time of the Second Vatican Council, have distinguished themselves in promoting the Rosary I would mention Blessed John XXIII[4] and above all Pope Paul VI, who in his Apostolic Exhortation *Marialis Cultus* emphasized, in the spirit of the Second Vatican Council, the Rosary's evangelical character and its Christocentric inspiration. I myself have often encouraged the frequent recitation of the Rosary. From my youthful years this prayer has held an important place in my spiritual life. I was powerfully reminded of this during my recent visit to Poland, and in particular at the Shrine of Kalwaria. The Rosary has accompanied me in moments of joy and in moments of difficulty. To it I have entrusted any number of concerns; in it I have always found comfort. Twenty-four years ago, on 29 October 1978, scarcely two weeks after my election to the See of Peter, I frankly admitted: "The Rosary is my favourite prayer. A marvellous prayer! Marvellous in its simplicity and its depth. [...]. It can be said that the Rosary is, in some sense, a prayer-commentary on the final chapter of the Vatican II Constitution *Lumen Gentium*, a chapter which discusses the wondrous presence of the Mother of God in the mystery of Christ and the Church. Against the background of the words *Ave Maria* the principal events of the life of Jesus Christ pass before the eyes of the soul. They take shape in the complete series of the joyful, sorrowful and glorious myster-

---

3   Cf. *Acta Leonis XIII*, 3 (1884), 280-289.

4   Particularly worthy of note is his Apostolic Epistle on the Rosary *Il religioso convegno* (29 September 1961): AAS 53 (1961), 641-647.

ies, and they put us in living communion with Jesus through—we might say—the heart of his Mother. At the same time our heart can embrace in the decades of the Rosary all the events that make up the lives of individuals, families, nations, the Church, and all mankind. Our personal concerns and those of our neighbour, especially those who are closest to us, who are dearest to us. Thus the simple prayer of the Rosary marks the rhythm of human life".[5]

With these words, dear brothers and sisters, I set *the first year of my Pontificate* within the daily rhythm of the Rosary. Today, *as I begin the twenty-fifth year of my service as the Successor of Peter*, I wish to do the same. How many graces have I received in these years from the Blessed Virgin through the Rosary: *Magnificat anima mea Dominum!* I wish to lift up my thanks to the Lord in the words of his Most Holy Mother, under whose protection I have placed my Petrine ministry: *Totus Tuus!*

October 2002—October 2003: The Year of the Rosary

3. Therefore, in continuity with my reflection in the Apostolic Letter *Novo Millennio Ineunte*, in which, after the experience of the Jubilee, I invited the people of God to "start afresh from Christ",[6] I have felt drawn to offer a reflection on the Rosary, as a kind of Marian complement to that Letter and an exhortation to contemplate the face of Christ in union with, and at the school of, his Most Holy Mother. To recite the Rosary is nothing other than to *contemplate with Mary the face of Christ*. As a way of highlighting this invitation, prompted by the forthcoming 120th anniversary of the aforementioned Encyclical of Leo XIII, I desire that during the course of this year the Rosary should be especially emphasized and promoted in the various Christian communities. I therefore proclaim the year from October 2002 to October 2003 *the Year of the Rosary*.

I leave this pastoral proposal to the initiative of each ecclesial community. It is not my intention to encumber but rather to complete and consolidate pastoral programmes of the Particular Churches. I am confident that

---

[5]   Angelus: *Insegnamenti di Giovanni Paolo II*, I (1978): 75-76.

[6]   AAS 93 (2001), 285.

the proposal will find a ready and generous reception. The Rosary, re-claimed in its full meaning, goes to the very heart of Christian life; it offers a familiar yet fruitful spiritual and educational opportunity for personal contemplation, the formation of the People of God, and the new evangeli-zation. I am pleased to reaffirm this also in the joyful remembrance of another anniversary: the fortieth anniversary of the opening of the Second Vatican Ecumenical Council on October 11, 1962, the "great grace" dis-posed by the Spirit of God for the Church in our time.[7]

Objections to the Rosary

4. The timeliness of this proposal is evident from a number of consid-erations. First, the urgent need to counter a certain crisis of the Rosary, which in the present historical and theological context can risk being wrongly devalued, and therefore no longer taught to the younger genera-tion. There are some who think that the centrality of the Liturgy, rightly stressed by the Second Vatican Ecumenical Council, necessarily entails giving lesser importance to the Rosary. Yet, as Pope Paul VI made clear, not only does this prayer not conflict with the Liturgy, *it sustains it*, since it serves as an excellent introduction and a faithful echo of the Liturgy, enabling people to participate fully and interiorly in it and to reap its fruits in their daily lives.

Perhaps too, there are some who fear that the Rosary is somehow unecumenical because of its distinctly Marian character. Yet the Rosary clearly belongs to the kind of veneration of the Mother of God described by the Council: a devotion directed to the Christological centre of the Christian faith, in such a way that "when the Mother is honoured, the Son...is duly known, loved and glorified".[8] If properly revitalized, the Rosary is an aid and certainly not a hindrance to ecumenism!

---

[7]   During the years of preparation for the Council, Pope John XXIII did not fail to encourage the Christian community to recite the Rosary for the success of this ecclesial event: cf. Letter to the Cardinal Vicar (28 September 1960): AAS 52 (1960), 814-816.

[8]   Dogmatic Constitution on the Church *Lumen Gentium*, 66.

A path of contemplation

5. But the most important reason for strongly encouraging the practice of the Rosary is that it represents a most effective means of fostering among the faithful that *commitment to the contemplation of the Christian mystery* which I have proposed in the Apostolic Letter *Novo Millennio Ineunte* as a genuine "training in holiness": "What is needed is a Christian life distinguished above all in the *art of prayer*".[9] Inasmuch as contemporary culture, even amid so many indications to the contrary, has witnessed the flowering of a new call for spirituality, due also to the influence of other religions, it is more urgent than ever that our Christian communities should become "genuine schools of prayer".[10]

The Rosary belongs among the finest and most praiseworthy traditions of Christian contemplation. Developed in the West, it is a typically meditative prayer, corresponding in some way to the "prayer of the heart" or "Jesus prayer" which took root in the soil of the Christian East.

Prayer for peace and for the family

6. A number of historical circumstances also make a revival of the Rosary quite timely. First of all, the need to implore from God *the gift of peace*. The Rosary has many times been proposed by my predecessors and myself as a prayer for peace. At the start of a millennium which began with the terrifying attacks of 11 September 2001, a millennium which witnesses every day innumerous parts of the world fresh scenes of bloodshed and violence, to rediscover the Rosary means to immerse oneself in contemplation of the mystery of Christ who "is our peace", since he made "the two of us one, and broke down the dividing wall of hostility" (*Eph* 2:14). Consequently, one cannot recite the Rosary without feeling caught up in a clear commitment to advancing peace, especially in the land of Jesus, still so sorely afflicted and so close to the heart of every Christian.

A similar need for commitment and prayer arises in relation to another critical contemporary issue: *the family*, the primary cell of society, increas-

---

[9]   No. 32: AAS 93 (2001), 288.

[10]   *Ibid.*, 33: loc. cit., 289.

ingly menaced by forces of disintegration on both the ideological and practical planes, so as to make us fear for the future of this fundamental and indispensable institution and, with it, for the future of society as a whole. The revival of the Rosary in Christian families, within the context of a broader pastoral ministry to the family, will be an effective aid to countering the devastating effects of this crisis typical of our age.

"Behold, your Mother!" (Jn 19:27)

7. Many signs indicate that still today the Blessed Virgin desires to exercise through this same prayer that maternal concern to which the dying Redeemer entrusted, in the person of the beloved disciple, all the sons and daughters of the Church: "Woman, behold your son!" (*Jn*19:26). Well-known are the occasions in the nineteenth and the twentieth centuries on which the Mother of Christ made her presence felt and her voice heard, in order to exhort the People of God to this form of contemplative prayer. I would mention in particular, on account of their great influence on the lives of Christians and the authoritative recognition they have received from the Church, the apparitions of Lourdes and of Fatima;[11] these shrines continue to be visited by great numbers of pilgrims seeking comfort and hope.

Following the witnesses

8. It would be impossible to name all the many Saints who discovered in the Rosary a genuine path to growth in holiness. We need but mention Saint Louis Marie Grignion de Montfort, the author of an excellent work on the Rosary,[12] and, closer to ourselves, Padre Pio of Pietrelcina, whom I recently had the joy of canonizing. As a true apostle of the Rosary, Blessed Bartolo Longo had a special charism. His path to holiness rested on an inspiration heard in the depths of his heart: "Whoever spreads the Rosary

---

[11] It is well-known and bears repeating that private revelations are not the same as public revelation, which is binding on the whole Church. It is the task of the Magisterium to discern and recognize the authenticity and value of private revelations for the piety of the faithful.

[12] *The Secret of the Rosary.*

is saved!".[13] As a result, he felt called to build a Church dedicated to Our Lady of the Holy Rosary in Pompei, against the background of the ruins of the ancient city, which scarcely heard the proclamation of Christ before being buried in 79 A.D. during an eruption of Mount Vesuvius, only to emerge centuries later from its ashes as a witness to the lights and shadows of classical civilization. By his whole life's work and especially by the practice of the "Fifteen Saturdays", Bartolo Longo promoted the Christocentric and contemplative heart of the Rosary, and received great encouragement and support from Leo XIII, the "Pope of the Rosary".

CHAPTER I
CONTEMPLATING CHRIST WITH MARY

A face radiant as the sun

9. "And he was transfigured before them, and his face shone like the sun" (*Mt* 17:2). The Gospel scene of Christ's transfiguration, in which the three Apostles Peter, James and John appear entranced by the beauty of the Redeemer, can be seen as *an icon of Christian contemplation*. To look upon the face of Christ, to recognize its mystery amid the daily events and the sufferings of his human life, and then to grasp the divine splendour definitively revealed in the Risen Lord, seated in glory at the right hand of the Father: this is the task of every follower of Christ and therefore the task of each one of us. In contemplating Christ's face we become open to receiving the mystery of Trinitarian life, experiencing ever anew the love of the Father and delighting in the joy of the Holy Spirit. Saint Paul's words can then be applied to us: "Beholding the glory of the Lord, we are being changed into his likeness, from one degree of glory to another; for this comes from the Lord who is the Spirit" (*2Cor* 3:18).

Mary, model of contemplation

10. The contemplation of Christ has an *incomparable model* in Mary. In a unique way the face of the Son belongs to Mary. It was in her womb

---

[13]   Blessed Bartolo Longo, *Storia del Santuario di Pompei*, Pompei, 1990, 59.

that Christ was formed, receiving from her a human resemblance which points to an even greater spiritual closeness. No one has ever devoted himself to the contemplation of the face of Christ as faithfully as Mary. The eyes of her heart already turned to him at the Annunciation, when she conceived him by the power of the Holy Spirit. In the months that followed she began to sense his presence and to picture his features. When at last she gave birth to him in Bethlehem, her eyes were able to gaze tenderly on the face of her Son, as she "wrapped him in swaddling cloths, and laid him in a manger" (*Lk*2:7).

Thereafter Mary's gaze, ever filled with adoration and wonder, would never leave him. At times it would be *a questioning look*, as in the episode of the finding in the Temple: "Son, why have you treated us so?" (*Lk* 2:48); it would always be *a penetrating gaze*, one capable of deeply understanding Jesus, even to the point of perceiving his hidden feelings and anticipating his decisions, as at Cana (cf. *Jn* 2:5). At other times it would be *a look of sorrow*, especially beneath the Cross, where her vision would still be that of a mother giving birth, for Mary not only shared the passion and death of her Son, she also received the new son given to her in the beloved disciple (cf. *Jn* 19:26-27). On the morning of Easter hers would be *a gaze radiant with the joy of the Resurrection*, and finally, on the day of Pentecost, *a gaze afire* with the outpouring of the Spirit (cf. *Acts* 1:14).

Mary's memories

11. Mary lived with her eyes fixed on Christ, treasuring his every word: "She kept all these things, pondering them in her heart" (*Lk* 2:19; cf. 2:51). The memories of Jesus, impressed upon her heart, were always with her, leading her to reflect on the various moments of her life at her Son's side. In a way those memories were to be the "rosary" which she recited uninterruptedly throughout her earthly life.

Even now, amid the joyful songs of the heavenly Jerusalem, the reasons for her thanksgiving and praise remain unchanged. They inspire her maternal concern for the pilgrim Church, in which she continues to relate her personal account of the Gospel. *Mary constantly sets before the faithful the "mysteries" of her Son*, with the desire that the contemplation of those mysteries will release all their saving power. In the recitation of the

Rosary, the Christian community enters into contact with the memories and the contemplative gaze of Mary.

The Rosary, a contemplative prayer

12. The Rosary, precisely because it starts with Mary's own experience, is *an exquisitely contemplative prayer*. Without this contemplative dimension, it would lose its meaning, as Pope Paul VI clearly pointed out: "Without contemplation, the Rosary is a body without a soul, and its recitation runs the risk of becoming a mechanical repetition of formulas, in violation of the admonition of Christ: 'In praying do not heap up empty phrases as the Gentiles do; for they think they will be heard for their many words' (*Mt* 6:7). By its nature the recitation of the Rosary calls for a quiet rhythm and a lingering pace, helping the individual to meditate on the mysteries of the Lord's life as seen through the eyes of her who was closest to the Lord. In this way the unfathomable riches of these mysteries are disclosed".[14]

It is worth pausing to consider this profound insight of Paul VI, in order to bring out certain aspects of the Rosary which show that it is really a form of Christocentric contemplation.

Remembering Christ with Mary

13. Mary's contemplation is above all *a remembering*. We need to understand this word in the biblical sense of remembrance (*zakar*) as a making present of the works brought about by God in the history of salvation. The Bible is an account of saving events culminating in Christ himself. These events not only belong to "yesterday"; *they are also part of the "today" of salvation*. This making present comes about above all in the Liturgy: what God accomplished centuries ago did not only affect the direct witnesses of those events; it continues to affect people in every age with its gift of grace. To some extent this is also true of every other devout approach to those events: to "remember" them in a spirit of faith and love

---

[14] Apostolic Exhortation *Marialis Cultus* (2 February 1974), 47: AAS (1974), 156.

is to be open to the grace which Christ won for us by the mysteries of his life, death and resurrection.

Consequently, while it must be reaffirmed with the Second Vatican Council that the Liturgy, as the exercise of the priestly office of Christ and an act of public worship, is "the summit to which the activity of the Church is directed and the font from which all its power flows",[15] it is also necessary to recall that the spiritual life "is not limited solely to participation in the liturgy. Christians, while they are called to prayer in common, must also go to their own rooms to pray to their Father in secret (cf. *Mt* 6:6); indeed, according to the teaching of the Apostle, they must pray without ceasing (cf.*1 Thes* 5:17)".[16] The Rosary, in its own particular way, is part of this varied panorama of "ceaseless" prayer. If the Liturgy, as the activity of Christ and the Church, is *a saving action par excellence*, the Rosary too, as a "meditation" with Mary on Christ, is *a salutary contemplation*. By immersing us in the mysteries of the Redeemer's life, it ensures that what he has done and what the liturgy makes present is profoundly assimilated and shapes our existence.

Learning Christ from Mary

14. Christ is the supreme Teacher, the revealer and the one revealed. It is not just a question of learning what he taught but of *"learning him"*. In this regard could we have any better teacher than Mary? From the divine standpoint, the Spirit is the interior teacher who leads us to the full truth of Christ (cf. *Jn* 14:26; 15:26; 16:13). But among creatures no one knows Christ better than Mary; no one can introduce us to a profound knowledge of his mystery better than his Mother.

The first of the "signs" worked by Jesus—the changing of water into wine at the marriage in Cana—clearly presents Mary in the guise of a teacher, as she urges the servants to do what Jesus commands (cf. *Jn* 2:5). We can imagine that she would have done likewise for the disciples after Jesus' Ascension, when she joined them in awaiting the Holy Spirit and

---

[15] Constitution on the Sacred Liturgy *Sacrosanctum Concilium*, 10.

[16] *bid.*, 12.

supported them in their first mission. Contemplating the scenes of the Rosary in union with Mary is a means of learning from her to "read" Christ, to discover his secrets and to understand his message.

This school of Mary is all the more effective if we consider that she teaches by obtaining for us in abundance the gifts of the Holy Spirit, even as she offers us the incomparable example of her own "pilgrimage of faith".[17] As we contemplate each mystery of her Son's life, she invites us to do as she did at the Annunciation: to ask humbly the questions which open us to the light, in order to end with the obedience of faith: "Behold I am the handmaid of the Lord; be it done to me according to your word" (*Lk* 1:38).

Being conformed to Christ with Mary

15. Christian spirituality is distinguished by the disciple's commitment to become conformed ever more fully to his Master (cf. *Rom* 8:29; *Phil* 3:10,12). The outpouring of the Holy Spirit in Baptism grafts the believer like a branch onto the vine which is Christ (cf. *Jn* 15:5) and makes him a member of Christ's mystical Body (cf. *1Cor* 12:12; *Rom* 12:5). This initial unity, however, calls for a growing assimilation which will increasingly shape the conduct of the disciple in accordance with the "mind" of Christ: "Have this mind among yourselves, which was in Christ Jesus" (*Phil* 2:5). In the words of the Apostle, we are called "to put on the Lord Jesus Christ" (cf. *Rom* 13:14; *Gal* 3:27).

In the spiritual journey of the Rosary, based on the constant contemplation—in Mary's company—of the face of Christ, this demanding ideal of being conformed to him is pursued through an association which could be described in terms of friendship. We are thereby enabled to enter naturally into Christ's life and as it were to share his deepest feelings. In this regard Blessed Bartolo Longo has written: "Just as two friends, frequently in each other's company, tend to develop similar habits, so too, by holding familiar converse with Jesus and the Blessed Virgin, by meditating on the mysteries of the Rosary and by living the same life in Holy Communion,

---

[17] Second Vatican Ecumenical Council, Dogmatic Constitution on the Church *Lumen Gentium*, 58.

we can become, to the extent of our lowliness, similar to them and can learn from these supreme models a life of humility, poverty, hiddenness, patience and perfection".[18]

In this process of being conformed to Christ in the Rosary, we entrust ourselves in a special way to the maternal care of the Blessed Virgin. She who is both the Mother of Christ and a member of the Church, indeed her "pre-eminent and altogether singular member",[19] is at the same time the "Mother of the Church". As such, she continually brings to birth children for the mystical Body of her Son. She does so through her intercession, imploring upon them the inexhaustible outpouring of the Spirit. Mary is *the perfect icon of the motherhood of the Church.*

The Rosary mystically transports us to Mary's side as she is busy watching over the human growth of Christ in the home of Nazareth. This enables her to train us and to mold us with the same care, until Christ is "fully formed" in us (cf. *Gal* 4:19). This role of Mary, totally grounded in that of Christ and radically subordinated to it, "in no way obscures or diminishes the unique mediation of Christ, but rather shows its power".[20] This is the luminous principle expressed by the Second Vatican Council which I have so powerfully experienced in my own life and have made the basis of my episcopal motto: *Totus Tuus.*[21] The motto is of course inspired by the teaching of Saint Louis Marie Grignion de Montfort, who explained in the following words Mary's role in the process of our configuration to Christ: *"Our entire perfection consists in being conformed, united and consecrated to Jesus Christ.* Hence the most perfect of all devotions is undoubtedly that which conforms, unites and consecrates us most perfectly to Jesus Christ. Now, since Mary is of all creatures the one most conformed to

---

[18] *I Quindici Sabati del Santissimo Rosario*, 27th ed., Pompei, 1916, 27.

[19] Second Vatican Ecumenical Council, Dogmatic Constitution on the Church *Lumen Gentium*, 53.

[20] *Ibid.*, 60.

[21] Cf. First Radio Address *Urbi et Orbi* (17 October 1978): AAS 70 (1978), 927.

Jesus Christ, it follows that among all devotions that which most conse-crates and conforms a soul to our Lord is devotion to Mary, his Holy Mother, and that the more a soul is consecrated to her the more will it be consecrated to Jesus Christ".[22] Never as in the Rosary do the life of Jesus and that of Mary appear so deeply joined. Mary lives only in Christ and for Christ!

Praying to Christ with Mary

16. Jesus invited us to turn to God with insistence and the confidence that we will be heard: "Ask, and it will be given to you; seek, and you will find; knock, and it will be opened to you" (*Mt* 7:7). The basis for this power of prayer is the goodness of the Father, but also the mediation of Christ himself (cf. *1Jn* 2:1) and the working of the Holy Spirit who "inter-cedes for us" according to the will of God (cf. *Rom* 8:26-27). For "we do not know how to pray as we ought" (*Rom* 8:26), and at times we are not heard "because we ask wrongly" (cf. *Jas* 4:2-3).

In support of the prayer which Christ and the Spirit cause to rise in our hearts, Mary intervenes with her maternal intercession. "The prayer of the Church is sustained by the prayer of Mary".[23] If Jesus, the one Mediator, is the Way of our prayer, then Mary, his purest and most transparent reflec-tion, shows us the Way. "Beginning with Mary's unique cooperation with the working of the Holy Spirit, the Churches developed their prayer to the Holy Mother of God, centering it on the person of Christ manifested in his mysteries".[24] At the wedding of Cana the Gospel clearly shows the power of Mary's intercession as she makes known to Jesus the needs of others: "They have no wine" (*Jn* 2:3).

The Rosary is both meditation and supplication. Insistent prayer to the Mother of God is based on confidence that her maternal intercession can obtain all things from the heart of her Son. She is "all-powerful by grace", to use the bold expression, which needs to be properly understood, of

---

[22] *Treatise on True Devotion to the Blessed Virgin Mary.*

[23] *Catechism of the Catholic Church*, 2679.

[24] *Ibid.*, 2675.

Blessed Bartolo Longo in his *Supplication to Our Lady*.[25] This is a conviction which, beginning with the Gospel, has grown ever more firm in the experience of the Christian people. The supreme poet Dante expresses it marvellously in the lines sung by Saint Bernard: "Lady, thou art so great and so powerful, that whoever desires grace yet does not turn to thee, would have his desire fly without wings".[26] When in the Rosary we plead with Mary, the sanctuary of the Holy Spirit (cf. *Lk* 1:35), she intercedes for us before the Father who filled her with grace and before the Son born of her womb, praying with us and for us.

Proclaiming Christ with Mary

17. The Rosary is also *a path of proclamation and increasing knowledge*, in which the mystery of Christ is presented again and again at different levels of the Christian experience. Its form is that of a prayerful and contemplative presentation, capable of forming Christians according to the heart of Christ. When the recitation of the Rosary combines all the elements needed for an effective meditation, especially in its communal celebration in parishes and shrines, it can present *a significant catechetical opportunity* which pastors should use to advantage. In this way too Our Lady of the Rosary continues her work of proclaiming Christ. The history of the Rosary shows how this prayer was used in particular by the Dominicans at a difficult time for the Church due to the spread of heresy. Today we are facing new challenges. Why should we not once more have recourse to the Rosary, with the same faith as those who have gone before us? The Rosary retains all its power and continues to be a valuable pastoral resource for every good evangelizer.

---

[25] The *Supplication to the Queen of the Holy Rosary* was composed by Blessed Bartolo Longo in 1883 in response to the appeal of Pope Leo XIII, made in his first Encyclical on the Rosary, for the spiritual commitment of all Catholics in combating social ills. It is solemnly recited twice yearly, in May and October.

[26] *Divina Commedia*, Paradiso XXXIII, 13-15.

CHAPTER II
MYSTERIES OF CHRIST–
MYSTERIES OF HIS MOTHER

The Rosary, "a compendium of the Gospel"

18. The only way to approach the contemplation of Christ's face is by listening in the Spirit to the Father's voice, since "no one knows the Son except the Father" (*Mt* 11:27). In the region of Caesarea Philippi, Jesus responded to Peter's confession of faith by indicating the source of that clear intuition of his identity: "Flesh and blood has not revealed this to you, but my Father who is in heaven" (*Mt* 16:17). What is needed, then, is a revelation from above. In order to receive that revelation, attentive listening is indispensable: "Only *the experience of silence and prayer* offers the proper setting for the growth and development of a true, faithful and consistent knowledge of that mystery".[27]

The Rosary is one of the traditional paths of Christian prayer directed to the contemplation of Christ's face. Pope Paul VI described it in these words: "As a Gospel prayer, centred on the mystery of the redemptive Incarnation, the Rosary is a prayer with a clearly Christological orientation. Its most characteristic element, in fact, the litany- like succession of *Hail Marys*, becomes in itself an unceasing praise of Christ, who is the ultimate object both of the Angel's announcement and of the greeting of the Mother of John the Baptist: 'Blessed is the fruit of your womb' (*Lk* 1:42). We would go further and say that the succession of *Hail Marys* constitutes the warp on which is woven the contemplation of the mysteries. The Jesus that each *Hail Mary* recalls is the same Jesus whom the succession of mysteries proposes to us now as the Son of God, now as the Son of the Virgin".[28]

---

[27] John Paul II, Apostolic Letter *Novo Millennio Ineunte* (6 January 2001), 20: AAS 93 (2001), 279.

[28] Apostolic Exhortation *Marialis Cultus* (2 February 1974), 46: AAS 6 (1974), 155.

A proposed addition to the traditional pattern

19. Of the many mysteries of Christ's life, only a few are indicated by the Rosary in the form that has become generally established with the seal of the Church's approval. The selection was determined by the origin of the prayer, which was based on the number 150, the number of the Psalms in the Psalter.

I believe, however, that to bring out fully the Christological depth of the Rosary it would be suitable to make an addition to the traditional pattern which, while left to the freedom of individuals and communities, could broaden it to include *the mysteries of Christ's public ministry between his Baptism and his Passion*. In the course of those mysteries we contemplate important aspects of the person of Christ as the definitive revelation of God. Declared the beloved Son of the Father at the Baptism in the Jordan, Christ is the one who announces the coming of the Kingdom, bears witness to it in his works and proclaims its demands. It is during the years of his public ministry that *the mystery of Christ is most evidently a mystery of light:* "While I am in the world, I am the light of the world" (*Jn* 9:5).

Consequently, for the Rosary to become more fully a "compendium of the Gospel", it is fitting to add, following reflection on the Incarnation and the hidden life of Christ (*the joyful mysteries*) and before focusing on the sufferings of his Passion (*the sorrowful mysteries*) and the triumph of his Resurrection (*the glorious mysteries*), a meditation on certain particularly significant moments in his public ministry (*the mysteries of light*). This addition of these new mysteries, without prejudice to any essential aspect of the prayer's traditional format, is meant to give it fresh life and to enkindle renewed interest in the Rosary's place within Christian spirituality as a true doorway to the depths of the Heart of Christ, ocean of joy and of light, of suffering and of glory.

The Joyful Mysteries

20. The first five decades, the "joyful mysteries", are marked by *the joy radiating from the event of the Incarnation*. This is clear from the very first mystery, the Annunciation, where Gabriel's greeting to the Virgin of Nazareth is linked to an invitation to messianic joy: "Rejoice, Mary". The whole of salvation history, in some sense the entire history of the world,

has led up to this greeting. If it is the Father's plan to unite all things in Christ (cf. *Eph* 1:10), then the whole of the universe is in some way touched by the divine favour with which the Father looks upon Mary and makes her the Mother of his Son. The whole of humanity, in turn, is embraced by the *fiat* with which she readily agrees to the will of God.

Exultation is the keynote of the encounter with Elizabeth, where the sound of Mary's voice and the presence of Christ in her womb cause John to "leap for joy" (cf. *Lk* 1:44). Gladness also fills the scene in Bethlehem, when the birth of the divine Child, the Saviour of the world, is announced by the song of the angels and proclaimed to the shepherds as "news of great joy" (*Lk* 2:10).

The final two mysteries, while preserving this climate of joy, already point to the drama yet to come. The Presentation in the Temple not only expresses the joy of the Child's consecration and the ecstasy of the aged Simeon; it also records the prophecy that Christ will be a "sign of contradiction" for Israel and that a sword will pierce his mother's heart (cf *Lk* 2:34-35). Joy mixed with drama marks the fifth mystery, the finding of the twelve-year-old Jesus in the Temple. Here he appears in his divine wisdom as he listens and raises questions, already in effect one who "teaches". The revelation of his mystery as the Son wholly dedicated to his Father's affairs proclaims the radical nature of the Gospel, in which even the closest of human relationships are challenged by the absolute demands of the Kingdom. Mary and Joseph, fearful and anxious, "did not understand" his words (*Lk* 2:50).

To meditate upon the "joyful" mysteries, then, is to enter into the ultimate causes and the deepest meaning of Christian joy. It is to focus on the realism of the mystery of the Incarnation and on the obscure foreshadowing of the mystery of the saving Passion. Mary leads us to discover the secret of Christian joy, reminding us that Christianity is, first and foremost, *euangelion*, "good news", which has as its heart and its whole content the person of Jesus Christ, the Word made flesh, the one Saviour of the world.

The Mysteries of Light

21. Moving on from the infancy and the hidden life in Nazareth to the public life of Jesus, our contemplation brings us to those mysteries which

may be called in a special way "mysteries of light". Certainly the whole mystery of Christ is a mystery of light. He is the "light of the world" (*Jn* 8:12). Yet this truth emerges in a special way during the years of his public life, when he proclaims the Gospel of the Kingdom. In proposing to the Christian community five significant moments—"luminous" mysteries— during this phase of Christ's life, I think that the following can be fittingly singled out: (1) his Baptism in the Jordan, (2) his self-manifestation at the wedding of Cana, (3) his proclamation of the Kingdom of God, with his call to conversion, (4) his Transfiguration, and finally, (5) his institution of the Eucharist, as the sacramental expression of the Paschal Mystery.

Each of these mysteries is *a revelation of the Kingdom now present in the very person of Jesus.* The Baptism in the Jordan is first of all a mystery of light. Here, as Christ descends into the waters, the innocent one who became "sin" for our sake (cf. *2Cor* 5:21), the heavens open wide and the voice of the Father declares him the beloved Son (cf. *Mt* 3:17 and parallels), while the Spirit descends on him to invest him with the mission which he is to carry out. Another mystery of light is the first of the signs, given at Cana (cf. *Jn* 2:1- 12), when Christ changes water into wine and opens the hearts of the disciples to faith, thanks to the intervention of Mary, the first among believers. Another mystery of light is the preaching by which Jesus proclaims the coming of the Kingdom of God, calls to conversion (cf. *Mk* 1:15) and forgives the sins of all who draw near to him in humble trust (cf. *Mk* 2:3-13; *Lk* 7:47- 48): the inauguration of that ministry of mercy which he continues to exercise until the end of the world, particularly through the Sacrament of Reconciliation which he has entrusted to his Church (cf. *Jn* 20:22-23). The mystery of light *par excellence* is the Transfiguration, tra- ditionally believed to have taken place on Mount Tabor. The glory of the Godhead shines forth from the face of Christ as the Father commands the astonished Apostles to "listen to him" (cf. *Lk* 9:35 and parallels) and to prepare to experience with him the agony of the Passion, so as to come with him to the joy of the Resurrection and a life transfigured by the Holy Spirit. A final mystery of light is the institution of the Eucharist, in which Christ offers his body and blood as food under the signs of bread and wine, and testifies "to the end" his love for humanity (*Jn* 13:1), for whose salvation he will offer himself in sacrifice.

In these mysteries, apart from the miracle at Cana, *the presence of Mary remains in the background.* The Gospels make only the briefest reference to her occasional presence at one moment or other during the preaching of Jesus (cf. *Mk* 3:31-5; *Jn* 2:12), and they give no indication that she was present at the Last Supper and the institution of the Eucharist. Yet the role she assumed at Cana in some way accompanies Christ throughout his ministry. The revelation made directly by the Father at the Baptism in the Jordan and echoed by John the Baptist is placed upon Mary's lips at Cana, and it becomes the great maternal counsel which Mary addresses to the Church of every age: "Do whatever he tells you" (*Jn* 2:5). This counsel is a fitting introduction to the words and signs of Christ's public ministry and it forms the Marian foundation of all the "mysteries of light".

The Sorrowful Mysteries

22. The Gospels give great prominence to the sorrowful mysteries of Christ. From the beginning Christian piety, especially during the Lenten devotion of the *Way of the Cross*, has focused on the individual moments of the Passion, realizing that here is found *the culmination of the revelation of God's love* and the source of our salvation. The Rosary selects certain moments from the Passion, inviting the faithful to contemplate them in their hearts and to relive them. The sequence of meditations begins with Gethsemane, where Christ experiences a moment of great anguish before the will of the Father, against which the weakness of the flesh would be tempted to rebel. There Jesus encounters all the temptations and confronts all the sins of humanity, in order to say to the Father: "Not my will but yours be done" (*Lk* 22:42 and parallels). This "Yes" of Christ reverses the "No" of our first parents in the Garden of Eden. And the cost of this faithfulness to the Father's will is made clear in the following mysteries; by his scourging, his crowning with thorns, his carrying the Cross and his death on the Cross, the Lord is cast into the most abject suffering: *Ecce homo!*

This abject suffering reveals not only the love of God but also the meaning of man himself.

Ecce homo: the meaning, origin and fulfilment of man is to be found in Christ, the God who humbles himself out of love "even unto death, death on a cross" (*Phil* 2:8). The sorrowful mysteries help the believer to relive the death of Jesus, to stand at the foot of the Cross beside Mary, to enter with her into the depths of God's love for man and to experience all its life-giving power.

The Glorious Mysteries

23. "The contemplation of Christ's face cannot stop at the image of the Crucified One. He is the Risen One!"[29] The Rosary has always expressed this knowledge born of faith and invited the believer to pass beyond the darkness of the Passion in order to gaze upon Christ's glory in the Resurrection and Ascension. Contemplating the Risen One, Christians *rediscover the reasons for their own faith* (cf. *1Cor* 15:14) and relive the joy not only of those to whom Christ appeared—the Apostles, Mary Magdalene and the disciples on the road to Emmaus—but also *the joy of Mary*, who must have had an equally intense experience of the new life of her glorified Son. In the Ascension, Christ was raised in glory to the right hand of the Father, while Mary herself would be raised to that same glory in the Assumption, enjoying beforehand, by a unique privilege, the destiny reserved for all the just at the resurrection of the dead. Crowned in glory—as she appears in the last glorious mystery—Mary shines forth as Queen of the Angels and Saints, the anticipation and the supreme realization of the eschatological state of the Church.

At the centre of this unfolding sequence of the glory of the Son and the Mother, the Rosary sets before us the third glorious mystery, Pentecost, which reveals the face of the Church as a family gathered together with Mary, enlivened by the powerful outpouring of the Spirit and ready for the mission of evangelization. The contemplation of this scene, like that of the other glorious mysteries, ought to lead the faithful to an ever greater appreciation of their new life in Christ, lived in the heart of the Church, a life of which the scene of Pentecost itself is the great "icon".

---

[29] John Paul II, Apostolic Letter *Novo Millennio Ineunte* (6 January 2001), 28: AAS 93 (2001), 284.

The glorious mysteries thus lead the faithful to *greater hope for the eschatological goal* towards which they journey as members of the pilgrim People of God in history. This can only impel them to bear courageous witness to that "good news" which gives meaning to their entire existence.

From "mysteries" to the "Mystery": Mary's way

24. The cycles of meditation proposed by the Holy Rosary are by no means exhaustive, but they do bring to mind what is essential and they awaken in the soul a thirst for a knowledge of Christ continually nourished by the pure source of the Gospel. Every individual event in the life of Christ, as narrated by the Evangelists, is resplendent with the Mystery that surpasses all understanding (cf. *Eph* 3:19): the Mystery of the Word made flesh, in whom "all the fullness of God dwells bodily" (*Col* 2:9). For this reason the *Catechism of the Catholic Church* places great emphasis on the mysteries of Christ, pointing out that "everything in the life of Jesus is a sign of his Mystery".[30] The *"duc in altum"* of the Church of the third millennium will be determined by the ability of Christians to enter into the "perfect knowledge of God's mystery, of Christ, in whom are hidden all the treasures of wisdom and knowledge" (*Col* 2:2-3). The Letter to the Ephesians makes this heartfelt prayer for all the baptized: "May Christ dwell in your hearts through faith, so that you, being rooted and grounded in love, may have power…to know the love of Christ which surpasses knowledge, that you may be filled with all the fullness of God" (3:17-19).

The Rosary is at the service of this ideal; it offers the "secret" which leads easily to a profound and inward knowledge of Christ. We might call it *Mary's way*. It is the way of the example of the Virgin of Nazareth, a woman of faith, of silence, of attentive listening. It is also the way of a Marian devotion inspired by knowledge of the inseparable bond between Christ and his Blessed Mother: *the mysteries of Christ* are also in some sense *the mysteries of his Mother*, even when they do not involve her directly, for she lives from him and through him. By making our own the words of the Angel Gabriel and Saint Elizabeth contained in the *Hail*

---

[30] No. 515.

Mary, we find ourselves constantly drawn to seek out afresh in Mary, in her arms and in her heart, the "blessed fruit of her womb" (cf *Lk* 1:42).

Mystery of Christ, mystery of man

25. In my testimony of 1978 mentioned above, where I described the Rosary as my favourite prayer, I used an idea to which I would like to return. I said then that "the simple prayer of the Rosary marks the rhythm of human life".[31]

In the light of what has been said so far on the mysteries of Christ, it is not difficult to go deeper into this *anthropological significance* of the Rosary, which is far deeper than may appear at first sight. Anyone who contemplates Christ through the various stages of his life cannot fail to perceive in him *the truth about man*. This is the great affirmation of the Second Vatican Council which I have so often discussed in my own teaching since the Encyclical Letter *Redemptor Hominis*: "it is only in the mystery of the Word made flesh that the mystery of man is seen in its true light".[32] The Rosary helps to open up the way to this light. Following in the path of Christ, in whom man's path is "recapitulated",[33] revealed and redeemed, believers come face to face with the image of the true man. Contemplating Christ's birth, they learn of the sanctity of life; seeing the household of Nazareth, they learn the original truth of the family according to God's plan; listening to the Master in the mysteries of his public ministry, they find the light which leads them to enter the Kingdom of God; and following him on the way to Calvary, they learn the meaning of salvific suffering. Finally, contemplating Christ and his Blessed Mother in glory, they see the goal towards which each of us is called, if we allow ourselves to be healed and transformed by the Holy Spirit. It could be said that each mystery of the Rosary, carefully meditated, sheds light on the mystery of man.

---

[31] Angelus Message of 29 October 1978 : *Insegnamenti*, I (1978), 76.

[32] Second Vatican Ecumenical Council, Pastoral Constitution on the Church in the Modern World *Gaudium et Spes*, 22.

[33] Cf. Saint Irenaeus of Lyons, *Adversus Haereses*, III, 18, 1: PG 7, 932.

At the same time, it becomes natural to bring to this encounter with the sacred humanity of the Redeemer all the problems, anxieties, labours and endeavours which go to make up our lives. "Cast your burden on the Lord and he will sustain you" (*Ps* 55:23). To pray the Rosary is to hand over our burdens to the merciful hearts of Christ and his Mother. Twenty-five years later, thinking back over the difficulties which have also been part of my exercise of the Petrine ministry, I feel the need to say once more, as a warm invitation to everyone to experience it personally: the Rosary does indeed "mark the rhythm of human life", bringing it into harmony with the "rhythm" of God's own life, in the joyful communion of the Holy Trinity, our life's destiny and deepest longing.

CHAPTER III
"FOR ME, TO LIVE IS CHRIST"

The Rosary, a way of assimilating the mystery

26. Meditation on the mysteries of Christ is proposed in the Rosary by means of a method designed to assist in their assimilation. It is a method *based on repetition*. This applies above all to the *Hail Mary*, repeated ten times in each mystery. If this repetition is considered superficially, there could be a temptation to see the Rosary as a dry and boring exercise. It is quite another thing, however, when the Rosary is thought of as an out-pouring of that love which tirelessly returns to the person loved with ex-pressions similar in their content but ever fresh in terms of the feeling pervading them.

In Christ, God has truly assumed a "heart of flesh". Not only does God have a divine heart, rich in mercy and in forgiveness, but also a hu-man heart, capable of all the stirrings of affection. If we needed evidence for this from the Gospel, we could easily find it in the touching dialogue between Christ and Peter after the Resurrection: "Simon, son of John, do you love me?" Three times this question is put to Peter, and three times he gives the reply: "Lord, you know that I love you" (cf. *Jn* 21:15-17). Over and above the specific meaning of this passage, so important for Peter's mission, none can fail to recognize the beauty of this triple repetition, in which the insistent request and the corresponding reply are expressed in terms familiar from the universal experience of human love. To understand the Rosary, one has to enter into the psychological dynamic proper to love.

One thing is clear: although the repeated *Hail Mary* is addressed directly to Mary, it is to Jesus that the act of love is ultimately directed, with her and through her. The repetition is nourished by the desire to be conformed ever more completely to Christ, the true programme of the Christian life. Saint Paul expressed this project with words of fire: "For me to live is Christ and to die is gain" (*Phil* 1:21). And again: "It is no longer I that live, but Christ lives in me" (*Gal* 2:20). The Rosary helps us to be conformed ever more closely to Christ until we attain true holiness.

A valid method...

27. We should not be surprised that our relationship with Christ makes use of a method. God communicates himself to us respecting our human nature and its vital rhythms. Hence, while Christian spirituality is familiar with the most sublime forms of mystical silence in which images, words and gestures are all, so to speak, superseded by an intense and ineffable union with God, it normally engages the whole person in all his complex psychological, physical and relational reality.

This becomes apparent *in the Liturgy.* Sacraments and sacramentals are structured as a series of rites which bring into play all the dimensions of the person. The same applies to non-liturgical prayer. This is confirmed by the fact that, in the East, the most characteristic prayer of Christological meditation, centred on the words "Lord Jesus Christ, Son of God, have mercy on me, a sinner"[34] is traditionally linked to the rhythm of breathing; while this practice favours perseverance in the prayer, it also in some way embodies the desire for Christ to become the breath, the soul and the "all" of one's life.

...which can nevertheless be improved

28. I mentioned in my Apostolic Letter *Novo Millennio Ineunte* that the West is now experiencing *a renewed demand for meditation*, which at

---

[34]   *Catechism of the Catholic Church*, 2616.

times leads to a keen interest in aspects of other religions.[35] Some Christians, limited in their knowledge of the Christian contemplative tradition, are attracted by those forms of prayer. While the latter contain many elements which are positive and at times compatible with Christian experience, they are often based on ultimately unacceptable premises. Much in vogue among these approaches are methods aimed at attaining a high level of spiritual concentration by using techniques of a psychophysical, repetitive and symbolic nature. The Rosary is situated within this broad gamut of religious phenomena, but it is distinguished by characteristics of its own which correspond to specifically Christian requirements.

In effect, the Rosary is simply *a method of contemplation*. As a method, it serves as a means to an end and cannot become an end in itself. All the same, as the fruit of centuries of experience, this method should not be undervalued. In its favour one could cite the experience of countless Saints. This is not to say, however, that the method cannot be improved. Such is the intent of the addition of the new series of *mysteria lucis* to the overall cycle of mysteries and of the few suggestions which I am proposing in this Letter regarding its manner of recitation. These suggestions, while respecting the well-established structure of this prayer, are intended to help the faithful to understand it in the richness of its symbolism and in harmony with the demands of daily life. Otherwise there is a risk that the Rosary would not only fail to produce the intended spiritual effects, but even that the beads, with which it is usually said, could come to be regarded as some kind of amulet or magic object, thereby radically distorting their meaning and function.

Announcing each mystery

29. Announcing each mystery, and perhaps even using a suitable icon to portray it, is as it were *to open up a scenario* on which to focus our attention. The words direct the imagination and the mind towards a particular episode or moment in the life of Christ. In the Church's traditional spirituality, the veneration of icons and the many devotions appealing to the senses, as well as the method of prayer proposed by Saint Ignatius of

---

[35]   Cf. No. 33: AAS 93 (2001), 289.

Loyola in the Spiritual Exercises, make use of visual and imaginative elements (the *compositio loci*), judged to be of great help in concentrating the mind on the particular mystery. This is a methodology, moreover, which *corresponds to the inner logic of the Incarnation:* in Jesus, God wanted to take on human features. It is through his bodily reality that we are led into contact with the mystery of his divinity.

This need for concreteness finds further expression in the announcement of the various mysteries of the Rosary. Obviously these mysteries neither replace the Gospel nor exhaust its content. The Rosary, therefore, is no substitute for *lectio divina*; on the contrary, it presupposes and promotes it. Yet, even though the mysteries contemplated in the Rosary, even with the addition of the *mysteria lucis*, do no more than outline the fundamental elements of the life of Christ, they easily draw the mind to a more expansive reflection on the rest of the Gospel, especially when the Rosary is prayed in a setting of prolonged recollection.

Listening to the word of God

30. In order to supply a Biblical foundation and greater depth to our meditation, it is helpful to follow the announcement of the mystery with *the proclamation of a related Biblical passage*, long or short, depending on the circumstances. No other words can ever match the efficacy of the inspired word. As we listen, we are certain that this is the word of God, spoken for today and spoken "for me".

If received in this way, the word of God can become part of the Rosary's methodology of repetition without giving rise to the ennui derived from the simple recollection of something already well known. It is not a matter of recalling information but of *allowing God to speak.* In certain solemn communal celebrations, this word can be appropriately illustrated by a brief commentary.

Silence

31. *Listening and meditation are nourished by silence.* After the announcement of the mystery and the proclamation of the word, it is fitting to pause and focus one's attention for a suitable period of time on the mystery concerned, before moving into vocal prayer. A discovery of the

importance of silence is one of the secrets of practicing contemplation and meditation. One drawback of a society dominated by technology and the mass media is the fact that silence becomes increasingly difficult to achieve. Just as moments of silence are recommended in the Liturgy, so too in the recitation of the Rosary it is fitting to pause briefly after listening to the word of God, while the mind focuses on the content of a particular mystery.

The "Our Father"

32. After listening to the word and focusing on the mystery, it is natural for *the mind to be lifted up towards the Father*. In each of his mysteries, Jesus always leads us to the Father, for as he rests in the Father's bosom (cf. *Jn* 1:18) he is continually turned towards him. He wants us to share in his intimacy with the Father, so that we can say with him: "Abba, Father" (*Rom* 8:15; *Gal* 4:6). By virtue of his relationship to the Father he makes us brothers and sisters of himself and of one another, communicating to us the Spirit which is both his and the Father's. Acting as a kind of foundation for the Christological and Marian meditation which unfolds in the repetition of the *Hail Mary*, the *Our Father* makes meditation upon the mystery, even when carried out in solitude, an ecclesial experience.

The ten "Hail Marys"

33. This is the most substantial element in the Rosary and also the one which makes it a Marian prayer *par excellence*. Yet when the *Hail Mary* is properly understood, we come to see clearly that its Marian character is not opposed to its Christological character, but that it actually emphasizes and increases it. The first part of the *Hail Mary*, drawn from the words spoken to Mary by the Angel Gabriel and by Saint Elizabeth, is a contemplation in adoration of the mystery accomplished in the Virgin of Nazareth. These words express, so to speak, the wonder of heaven and earth; they could be said to give us a glimpse of God's own wonderment as he contemplates his "masterpiece"—the Incarnation of the Son in the womb of the Virgin Mary. If we recall how, in the Book of Genesis, God "saw all that he had made" (*Gen* 1:31), we can find here an echo of that "pathos with which God, at the dawn of creation, looked upon the work of his

hands".[36] The repetition of the *Hail Mary* in the Rosary gives us a share in God's own wonder and pleasure: in jubilant amazement we acknowledge the greatest miracle of history. Mary's prophecy here finds its fulfilment: "Henceforth all generations will call me blessed" (*Lk* 1:48).

The centre of gravity in the *Hail Mary*, the hinge as it were which joins its two parts, is *the name of Jesus*. Sometimes, in hurried recitation, this centre of gravity can be overlooked, and with it the connection to the mystery of Christ being contemplated. Yet it is precisely the emphasis given to the name of Jesus and to his mystery that is the sign of a meaningful and fruitful recitation of the Rosary. Pope Paul VI drew attention, in his Apostolic Exhortation *Marialis Cultus*, to the custom in certain regions of highlighting the name of Christ by the addition of a clause referring to the mystery being contemplated.[37] This is a praiseworthy custom, especially during public recitation. It gives forceful expression to our faith in Christ, directed to the different moments of the Redeemer's life. It is at once *a profession of faith* and an aid in concentrating our meditation, since it facilitates the process of assimilation to the mystery of Christ inherent in the repetition of the *Hail Mary*. When we repeat the name of Jesus—the only name given to us by which we may hope for salvation (cf. *Acts* 4:12)—in close association with the name of his Blessed Mother, almost as if it were done at her suggestion, we set out on a path of assimilation meant to help us enter more deeply into the life of Christ.

From Mary's uniquely privileged relationship with Christ, which makes her the Mother of God, *Theotókos*, derives the forcefulness of the appeal we make to her in the second half of the prayer, as we entrust to her maternal intercession our lives and the hour of our death.

---

[36] John Paul II, *Letter to Artists* (4 April 1999), 1: AAS 91 (1999), 1155.

[37] Cf. No. 46: AAS 66 (1974), 155. This custom has also been recently praised by the Congregation for Divine Worship and for the Discipline of the Sacraments in its *Direttorio su pietà popolare e liturgia. Principi e orientamenti* (17 December 2001), 201, Vatican City, 2002, 165.

The "Gloria"

34. Trinitarian doxology is the goal of all Christian contemplation. For Christ is the way that leads us to the Father in the Spirit. If we travel this way to the end, we repeatedly encounter the mystery of the three divine Persons, to whom all praise, worship and thanksgiving are due. It is important that the *Gloria, the high-point of contemplation*, be given due prominence in the Rosary. In public recitation it could be sung, as a way of giving proper emphasis to the essentially Trinitarian structure of all Christian prayer.

To the extent that meditation on the mystery is attentive and profound, and to the extent that it is enlivened—from one *Hail Mary* to another—by love for Christ and for Mary, the glorification of the Trinity at the end of each decade, far from being a perfunctory conclusion, takes on its proper contemplative tone, raising the mind as it were to the heights of heaven and enabling us in some way to relive the experience of Tabor, a foretaste of the contemplation yet to come: "It is good for us to be here!" (*Lk* 9:33).

The concluding short prayer

35. In current practice, the Trinitarian doxology is followed by a brief concluding prayer which varies according to local custom. Without in any way diminishing the value of such invocations, it is worthwhile to note that the contemplation of the mysteries could better express their full spiritual fruitfulness if an effort were made to conclude each mystery with *a prayer for the fruits specific to that particular mystery*. In this way the Rosary would better express its connection with the Christian life. One fine liturgical prayer suggests as much, inviting us to pray that, by meditation on the mysteries of the Rosary, we may come to "imitate what they contain and obtain what they promise".[38]

Such a final prayer could take on a legitimate variety of forms, as indeed it already does. In this way the Rosary can be better adapted to

---

[38] "*...concede, quaesumus, ut haec mysteria sacratissimo beatae Mariae Virginis Rosario recolentes, et imitemur quod continent, et quod promittunt assequamur*". Missale Romanum 1960, in festo B.M. Virginis a Rosario.

different spiritual traditions and different Christian communities. It is to be hoped, then, that appropriate formulas will be widely circulated, after due pastoral discernment and possibly after experimental use in centres and shrines particularly devoted to the Rosary, so that the People of God may benefit from an abundance of authentic spiritual riches and find nourishment for their personal contemplation.

The Rosary beads

36. The traditional aid used for the recitation of the Rosary is the set of beads. At the most superficial level, the beads often become a simple counting mechanism to mark the succession of *Hail Marys*. Yet they can also take on a symbolism which can give added depth to contemplation.

Here the first thing to note is the way *the beads converge upon the Crucifix*, which both opens and closes the unfolding sequence of prayer. The life and prayer of believers is centred upon Christ. Everything begins from him, everything leads towards him, everything, through him, in the Holy Spirit, attains to the Father.

As a counting mechanism, marking the progress of the prayer, the beads evoke the unending path of contemplation and of Christian perfection. Blessed Bartolo Longo saw them also as a "chain" which links us to God. A chain, yes, but a sweet chain; for sweet indeed is the bond to God who is also our Father. A "filial" chain which puts us in tune with Mary, the "handmaid of the Lord" (*Lk* 1:38) and, most of all, with Christ himself, who, though he was in the form of God, made himself a "servant" out of love for us (*Phil* 2:7).

A fine way to expand the symbolism of the beads is to let them remind us of our many relationships, of the bond of communion and fraternity which unites us all in Christ.

The opening and closing

37. At present, in different parts of the Church, there are many ways to introduce the Rosary. In some places, it is customary to begin with the opening words of Psalm 70: "O God, come to my aid; O Lord, make haste to help me", as if to nourish in those who are praying a humble awareness of their own insufficiency. In other places, the Rosary begins with the

recitation of the Creed, as if to make the profession of faith the basis of the contemplative journey about to be undertaken. These and similar customs, to the extent that they prepare the mind for contemplation, are all equally legitimate. The Rosary is then ended with a prayer for the intentions of the Pope, as if to expand the vision of the one praying to embrace all the needs of the Church. It is precisely in order to encourage this ecclesial dimension of the Rosary that the Church has seen fit to grant indulgences to those who recite it with the required dispositions.

If prayed in this way, the Rosary truly becomes a spiritual itinerary in which Mary acts as Mother, Teacher and Guide, sustaining the faithful by her powerful intercession. Is it any wonder, then, that the soul feels the need, after saying this prayer and experiencing so profoundly the mother-hood of Mary, to burst forth in praise of the Blessed Virgin, either in that splendid prayer the *Salve Regina* or in the *Litany of Loreto*? This is the crowning moment of an inner journey which has brought the faithful into living contact with the mystery of Christ and his Blessed Mother.

Distribution over time

38. The Rosary can be recited in full every day, and there are those who most laudably do so. In this way it fills with prayer the days of many a contemplative, or keeps company with the sick and the elderly who have abundant time at their disposal. Yet it is clear—and this applies all the more if the new series of *mysteria lucis* is included—that many people will not be able to recite more than a part of the Rosary, according to a certain weekly pattern. This weekly distribution has the effect of giving the different days of the week a certain spiritual "colour", by analogy with the way in which the Liturgy colours the different seasons of the liturgical year.

According to current practice, Monday and Thursday are dedicated to the "joyful mysteries", Tuesday and Friday to the "sorrowful mysteries", and Wednesday, Saturday and Sunday to the "glorious mysteries". Where might the "mysteries of light" be inserted? If we consider that the "glorious mysteries" are said on both Saturday and Sunday, and that Saturday has always had a special Marian flavour, the second weekly meditation on the "joyful mysteries", mysteries in which Mary's presence is especially pronounced, could be moved to Saturday. Thursday would then be free for meditating on the "mysteries of light".

This indication is not intended to limit a rightful freedom in personal and community prayer, where account needs to be taken of spiritual and pastoral needs and of the occurrence of particular liturgical celebrations which might call for suitable adaptations. What is really important is that the Rosary should always be seen and experienced as a path of contemplation. In the Rosary, in a way similar to what takes place in the Liturgy, the Christian week, centred on Sunday, the day of Resurrection, becomes a journey through the mysteries of the life of Christ, and he is revealed in the lives of his disciples as the Lord of time and of history.

CONCLUSION

"Blessed Rosary of Mary, sweet chain linking us to God"

39. What has been said so far makes abundantly clear the richness of this traditional prayer, which has the simplicity of a popular devotion but also the theological depth of a prayer suited to those who feel the need for deeper contemplation.

The Church has always attributed particular efficacy to this prayer, entrusting to the Rosary, to its choral recitation and to its constant practice, the most difficult problems. At times when Christianity itself seemed under threat, its deliverance was attributed to the power of this prayer, and Our Lady of the Rosary was acclaimed as the one whose intercession brought salvation.

Today I willingly entrust to the power of this prayer—as I mentioned at the beginning—the cause of peace in the world and the cause of the family.

Peace

40. The grave challenges confronting the world at the start of this new Millennium lead us to think that only an intervention from on high, capable of guiding the hearts of those living in situations of conflict and those governing the destinies of nations, can give reason to hope for a brighter future.

The Rosary is by its nature a prayer for peace, since it consists in the contemplation of Christ, the Prince of Peace, the one who is "our peace" (*Eph* 2:14). Anyone who assimilates the mystery of Christ—and this is clearly the goal of the Rosary—learns the secret of peace and makes it his life's project. Moreover, by virtue of its meditative character, with the tranquil succession of *Hail Marys*, the Rosary has a peaceful effect on those who pray it, disposing them to receive and experience in their innermost depths, and to spread around them, that true peace which is the special gift of the Risen Lord (cf. *Jn* 14:27; 20.21).

The Rosary is also a prayer for peace because of the fruits of charity which it produces. When prayed well in a truly meditative way, the Rosary leads to an encounter with Christ in his mysteries and so cannot fail to draw attention to the face of Christ in others, especially in the most afflicted. How could one possibly contemplate the mystery of the Child of Bethlehem, in the joyful mysteries, without experiencing the desire to welcome, defend and promote life, and to shoulder the burdens of suffering children all over the world? How could one possibly follow in the footsteps of Christ the Revealer, in the mysteries of light, without resolving to bear witness to his "Beatitudes" in daily life? And how could one contemplate Christ carrying the Cross and Christ Crucified, without feeling the need to act as a "Simon of Cyrene" for our brothers and sisters weighed down by grief or crushed by despair? Finally, how could one possibly gaze upon the glory of the Risen Christ or of Mary Queen of Heaven, without yearning to make this world more beautiful, more just, more closely conformed to God's plan?

In a word, by focusing our eyes on Christ, the Rosary also makes us peacemakers in the world. By its nature as an insistent choral petition in harmony with Christ's invitation to "pray ceaselessly" (*Lk* 18:1), the Rosary allows us to hope that, even today, the difficult "battle" for peace can be won. Far from offering an escape from the problems of the world, the Rosary obliges us to see them with responsible and generous eyes, and obtains for us the strength to face them with the certainty of God's help and the firm intention of bearing witness in every situation to "love, which binds everything together in perfect harmony" (*Col* 3:14).

The family: parents...

41. As a prayer for peace, the Rosary is also, and always has been, *a prayer of and for the family.* At one time this prayer was particularly dear to Christian families, and it certainly brought them closer together. It is important not to lose this precious inheritance. We need to return to the practice of family prayer and prayer for families, continuing to use the Rosary.

In my Apostolic Letter *Novo Millennio Ineunte* I encouraged the celebration of the *Liturgy of the Hours* by the lay faithful in the ordinary life of parish communities and Christian groups;[39] I now wish to do the same for the Rosary. These two paths of Christian contemplation are not mutually exclusive; they complement one another. I would therefore ask those who devote themselves to the pastoral care of families to recommend heartily the recitation of the Rosary.

The family that prays together stays together. The Holy Rosary, by age-old tradition, has shown itself particularly effective as a prayer which brings the family together. Individual family members, in turning their eyes towards Jesus, also regain the ability to look one another in the eye, to communicate, to show solidarity, to forgive one another and to see their covenant of love renewed in the Spirit of God.

Many of the problems facing contemporary families, especially in economically developed societies, result from their increasing difficulty in communicating. Families seldom manage to come together, and the rare occasions when they do are often taken up with watching television. To return to the recitation of the family Rosary means filling daily life with very different images, images of the mystery of salvation: the image of the Redeemer, the image of his most Blessed Mother. The family that recites the Rosary together reproduces something of the atmosphere of the household of Nazareth: its members place Jesus at the centre, they share his joys and sorrows, they place their needs and their plans in his hands, they draw from him the hope and the strength to go on.

---

[39] Cf. No. 34: AAS 93 (2001), 290.

...and children

42. It is also beautiful and fruitful to entrust to this prayer *the growth and development of children.* Does the Rosary not follow the life of Christ, from his conception to his death, and then to his Resurrection and his glory? Parents are finding it ever more difficult to follow the lives of their children as they grow to maturity. In a society of advanced technology, of mass communications and globalization, everything has become hurried, and the cultural distance between generations is growing ever greater. The most diverse messages and the most unpredictable experiences rapidly make their way into the lives of children and adolescents, and parents can become quite anxious about the dangers their children face. At times parents suffer acute disappointment at the failure of their children to resist the seductions of the drug culture, the lure of an unbridled hedonism, the temptation to violence, and the manifold expressions of meaninglessness and despair.

To pray the Rosary *for children*, and even more, *with children*, training them from their earliest years to experience this daily "pause for prayer" with the family, is admittedly not the solution to every problem, but it is a spiritual aid which should not be underestimated. It could be objected that the Rosary seems hardly suited to the taste of children and young people of today. But perhaps the objection is directed to an impoverished method of praying it. Furthermore, without prejudice to the Rosary's basic structure, there is nothing to stop children and young people from praying it— either within the family or in groups—with appropriate symbolic and practical aids to understanding and appreciation. Why not try it? With God's help, a pastoral approach to youth which is positive, impassioned and creative—as shown by the World Youth Days!—is capable of achieving quite remarkable results. If the Rosary is well presented, I am sure that young people will once more surprise adults by the way they make this prayer their own and recite it with the enthusiasm typical of their age group.

The Rosary, a treasure to be rediscovered

43. Dear brothers and sisters! A prayer so easy and yet so rich truly deserves to be rediscovered by the Christian community. Let us do so, especially this year, as a means of confirming the direction outlined in my Apostolic Letter *Novo Millennio Ineunte*, from which the pastoral plans of

so many particular Churches have drawn inspiration as they look to the immediate future.

I turn particularly to you, my dear Brother Bishops, priests and deacons, and to you, pastoral agents in your different ministries: through your own personal experience of the beauty of the Rosary, may you come to promote it with conviction.

I also place my trust in you, theologians: by your sage and rigorous reflection, rooted in the word of God and sensitive to the lived experience of the Christian people, may you help them to discover the Biblical foundations, the spiritual riches and the pastoral value of this traditional prayer.

I count on you, consecrated men and women, called in a particular way to contemplate the face of Christ at the school of Mary.

I look to all of you, brothers and sisters of every state of life, to you, Christian families, to you, the sick and elderly, and to you, young people: *confidently take up the Rosary once again.* Rediscover the Rosary in the light of Scripture, in harmony with the Liturgy, and in the context of your daily lives.

May this appeal of mine not go unheard! At the start of the twenty-fifth year of my Pontificate, I entrust this Apostolic Letter to the loving hands of the Virgin Mary, *prostrating myself in spirit before her image in the splendid Shrine built for her by Blessed Bartolo Longo*, the apostle of the Rosary. I willingly make my own the touching words with which he concluded his well-known *Supplication to the Queen of the Holy Rosary*: "O Blessed Rosary of Mary, sweet chain which unites us to God, bond of love which unites us to the angels, tower of salvation against the assaults of Hell, safe port in our universal shipwreck, we will never abandon you. You will be our comfort in the hour of death: yours our final kiss as life ebbs away. And the last word from our lips will be your sweet name, O Queen of the Rosary of Pompei, O dearest Mother, O Refuge of Sinners, O Sovereign Consoler of the Afflicted. May you be everywhere blessed, today and always, on earth and in heaven".

From the Vatican, on the 16th day of October in the year 2002, the beginning of the twenty-fifth year of my Pontificate.

JOHN PAUL II

Where Did the Rosary Come From?

Its History and Lore

Richard Gribble, CSC

Closely allied with the Battle of Lepanto in 1571 was the universal "telling" of the rosary to save Christian Europe from being overwhelmed by the approaching Turkish fleet. Had the Turks won, all Europe would have become Muslim. Despite the great dread of defeat, a stunning victory was achieved and ever since then October 7 has been celebrated as Our Lady of Victory.

A rather simple and humble story tells of a priest in his efforts to exhort young girls in the imitation of the Virgin Mary. Speaking of the Annunciation, the priest asked his charges, "What do you think Mary was doing when the angel Gabriel appeared to her? Was she cleaning the house, gossiping with neighbors or reading? No! What else would she have been doing but sitting quietly in her room saying her beads." The picture derived from this story makes it appear that the rosary has always been a party of Christian piety and devotion. Although the story stretches reality, it is true that since the fifteenth century the rosary has found sufficient honor and tribute to establish it as a fixture within the spiritual practice of most Roman Catholics. The roots of this popular prayer are rich and can be found in an evolutionary process which combined legend, devotion, and official church recognition.

As the apocryphal story above indicates, much legend and lore is associated with the rosary in its long history as part of Catholic devotion. Two basic hypotheses exist to explain the origins of the rosary. The first, offered by the "development of religion" theory, states that the Christian rosary came to Europe from the influence of prayer counters used in Eastern religions, as the Crusaders brought some Islamic practices, such as the use of prayer beads, into Christianity. The other hypothesis of the rosary's origin is that the devotion came to us essentially complete from the hands of Saint Dominic, who has been instructed by the Blessed Mother on its use and efficacy.

Although some merits can be found in each of these theories, neither of them can be adequately supported from the historical record. Hindus and Buddhists have used prayer beads since before the time of Christ. Yet, there is no demonstrable data which links the beads of these Eastern religions to those of Christianity. The theory that crusaders introduced the rosary to the West from the influence of Islam is also more conjecture than fact.

The long-standing tradition that Dominic was given the rosary by Mary actually began 200 years after the saint's death. Blessed Alanus de Rupe, a fellow Dominican, wrote an account in 1460 in which Mary appeared to Dominic, who was dejected from his failure to convert the Cathars. The Blessed Mother told him that intellectual thinking and preaching were not required against the Cathars, but rather the successful use and promotion of her psalter. She then entrusted to him the rosary, gave him instructions for its use, and revealed it devotion. The story possessed every reason for acceptance, especially its association with a well-known saint. Papal documents supported this theory into the twentieth century. Even the learned John Henry Cardinal Newman explicitly supported the tradition.

The Dominican tradition was not seriously challenged until the eighteenth-century work of the Bollandists, a group of Dutch Jesuits who researched the lives of the saints. These scholars could find no evidence to link the rosary to Saint Dominic in their painstaking work to separate fact from fiction with respect to the saints. In the twentieth century the learned Jesuit Herbert Thurston also challenged the prevailing tradition of the Dominican origin of the rosary. His work created a battle between those who defended the tradition and those who sought new answers concerning the rosary.

The historical record best supports the concept that the rosary evolved into its present form. The elements of prayer beads and the tradition of Saint Dominic are integral to this development, but they are two elements to a vastly larger picture, a portrait which encompasses the evolution of prayers, the practice of piety, and the fulfillment of the age old adage, Lex orandi, lex credendi ("The rule of prayer is the rule of belief").

The story of the rosary begins with the desert fathers in their attempts to say their prayers faithfully. These anchorites used stones or pebbles to count their daily petitions to God. One stone would be discarded from a bag or pouch with each prayer said, so that the number to be recited could be accurately counted. As time passed, more permanent devices, such as a knotted cord or a notched piece of wood, were used to count these daily prayers and devotions. Thus the concept of a prayer-counter has been with Christianity since the Patristic period.

Irish monks of the seventh century must be credited with the introduction of prayer groups for use in penance or devotion. Recitation of the 150 psalms, arranged in three groups of 50 (na tri coicat), was regularly assigned as penance and prayer for the monks. It was common practice for monks to pray two "fifties" for the repose of the soul of a benefactor or member of the community. "Fifties" were also assigned as corporal prayer.

Saint Columbia is the one who brought this practice of grouped psalms as prayer to the Continent.

In medieval times the recitation of the Psalms was a practice largely reserved for the literate. Thus, as often happens, conditions necessitated a change of practice. Those monks who were illiterate, or those who could read but had no access to a full text of the Latin psalms, began to substitute popular prayers, in remembrance of Christ, for the psalms. The practice became known as the Jesus Psalter. In order to bring order to the endless possibilities that resulted from substitution for the psalms, the Irish monks circa 800 began to promote the use of the Paternoster (Our Father) as a common prayer which could be assigned in the na tri coicat format for penance. This harmless shift to a universally known prayer, a change which allowed participation by all, was a major step in rosary development. This practice became common throughout Europe. Religious at Cluny (1096) were many times assigned 50 psalms or Our Fathers for the deceased. At the dawn of the eleventh century the use of three fifties of Our Fathers, known as the Little Psalter, prayed on cords or beads of some type, was widespread.

The replacement of the Our Father with the Hail Mary as the primary prayer of the rosary came about in the eleventh and twelfth centuries through a rather complex process. Several Archbishops of Canterbury composed "Psalters if 150 Praises of the Blessed Virgin." These no-corporal prayers were usually structured in the na tri coicat format. The Ave (Hail Mary) was the basic prayer of these special Marian psalters. Over time the Little Psalter and the beads became associated with the Blessed Virgin and her devotion.

The Ave used in these special psalters was not the prayer we know today. Prior to the fifteenth century, this praise of Mary was totally Scriptural in origin. The infancy narrative of Luke's Gospel is the root source of the Ave. At the annunciation the angel Gabriel proclaims, "Rejoice, O highly favored daughter! The Lord is with you." (1:28) Later, during the visitation, Mary's cousin Elizabeth states, "Blest are you among women and blest is the fruit of your womb" (1:42). The combined greeting of Scripture was used in the offertory of the Mass on the fourth Sunday of Advent, a Marian celebration, for the year 600. The prayer was also used in the Saturday Divine Office and the Little Office of the Blessed Virgin Mary from the thirteenth century.

Popular devotion led to an expansion of the prayer to its contemporary form. The word Jesus was initially added by Pope Urban IV in 1261. Additions, composed by Saint Anselm of Canterbury and the Catholic reformer Savonarola in the late-fifteenth century, are very close to the words used today. The Catechism produced at the Council of Trent (1545-63) officially reorganized the popular addition, "Holy Mary, Mother of God, pray for us sinners, now and at the hour of our death. Amen," which was then adopted by the revised Roman Breviary of 1568.

The basic structure of the rosary as we know it today stems from the fourteenth century and the work of Henry of Kalbar. Henry was the first to bracket the Marian Psalter with 15 Paters which stood like columns between groups of ten Aves. This German tradition came to England in the fifteenth century. Extant records show that students at Eton College in 1440 were required to recite daily the Psalter of the Blessed Virgin Mary, which consisted of 15 Our Fathers and 150 Hail Marys. Archeological evidence testifies to this same structure. Early-fifteenth century "rosaries" consists of strings of beads where each ten were separated by a larger "marker" bead. The rosary pendant used to pray the Apostles Creed, Our Father, three Hail Marys, and the Doxology, was developed from six-teenth and seventeenth century forms of the rosary. Two early seventeenth century Jesuit works, *The Garden of Our Blessed Lady* (1612) and *Sacri Rosarii Excercitiones* (1622), speak of the pendant as part of the rosary devotion.

Besides the Our Father, which is given us almost verbatim in our con-temporary use by Saint Mathew (6:9-13), and the aforementioned Hail Mary, the rosary uses three other prayers. The Doxology of Glory Be has origins which are older than all aspects of the rosary, save the Lord's Prayer. Invocation of the Trinity was common in the early Patristic period, bor-rowing from the Hebrew Scriptures' exhortation, "God be praised." As early as 529 at the Second Council of Vaison, the doxology as we recite it today was authorized to be said after all psalms in the psalter. The doxology's association with the rosary begins in the Renaissance period. One prayer book written circa 1500 asks that "the prayer of the Holy Trinity be added to every Our Father of the Psalter." In 1566 another prayer book called for the doxology to be said after each decade of Hail Marys. Oddly enough the doxology has never been officially recognized as part of the rosary. The document Supremi apostolatus of Leo XIII (1883), which outlined the essentials of the rosary, made no reference to the doxology universally recited by the faithful.

In the Patristic Church, Ambrose and Rufinus (circa 380) wrote ac-counts of the Apostles Creed and assigned its authorship to the apostles. Medieval tradition promoted this theory, saying it was written on the day of Pentecost, under the inspiration of the Holy Spirit. Contemporary schol-arship has shown the Apostles Creed to be one form of a baptismal creed used in fifth-century Rome. The creed is first mentioned as part of the rosary in the Libellus Perutilis, published in 1495. The author saw the creed as a hoop around which a garland of 50 Aves and associated Paters was woven. In the sixteenth century Cistercians were ordered to pray the Apostle Creed with the Aves and Paters of the Marian Psalter.

The Salve Regina or Hail Holy Queen entered into liturgical prayer from the Latin Church. In the thirteenth century Cistercians and Franciscans adopted its use in Compline (night prayer). From the fourteenth century it has been universally sung after Compline in the Latin rite breviary. The authorship of the prayer is uncertain. At least four people have been associated with its composition, including Saint Bernard of Clairvaux. The prayer's association with the rosary coincided with other events of the day. In 1568 Pope Pius V decreed that the Salve should be sung or recited after Vespers from Trinity Sunday to the first Sunday in Advent. Official papal recognition of the rosary at the same time suggests some connection, although there is no certainty.

On the surface the rosary appears to be a simple repetition of prayers with no direction. This is, however, not the case. The mysteries of the rosary, contemplated during the prayer's recitation, reside at the true heart of this devotion and make it a meditation upon the life of Christ and His mother Mary. Meditations associated with the prayers of the rosary began in the early fifteenth century. Dominic of Prussia in his book *Liber experientiarium* composed a set of 50 meditative clauses for each Ave recited in a typical "set of 50." The subject of these clauses embraced the entire life of Jesus and His relationship with Mary. These meditations were later expanded to 150 for each Ave of the entire rosary. These clauses, which were published in books because they were quite difficult to memorize, were appended to the Biblical (first half) of the Hail May. For example, the first Hail Mary read, "Hail Mary, full of Grace, the Lord is with thee. Blessed art thou among women and blessed is the fruit of thy womb, Jesus, whom thou didst conceive by the Holy Spirit, through the message of an angel. Amen."

The transition from 150 mysteries to the contemporary 15 began with Alberto da Castello in the early sixteenth century. In his 1521 book *Rosario della Gloriosa Virgine*, the word mystery is used for the first time in association with the rosary. The monograph keeps the 150 clauses but divides them into groups of ten and has them introduced by a Paternoster whose theme is consistent with the ten clauses which follow in the decade of Aves.

Several theories exist as to the precise origin of the 15 mysteries in their current configuration of five glorious, joyful, and sorrowful. Various forms of physical evidence show that the mysteries were placed in groups. An anonymous prayer book of 1483 lists the mysteries and divides them into three groups. An altarpiece in a Dominican convent in Frankfurt (1490) contains all 15 present mysteries. One of the original rosary books, *Unser Lieben Frauen Psalter,* contains three insert pages, each with five colored woodcuts of the present mysteries, save the coronation of Mary, which is subsumed into the Assumption. The 1573 text, *Rosario Della Sacratissima,* lists the mysteries in their present groupings.

Meditation on the rosary was championed by the Jesuits from the foundation of their Society. One book title is illustrative. In 1573 Gaspard Loarte, S.J. published *Advice and Suggestions on the Manner of Meditating on the Mysteries of the Rosary of the Blessed Virgin, Our Mother.* The work's influence must have been great, for it was rapidly translated from the original French to German, Latin, Spanish, and Portuguese.

Official Church recognition of the rosary as an approved devotion begins with the aforementioned Alanus de Rupe. As well as initiating the tradition of the Dominican origin of the rosary, Blessed Alanus founded the Confraternity of the Rosary in 1470. Before this time the rosary was an individual devotion of piety; there was no centralized effort to have the prayer recognized. De Rupe's organization was subsumed under a similar organization started by Jacob Sprenger in Cologne. This latter group grew rapidly. One report listed 500,000 members by 1479. Popularity was guaranteed for the Confraternity, since its requirements for membership were minimal: recitation of Our Lady's Psalter once per week and reception of Holy Communion on the first Sunday of the month. Sprenger's manual for the organization called for recitation of the complete psalter (15 decades) where, "after ten white roses they must insert one red rose," thus giving definition to the idea of one Pater followed by ten Aves.

The Confraternity of the Rosary brought the devotion to the forefront of Church practice. Almost 100 years later in 1571, Don Juan's great naval victory over the Turks at Lepanto was attributed to the rosary. Pius V declared that from that day, October 7, a commemoration of the rosary would be made in the Mass for that day. In 1573, at the request of the Dominican order, Pope Gregory XIII established the Feast of the Most Holy Rosary on the first Sunday in October. Initially the feast was granted only to churches which possessed an altar dedicated to the rosary. In 1671 Pope Clement X extended the feast to the universal Church. Today the feast is celebrated as an obligatory memorial on October 7. The official definition of the rosary is that given in the breviary for October 7: "The rosary is a certain form of prayer wherein we say 15 decades of Hail Marys with an Our Father between each, and recalling in pious meditation as many mysteries of our redemption as there are single [decades]."

Rosary devotion has been championed by many in the post-Reformation period. Saint Louis Marie de Montfort in his book *The Secret of the Most Holy Rosary* (1680) gave a brief history of the devotion. The text also served as a manual for the prayers' recitation. In the nineteenth century Pope Leo XIII wrote 12 encyclicals and other documents which promoted rosary devotion. Leo was the one who, in Supremi apostolatus, initiated the idea of October as a special month for devotion to the rosary. More recently Rather Patrick Peyton, CSC, traveled the world many times over in the promotion of family prayer centered on the rosary.

Contemporary Catholicism has seen an eclipse in rosary devotion. Yet this prayers' strong roots in the tradition of the Faith suggest that one day it will shine again brightly. Our appreciation for the historical roots of this special prayer and its mysteries can aid our personal renewal and help us to rediscover the efficacy and importance of Catholic devotional life.

Holy Cross Father, Richard Gribble, is the author of many books including *The History and Devotion of the Rosary* (Our Sunday Visitor). His latest work, the definitive biography of Fr. Patrick Peyton, (The family that prays together stays together) will be published soon.

The Fifteen Promises of the Blessed Virgin to Christians Who Faithfully Pray the Rosary

1. To all those who shall pray my Rosary devoutly, I promise my special protection and great graces.

2. Those who shall persevere in the recitation of my Rosary will receive some special grace.

3. The Rosary will be a very powerful armor against hell; it will destroy vice, deliver from sin and dispel heresy.

4. The rosary will make virtue and good works flourish, and will obtain for souls the most abundant divine mercies. It will draw the hearts of men from the love of the world and its vanities, and will lift them to the desire of eternal things. Oh, that souls would sanctify themselves by this means.

5. Those who trust themselves to me through the Holy Rosary will not perish.

6. Whoever recites my Rosary devoutly reflecting on the mysteries, shall never be overwhelmed by misfortune. He will not experience the anger of God nor will he perish by an unprovided death. The sinner will be converted; the just will persevere in grace and merit eternal life.

7. Those truly devoted to my Rosary shall not die without the sacraments of the Church.

8. Those who are faithful to recite my Rosary shall have during their life and at their death the light of God and the plenitude of His graces and will share in the merits of the blessed.

9. I will deliver promptly from purgatory souls devoted to my Rosary.

10. True children of my Rosary will enjoy great glory in heaven.

11. What you shall ask through my rosary you shall obtain.

12. To those who propagate my Rosary I promise aid in all their necessities.

13. I have obtained from my son that *all the members of the Rosary Confraternity* shall have as their intercessors, in life and in death, the entire celestial court.

14. Those who recite my Rosary faithfully are my beloved children, the brothers and sisters of Jesus Christ.

15. Devotion to my Rosary is a special sign of predestination.

Simple Directions for Praying the Rosary

Praying the rosary is a bit like riding a bike or tying your shoe. It's easy once you know how to do it, but difficult to "explain" how to do it. But I think the best way is just to start with the prayers written out for you and then make your way around the beads—step by step. If you try to get it perfectly, piously done you will only get discouraged. For the first time or two don't worry about anything but just doing the mechanics of the prayer. Like riding a bike you don't start enjoying the scenery until you can make the thing go!

So, if this is your first time praying the rosary. Keep it simple! You don't even need rosary beads to start—just something to help you count. Ten fingers, ten pennies, whatever is at hand.

Step one: Make the sign of the cross.

With your right hand touch your forehead and say "In the name of the Father" then drop your hand down to the middle of your chest and say, "the Son" and then touching first your left shoulder and then right say, "and the Holy Spirit. Amen"

Step two: Pray the Apostle's Creed.

If you are using rosary beads then this is said while holding the cross in your hand.

> I believe in God, the Father almighty,
> creator of heaven and earth.
>
> I believe in Jesus Christ, his only Son, our Lord.
>
> He was conceived by the power of the Holy Spirit
> and was born of the Virgin Mary.
>
> He suffered under Pontius Pilate,
> was crucified,
> died, and was buried.
>
> He descended into hell.
>
> On the third day he arose again.

He ascended into heaven
and is seated at the right hand
of the Father.

He will come again to judge
the living and the dead.

I believe in the Holy Spirit,
the Holy Catholic Church,
the communion of saints,
the forgiveness of sins,
the resurrection of the body,
and life everlasting. Amen

Step three: Pray the Our Father.

This is done on the first big bead next to the crucifix if you are using a regular rosary.

Our Father who art in heaven,
hallowed be thy name.

Thy kingdom come.
Thy will be done on earth,
as it is in heaven.

Give us this day our daily bread,
and forgive us our trespasses,
as we forgive those who trespass against us,
and lead us not into temptation,
but deliver us from evil. Amen.

Step four: Pray three Hail Marys.

One for each of the next three beads.

Hail Mary, full of grace,
the Lord is with you!

Blessed are you among women,
and blessed is the fruit of your womb, Jesus.

Holy Mary, Mother of God,
pray for us sinners,
now and at the hour of our death. Amen

Step five: On the next big bead you pray the Glory Be.
Glory be to the Father,
and to the Son,
and to the Holy Spirit;
as it was in the beginning,
is now, and will be forever. Amen

Hurray! You have prayed the first part of the rosary—all the prayers for the rest will consist of these last three prayers. You don't have to learn anything new to get the mechanics of the rosary understood. And once the mechanics are learned, just like riding the bike soon you will not even think about how to pray the rosary you will just do it!

You will find that praying the rosary will be different for you each and every time. Just like taking a walk—even though it may be the same path you always take, new things will always be before you. There are five simple meditations for each set of mysteries of the rosary. Don't make it complicated. Keep your thoughts simple and let the Holy Spirit guide you along new avenues of Spiritual experience. There are as many different reflections for the mysteries of the rosary as there are different snowflakes. Once you have prayed the rosary a few times, you might want to try praying it with meditations from someone else as found in a book or pamphlet to help you with new insights—but keeping it simple is just as good and powerful a way to pray.

There are now four different Mysteries of the Rosary. Each one allows you to meditate on the life of Jesus and Mary in a special way.

The Joyful Mysteries: Family Life—Jesus being born and growing up.

The Luminous Mysteries: Jesus public life—His preaching and miracles.

The Sorrowful Mysteries: Jesus dying for us.

The Glorious Mysteries: Jesus opening heaven for us!

How and when and where you pray the Rosary is entirely up to you. It's your prayer, your special time to spend with God. Many people like to rotate the mysteries and pray a different set of mysteries each day. Pope John Paul II suggested praying the following:

Joyful Mysteries on Monday and Saturday,
Sorrowful Mysteries on Tuesday and Friday,
Luminous Mysteries on Thursday,
Glorious Mysteries on Wednesday and Sunday.

Each set of mysteries consists of five chapters in the life of the Gospel. Starting with the Joyful Mysteries we break it down like this:

First Joyful Mystery
The Angel makes the Announcement to Mary.
Pray: One Our Father
Ten Hail Marys
One Glory Be

Second Joyful Mystery
Elizabeth greets Mary
Pray: One Our Father
Ten Hail Marys
One Glory Be

Third Joyful Mystery
Jesus is born in Bethlehem.
Pray: One Our Father
Ten Hail Mary's
One Glory Be

Fourth Joyful Mystery
Jesus is presented in the temple.
Pray: One Our Father
Ten Hail Marys
One Glory Be

Fifth Joyful Mystery
    Jesus is found in the temple.
    Pray: One Our Father
    Ten Hail Marys
    One Glory Be

You may want to finish the rosary by praying the Hail, Holy Queen:

    Hail, Holy Queen,
    Mother of Mercy!

    Our life, our sweetness,
    and our hope!
    to thee do we cry,
    poor banished children of Eve;
    to thee do we send up our sighs,
    mourning and weeping in this valley, of tears.

    Turn then, most gracious Advocate,
    thine eyes of mercy toward us;
    and after this our exile
    show unto us the blessed fruit
    of thy womb, Jesus.

    O clement, O loving,
    O sweet Virgin Mary.

Finish by making the sign of the Cross.
    In the name of the Father, and of the Son,
    and of the Holy Spirit. Amen.

If you do not have a rosary, and would like to receive one, there is a coupon for sending for a free one at the back of this book.

Meditations of the Rosary

The rosary is a meditative expression of prayer that calls us to praise God with our lips and draw near to him with our hearts. The Catechism of the Catholic Church says, "Meditation engages thought, imagination, emotion and desire. This mobilization of faculties is necessary in order to deepen our conversion of our heart, and strengthen our will to follow Christ. Christian prayer tries above all to meditate on the mysteries of Christ."

The rosary has four sets of mysteries: the joyful, the luminous, the sorrowful and the glorious. Each set of mysteries contains five separate decades, or ten prayers, and will take you once completely around the rosary beads. Begin by praying the introductory prayers.

Each decade consists of prayers found in the introductory prayers: Our Father, ten Hail Marys and one Glory Be. As you pray each decade with the Our Father prayer, think about the setting of the mystery: the sights, sounds and feelings of those in the story. As you pray through the ten Hail Marys let the story unfold before you, knowing that Christ is acting on your behalf. If you read the passages referred to in each mystery, the story will be fresh in you mind, allowing you to focus on important details and gain new insights. Finish each mystery with one Glory Be, an expression of thankfulness to God.

Introductory and Common Prayers

A. In the name of the Father, and of the Son and of the Holy Spirit. Amen. (Sign of the cross.)

B. I believe in God the Father almighty, creator of heaven and Earth. I believe in Jesus Christ, his only Son our Lord. He was conceived by the Holy Spirit and born of the Virgin Mary. He suffered under Pontius Pilate, was crucified, died, and was buried. He descended into hell. On the third day he rose again. He ascended into heaven and is seated at the right hand of the Father. He will come again to judge the living and the dead. I believe in the Holy Spirit, the holy Catholic Church, the communion of saints, the forgiveness of sins, the resurrection of the body, and life everlasting. Amen.

C. Our Father, who art in heaven, hallowed be they name; thy kingdom come; thy will be done, on Earth as it is in heaven. Give us this day our daily bread; and forgive us our trespasses, as we forgive those who trespass against us; and lead us not into temptation, but deliver us from evil. Amen.

D. Hail, Mary, full of grace, the Lord is with thee; blessed art thou among women and blessed is the fruit of thy womb, Jesus. Holy Mary, Mother of God, pray for us sinners, now and at the hour of our death. Amen.

E. Glory be to the Father, and to the Son, and to the Holy Spirit. As it was in the beginning, is now, and ever shall be, world without end. Amen.

The Joyful Mysteries

1. The Annunciation
    Luke 1,26-38. Verse 35: And the angel said to her, "The Holy Spirit will come upon you, and the power of the Most High will overshadow you; therefore the child to be born will be called holy, the Son of God."

2. The Visitation
    Luke 1,39-56. Verses 41-43: And when Elizabeth heard the greeting of Mary, the babe leaped in her womb; and Elizabeth was filled with the Holy Spirit and she exclaimed with a loud cry, "Blessed are you among women, and blessed is the fruit of your womb! And why is this granted me, that the mother of my Lord should come to me?"

3. The Nativity
    Luke 2,1-20. Verse 7: And she gave birth to her firstborn son and wrapped him in swaddling cloths, and laid him in a manger, because there was no place for them in the inn.

4. The Presentation of Jesus at the Temple
    Luke 2,21-38. Verses 28-32: (Simeon) took him up in his arms and blessed God and said, "Lord, now lettest thou thy servant depart in peace, according to thy word for mine eyes have seen thy salvation

which thou hast prepared in the presence of all peoples, a light for revelation to the Gentiles, and for glory to thy people Israel."

5. Finding Jesus in the Temple
    Luke 2,41-52. Verses 45-47: And when they did not find him, they returned to Jerusalem, seeking him. After three days they found him in the temple, sitting among the teachers, listening to them and asking them questions; and all who heard him were amazed at his understanding and his answers.

The Mysteries of Light

Text from Apostolic Letter Rosarium Virginis Mariae, Oct. 2002

1. Jesus' Baptism in the Jordon
    The Baptism in the Jordan is first of all a mystery of light. Here, as Christ descends into the waters, the innocent one who became "sin" for our sake (cf 2Cor 5:21), the heavens open wide and the voice of the Father declares him the beloved Son (cf. Mt 3:17 and parallels), while the Spirit descends on him to invest him with the mission which he is to carry out.

2. Jesus at the Wedding in Cana
    Another mystery of light is the first of the signs, given at Cana (cf. Jn 2:1-12), when Christ changes water into wine and opens the hearts of the disciples to faith, thanks to the intervention of Mary, the first among believers.

3. Jesus Proclaims the Kingdom of God
    Another mystery of light is the preaching by which Jesus proclaims the coming of the Kingdom of God, calls to conversion (cf. Mk 1:15) and forgives the sins of all who draw near to him in humble trust (cf. Mk 2:3-13; Lk 7:47-48): the inauguration of that ministry of mercy which he continues to exercise until the end of the world, particularly through the Sacrament of Reconciliation which he has entrusted to his church (cf. Jn 20:22-23).

4. The Transfiguration

   The mystery of light par excellence is the Transfiguration, traditionally believed to have taken place on the Mount Tabor. The glory of the
   Godhead shines forth from the face of Christ as the Father commands
   the astonished Apostles to "listen to him" (cf. Lk 9:35 and parallels)
   and to prepare to experience with him the agony of the Passion, so as
   to come with him to the joy of the Resurrection and a life transfigured
   by the Holy Spirit.

5. Institution of the Eucharist

   A final mystery of light is the institution of the Eucharist, in which
   Christ offers his body and blood as food under the signs of bread and
   wine, and testifies "to the end" his love for humanity (Jn 13:1), for
   whose salvation he will offer himself in sacrifice (Turn to the concluding Prayers).

The Sorrowful Mysteries

1. The Agony in the Garden

   Luke 22, 39-46. Verses 41-42, 44: And he withdrew from them about
   a stone's throw, and knelt down and prayed, "Father, if thou art willing, remove this cup from me; nevertheless not my will, but thine. Be
   done"…He was in such agony and he prayed so fervently that his
   sweat became like drops of blood falling on the ground.

2. The Scourging at the Pillar

   Matthew 27, 15-26. Verse 26: Then [Pilate] released for them Barabbas,
   and having scourged Jesus, delivered him to be crucified.

3. The Crowning with Thorns

   Matthew 27, 27-31. Verses 29-30: and plaiting a crown of thorns [the
   soldiers] put it on his head, and put a reed in his right hand. And kneeling before him they mocked him saying, "Hail, King of the Jews!"
   And they spat upon him, and took the reed and struck him on the
   head.

4. The Carrying of the Cross
   John 19, 16-17: Then he handed him over to them to be crucified. So they took Jesus, and he went out, bearing his own cross, to the place called the place of a skull, which is called in Hebrew Golgotha.

5. The Crucifixion
   Luke 23,33-49. Verses 44-46: It was now about the sixth hour, and there was darkness over the whole land until the ninth hour, while the sun's light failed; and the curtain of the temple was torn in two. Then Jesus, crying with a loud voice, said, "Father, into thy hands I commit my spirit!" And having said this he breathed his last (Turn to Concluding Prayers).

The Glorious Mysteries

1. The Resurrection
   Luke 24:1-12. Verses 5-7: …and as they were frightened and bowed their faces to the ground, the men said to them, "Why do you seek the living among the dead? Remember how he told you, while he was still in Galilee, that the Son of man must be delivered into the hands of sinful men, and be crucified, and on the third day rise."

2. The Ascension
   Acts 1, 6-12. Verse 9-11: And when he had said this, as they were looking on, he was lifted up, and a cloud took him out of their sight. And while they were gazing into heaven as he went, behold, two men stood by them in white robes and said, "Men of Galilee, why do you stand looking into heaven? This Jesus, who was taken up from you into heaven, will come in the same way as you saw him go into heaven."

3. The Descent of the Holy Spirit
   Acts 2,1-13. Verses 2-4: And suddenly a sound came from heaven like the rush of a mighty wind, and it filled all the house where they were sitting. And there appeared to them tongues as of fire, distributed and resting on each one of them. And they were all filled with the Holy

Spirit and began to speak in other tongues, as the Spirit gave them utterance.

4. The Assumption of Mary
    Universal Catechism, par. 974: The Most Blessed Virgin Mary, when the course of her earthly life was completed, was taken up body and soul into the glory of heaven, where she already shares in the glory of her Son's Resurrection, anticipating the resurrection of all members of his Body.

5. The Coronation of Mary
    Revelation 12, 1: And a great portent appeared in heaven, a woman clothed with the sun, with the moon under her feet, and on her head a crown of twelve stars....

Concluding Prayers

F. Hail, Holy Queen, Mother of Mercy, our life, our sweetness, and our hope! To you we cry, poor banished children of Eve; to you we send up our sighs, mourning and weeping in this valley of tears. Turn then most gracious advocate, your eyes of mercy toward us; and after this our exile, show us to the blessed fruit of your womb, Jesus. O clement, O loving, O sweet Virgin Mary; Pray for us, O holy Mother of God. That we may be made worthy of the promises of Christ.

G. In the name of the Father, and of the Son, and of the Holy Spirit. Amen. (Sign of the cross.)

Contributed By Seth Murray
www.rosaryshop.com

Rosary Making Instructions

Directions to make a 5-decade Chain Rosary

This section describes the supplies, tools and techniques necessary to make a 5-decade chain rosary.

Tools

Your choice of rosary-making tools will depend on the type of rosaries you are making. In general, the quality of the tools being used can positively or negatively affect how easily and quickly a rosary can be made. Poor quality tools, even in the best of hands, can have poor, painful or frustrating results. High quality tools are relatively inexpensive and may last many years.

Chain rosaries—those made from stock wire or individual links—require at least a set of rosary pliers. These special pliers combine a side-cutter and round-nose pliers into a single unit. We strongly recommend the purchase of smooth-jaw chain nose pliers as well, without which some techniques are very difficult and rough on the fingers. When stone beads are used, it is also helpful to have a fine bead reamer on hand. Some stone beads may have irregular bores or be plugged by foreign objects. The drill holes can be quickly cleared by a decent reamer.

Supplies

    53 Hail Mary Beads
    6 Our Father Beads
    1 Center (optional)
    1 Crucifix or Cross
    1 or more Medals (optional)
    53 eyepins
    4+ jumprings and 1' chain

The supplies necessary for rosary making vary in cost from a few cents to over $100, depending on the type of chaplet you are making. Obviously, almost every chaplet requires a number of beads and a choice of a crucifix, cross, center and perhaps a medal (or several). Some chaplets omit one or more of these elements.

Chain chaplets require a combination of eyepins, jump rings and chain, or wire from which to manually make these. The eyepin, jumpring and chain dimensions vary, depending on the size of the rosary. The most common eyepin is one inch long and .028 inches in diameter. Common jumprings are 3-4mm. Rosary chain is called cable chain with a 2.5-3mm link. Other types of links are also used, but cable is fairly easy to get.

Techniques

Like any art, rosary-making consists of numerous basic techniques that may appear simple, but do require some practice to do consistently.

Connecting Eyepins

There is an eyepin going through every bead on a chain rosary. Eyepins can be purchased ready-to-use, or made by hand from a roll of wire. For this tutorial we will use the pre-manufactured ones.

1. "Fill" the eyepin by placing it through a bead.

2. Using the wire cutters built into the side of your rosary pliers (or another set of cutters), snip the wire so that about 3/8 of an inch of wire extends past the bead. With practice you will be able to judge the length of wire needed by sight. The overall length of the eyepin will vary depending on the size of the bead.

3. As close to the bead as you can, bend the wire back to make a 90 degree angle. Bend the wire in such a way that the second loop will be perpendicular to the first one on the other side of the bead. This will limit kinking in your completed rosary.

4. Move pliers down to the end of the wire so that the wire ends just a hair past the tips of your pliers. Grip the wire firmly with the pliers. Rotating

your wrist, roll the wire in toward the bead to make a nice even loop, leaving a small gap in the loop so that the next eyepin will be able to fit through it.

5. Place the eye of the next eyepin through the gap you just made.

6. Finish the loop with your pliers and gently squeeze the first eyepin closed. Try to tuck the end of the wire slightly into the hole of the bead. Leave no extra space between the wire loop and the bead (the bead should not be able to slide on the wire). This will make the rosary less likely to come apart with much use.

Simply repeat these steps as many times as are necessary to make the parts of your chaplet.

Connecting Chain

Chain can be purchased premade or made by hand from bulk rolls of wire. To connect the chain to your chaplet, first make sure your chain is the desired length (by cutting off any excess links). Open the eyepin or

jumpring by twisting the loop open to the side—do not open it by unrolling it. Place the chain link onto the open end and close the eyepin or jumpring by twisting the free end back into its loop. Squeeze it tight if necessary.

Using Jumprings and Split Rings

Jumprings and split rings are used to connect crucifixes, crosses, centers and medals to your chaplet. Jumprings are the most common connector. To use a jumpring, open it by twisting it open—do not pull the ends directly apart as this can introduce fractures into the ring, weakening it. Then simply attach the parts to the jumpring and close it by gently twisting it back into shape.

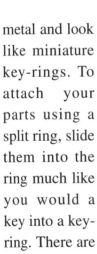

A split ring is significantly stronger than a jumpring. They are made from strong, spring-like

metal and look like miniature key-rings. To attach your parts using a split ring, slide them into the ring much like you would a key into a key-ring. There are special pliers available for doing this, but they are rarely necessary unless you work with a lot of very strong split rings. Toothpicks can help,

Contributed By Seth Murray
www.rosaryshop.com

*Note by Sister Patricia: I had originally planed to write this article myself—but in looking on the Internet I found a great site called the Rosary Shop that had these wonderful directions complete with pictures—and they had done such a great job I thought, hmmm, maybe they will let me use their material in this book? I called them up and they said, yes! But this article is only a small part of the free and wonderful directions you can find at www.rosaryshop.com to make rosaries. Not just the chain rosaries but also cord rosaries and flex-wire rosaries.

In fact just to give a free plug to the Rosary Shop—I think their web site has the most complete and detailed of all instructions for making rosaries that I have found. You can download their complete instructions for free or get them in a small booklet for only a few dollars.

Rosary Resources

Please visit www.rosary101.com for the latest information

Association of Marian Helpers
Eden Hill
Stockbridge, MA 01263
http://www.marian.org

The Blue Army of Our Lady of Fatima
P. O. Box 976
674 Mountain View Road
Washington, NJ 07882
http://www.bluearmy.com

Confraternity of the Most Holy Rosary
Domincans (An Archconfraternity)
The Rosary Center
P. O. Box 3617
Portland, OR 97208
http://www.rosary-center.org

Holy Cross Family Ministries
Patrick Peyton
518 Washington St.
North Easton, MA 02356-1200
http://www.familyrosary.org/main/
    rosary.php

Legion of Mary
Concilium Legionis Mariae
The International Centre of the
    Legion of Mary
De Montfort House
Morning Star Avenue
Brunswick Street
Dublin 7, Ireland
http://www.legion-of-mary.ie

Praying the Rosary Online

The Holy Rosary
http://www.theholyrosary.org

Virtual Rosary
http://www.virtualrosary.org

Rosary Prayer
http://rosary.virtualave.net

Perpetual Web Rosary
http://www.mich.com/~buffalo/
    rosary.html

Pray the Online Rosary
http://www.easterbrooks.com/personal/
    calendar/rosary.html

The Rosary Online
http://wordbytes.org/prayers/Rosary/
    index.html

Praying the Rosary – Real Audio
http://www.donabate.irishchurch.net/
    rosary/frame1.html

Rosary on TV

Boston Catholic Television
P. O. Box 9109
Newtonville, MA 02460-9109
http://www.catholictv.org

Catholic Familyland
3375 County Road 36
Bloomingdale, Ohio 43910
http://www.familyland.org

Rosary on TV/Radio

Eternal World Television Network
5817 Old Leeds Road
Birmingham, AL 35210
http://www.ewtn.com

Rosary on Radio/Internet

Boston Catholic Radio
75 Union Park Street
Boston, Massachusetts 02118
http://www.bostoncatholic.com

Canadian Catholic Radio
P.O. Box 7104
Windsor, Ontario N9C3Z1
http://www.canadiancatholicradio.ca

Radio Maria USA
601 Washington Street
Alexandria, LA 71301
http://www.radiomaria.org/usa

Radio Peace
PO Box 180
Tahoma, CA 96142
http://www.radiopeace.org

Saint Joseph Radio
P.O. Box 2983
Orange, California 92859
http://www.stjosephradio.org

Spirit FM 905
P.O. Box 18081
Tampa, FL 33679
http://spiritfm905.com

Rosary Videos

The Song of Bernadette
VHS (1945) (B&W)
Jennifer Jones, William Eythe
ASIN: 6300246981

The Miracle of Our Lady of Fatima
VHS (1952)
John Brahm, Gilbert Roland
ASIN: 6300270998

Wonders of the Vatican Library:
    The Rosary DVD
ASIN: B000066RUE

Think Good Thoughts
A tool for teaching the Rosary
#822833OV048E VHS 27 min.
Holy Cross Family Ministries

A Dedicated Man
#822833OV020E VHS 30 min.
Holy Cross Family Ministries

A Journey of Hope
The Rosary in the Latino Community
#822833OV027E VHS 55 min
Holy Cross Family Ministries

A Most Unusual Man
#822833OV019E VHS 60 min
Holy Cross Family Ministries

A World at Prayer
The Vision of Patrick Peyton, CSC
#822833OV026E VHS 25 min
Holy Cross Family Ministires

Living the Mysteries
#822833OV037E VHS 29 min
Holy Cross Family Ministries

Rosary Books

Mysteries of Light: Meditations on the Mysteries of the Rosary with John Paul II
by Pope John Paul II
ISBN: 076481060X
Liguori Publications

The Rosary Hour: The Private Prayers of Pope John Paul II
by Pope John Paul II
ISBN: 074344440X
Atria Books; (October 22, 2002)

The History and Devotion of the Rosary
by Richard E. Gribble
ASIN: 087973521X
Our Sunday Visitor; (September 1992)

The Rosary of Our Lady
by Romano Guardini
ISBN: 0918477786
Sophia Inst Pr; (July 1999)

The Power of the Rosary
by Albert J. M. Shamon
ISBN: 1891280104
CMJ Marian Publishers; Reprinted edition (June 2000)

The Essential Rosary: Prayers
by Caryll Houselander
ISBN: 0918477360
Sophia Inst Pr; (May 1996)

Praying the Rosary: The Joyful, Fruitful, Sorrowful, and Glorious Mysteries
by Warren F. Dicharry
ISBN: 0814624847
Liturgical Press; (March 1998)

The Seeker's Guide to the Rosary
by Elizabeth Kelly, Liz Kelly
ISBN: 0829415130
Loyola Press

Fifteen Mysteries in the Life of Jesus: Reflections
by Richard Hobbs
ISBN: 0818909013
Alba House; (June 2002)

"Calls" From the Message of Fatima
by Sister Lucia (the surviving seer of Fatima)
ISBN 9728524234
Distributed by The Ravengate Press

Father Peytons Rosary Prayer Book
by Patrick Peyton
ISBN: 1853901431
Veritas Publications

The Song of Bernadette
by Franz Werfel
ISBN: 0884117200
Aeonian Pr(Amerx); (June 1940)

Saint Bernadette Soubirous
by Francois Trochu
ISBN: 0895552531
Tan Books & Publishers, Inc.; (April 1993)

Rosary Audio

The Most Holy Rosary
by Scott Hahn CD
ISBN: 1570583765

The Rosary (including Mysteries of Light)
ACTA CD
ISBN 0-879460240-X

Pray the Rosary with Father Peyton
#822833OA025E Cassette
#82283CD025E CD
Holy Cross Family Ministries

The Joyful Hour
#822833OA26E Cassette
Holy Cross Family Ministries

The Triumphant Hour
#822833OA28E Cassette
Holy Cross Family Ministries

Rosary Making

Our Lady's Rosary Makers
P. O. Box 37080
Louisville, KY 40233
Ph: (502) 968-1434
http://www.olrm.win.net

The Rosary Shop (Online Store Only)
805 NW Alder Street
McMinnville, OR 97128
http://www.rosaryshop.com

Rosary Makers (Online Store Only)
http://rosarymakers.org

Saints & the Rosary

Bl. Alan de la Roche
St. Aloysius of Gonzaga
Bl. Bartolo Longo
St. Bernadette
St. Catherine of Bologna
St. Juan Diego
Bl. Jacinta & Bl. Francesco
St. Francis de Sales
St. Maximillian Kolbe
St. Louis de Montfort
St. Padre Pio

Popes & the Rosary

Pope Benedict XV
Pope Clement X
Pope Gregory XIII
Pope John XXIII
Pope John Paul II
Pope Leo XIII
Pope Paul VI
Pope Pius V
Pope Pius XI
Pope Pius XII

Holy Men & Women & the Rosary

Mother Teresa
Patrick Peyton

Authors by Location

INDEX

Give the Gift of
101 Inspirational Stories of the Rosary
to your Family and Friends

This book makes a great fund-raiser, door prize or gift for special events such as RCIA or Confirmation. Give for birthdays, Mother's Day, Father's Day or Christmas. Wonderful for College students, and if you have a loved one in the military, the message of Mary's protection in war is very comforting.

Visit Your Local Bookstore

or

Order Direct From:

Park Press Incorporated
355 North 6th Ave.
P.O. Box 475
Waite Park, MN 56387

Call Toll Free (888) 809-7473
Fax: (320) 255-8937

Need a Rosary?

We will be glad to send you a free rosary. The Holy Cross Family Ministries has given us a thousand rosaries to distribute free of charge to spread this wonderful devotion.

You can also get a free rosary for your church or parish group by going directly to the Holy Cross Family Ministries.

Holy Cross Family Ministries
518 Washington St.,
North Easton, MA 02356-1200
USA
1-800-299-PRAY (7729)

www.familyrosary.org